TRIBES OF INDIA, NEPAL TIBET BORDERLAND

TRIBES OF INDIA, NEPAL, TIBET BORDERLAND

A STUDY OF CULTURAL TRANSFORMATION

B.S. BISHT

GYAN

GYAN PUBLISHING HOUSE

NEW DELHI-110 002

Tribes of India, Nepal, Tibet Borderland
(Tribal Studies, Anthropology, Sociology, Development Economics)

Library of Congress Card No. 93-900313

ISBN: 978-81-212-0454-4

Reprinted in 2013 in India by
Gyan Publishing House
23, Main Ansari Road, Daryaganj,
New Delhi - 110002
Phones : 23282060, 23261060
Fax : (011) 23285914
E-mail : books@gyanbooks.com
Website: gyanbooks.com

Printed at: G. Print Process, Delhi

PREFACE

Having been acquainted with some folk-tales and legends about the tribal culture since my childhood, the longing for the exact and objective acquaintance of the tribal culture deepened and got mature with the maturity of my mind, and particularly during my field work for Ph.D. dissertation in 1980-81, when I was working on a little known tribe *i.e.* Rajis of Kumaun in Uttar Pradesh. Thanks to the 'longing' which ultimately induced me to come in close proximity of the five Scheduled Tribal Communities named; Bhotiyas, Buxas, Tharus, Rajis and Jaunsaris of Uttarakhand in Uttar Pradesh and also enabled to present a real canvas of the tribal culture in its changing scene. The present thesis may, therefore, be considered as the inevitable corollary of that very 'longing' which was implanted in the imaginary world of my early days of childhood and blossomed as a result of the scientific research through participant observation of the real culture of the tribals during the latter half of the eighties when I formulated this project with a view to test all those imaginations, legends and the folk-lores.

In fact, a diversified society like India, which consists of various castes, creeds, communities, linguistic groups and also encounters the numerous problems of social integration, communal harmony, culture contacts, regionalism and lingual agitation, the study of culture is of great importance not only from policy point of view but also in academic interest. With a view in mind, a thorough and candid effort has been made in presenting the research findings regarding the study of the tribal cultures of Uttarakhand, a border region of India which constitute the international boundary with Tibet and Nepal in its changing perspective.

Though in the field of cultural anthropology and sociology, the study of different tribal communities has been conducted by a number of scholars in India and abroad but so far as the study of the tribal culture of Uttarakhand in Uttar Pradesh is concerned, none of the scholars has made the cultural study in the holistic frame of reference. Hence, in view of the necessity of the academic interest an attempt has been made to study the culture of the five Scheduled Tribe Communities of Uttarakhand in a comparative cum holistic manner. As the Scheduled Tribe Communities under reference have no written script of their own, hence the research findings of the previous scholars, the government reports and other supplementary secondary information available through secondary sources have been taken into account as a base-line data for the analysis of the cultural transformation. The major social institutions of the tribal communities have been discussed in their changing perspective. The impact of the culture-contact as well as the various welfare schemes of the government has also been analysed in a scientific manner. The findings of the study is based on the information gathered through primary and secondary sources. In view of the systematic presentation of the research findings, the whole of the book has been divided into seven major chapters. The first chapter deals with the introduction of the problem, the second chapter consists of the conceptual analysis and the review of the literature, the third chapter is related with the analytical presentation of the methodology and the research design, while the rest of the chapters deal with the empirical portion of the study.

This work is indeed a beautiful bouquet, in which the different cultural aspects of the different tribal communities symbolize as the varieties of the flowers which have systematically been plucked (gathered) with the help of the various agencies and the resource persons and arrayed (arranged) scientifically as to make it more intelligible. In this regard my first and foremost thanks are due to 'God Shiva' (the Lord of Great Himalaya) the blessings of whom made possible my field study on the tribal communities residing in the most remote hilly, mountainous, rugged, forested and the abstruse Himalayan regions. Secondly, that part of the tribal population which constitute the field of my study is equally the claimant of my sincere thanks, who not only provided the real, intensive, and reliable information concerning to my research problem but also rendered every possible assistance which I really needed during the tiresome, tedious, however, pleasant moments of my stay with them without which the data collection was absolutely difficult if not impossible. As a matter of fact, the hospitality, in spite of being an outsider and a stranger I enjoyed among the tribal people was praise-worthy and an animated example of "Atithi Devo Bhava". How can I forget the warmth of the welcome given to me by the tribal people in general and the Bhotiyas, Tharus and Jaunsaris in particular. The invitation from the council of elders to hear the proceedings of the meeting, permission to join the 'Rang-Bang' by youths and offering of a cup of 'Chyakti' as the mark of honour by a virgin, in Bhotiya community, the presentation of a special tribal dance, Holi-songs by Tharus and the performance of the customary reception *i.e.* the washing of the feet and hands of mine at the threshold of the house and to repeat the same before and after the meal by young lady, and to accommodate myself as a family member, by Jaunsaris, are some of the unforgettable moments of my stay as a researcher with the tribal people which ultimately made easier the process of data collection and also provided every possible opportunity to understand intensively and comprehensively the different cultural patterns of the tribal from nearby. Hence, I am really thankful to the tribal people for all they did for me during my stay with them. Moreover, I would like to express my sincere thanks to Mr. Napalchyal, the Pharmacist at Darma, Dharchula, Mr. Nandan Singh Gwal, an under-graduate student, Mr. Jauhar Singh Nabiyal, President "Ran Sanskriti Parishad' Dharchula, Miss Gangotri Garbyal, (Retd. Principal), Manager, Narayan Ashram (all are Bhotiyas), Mr. Rameshwar Singh Rana, Mr. Kripal Singh Rana, Mr. Gopal Singh Rana (Tharus) and Mr. Guman Singh Chauhan an under-graduate student and Mr. Teeka Ram Joshi an innkeeper at Kalsi Gate, Dehradun (both are Khasas) and so many other tribal people who spent so many days with me during the field work of the respective communities and discussed over the cultural patterns of their own.

I also like to record my appreciation of the co-operation of the library staff, particularly of the ICSSR, New Delhi, J.N.U., New Delhi, Delhi University, Delhi and Lucknow University, Lucknow, who rendered me every possible library facilities. Even greater is my debt of gratitude to the sociologists, anthropologists, authors and so many scholars, whose scholarly research findings, thoughts and the models I used in my study. My sincere most thanks are due to my worshipful parents who told me about the doings, occupations and various cultural aspects of the tribal people who used to come to barter their products or things of daily needs in the village areas to quest the childish curiosity of mine which really cultivated the longing of knowing about the tribal people from nearby. My sincere thanks are due to my respectful brother Sri Hira Singh Bisht who indeed paved the way of my study and always encouraged to undertake this hard toil of studying the tribal people living in the abstruse, most remote and isolated forested regions and thus made possible the presentation of the untouched aspects of their cultural life in the present changing perspectives.

Last by no means least I extend my sincere love to my wife Mrs. Sarojani Bisht, for whom I have really no words of appreciation for the cooperation she rendered by taking up all the liabilities of the family and faced smilingly every problem and hardship in my absence. She is indeed the co-sharer of this work.

B.S. BISHT

CONTENTS

1

INTRODUCTION

Tribal culture is an integral part of India's cultural heritage. Hence, an adequate knowledge of tribal culture and its heritage is essentially important in the exploration of Indian culture, since the tribal culture alongwith the varied cultures of different ethnic groups constitutes the composite culture of India. The tribal population in India exhibits typical customs, traditions, religious beliefs, practices as well as the various forms of economy, and law and government. But the centuries old confinement of tribals into the isolation of dense forests and remote uninhabited areas has kept them away from the main-stream of social life. At the earliest stage of cultural evolution, the tribals were neither able to organize their socio-cultural life nor had they any particular pattern of social interaction. There was no system, nothing definite, except incoherent homogeneity among the people as well as their cultural complexes. But gradually, with the passage of time the experiences, realisation and the knowledge of the tribal people increased and subsequently they learnt to live and work together. Thus, the concept of social organization and its cultural system came into existence. Eventually, the state of an indefinite incoherent homogeneity among the people transformed into the state of definite coherent heterogeneity. However, the tribal culture which chiefly consists of material and non-material cultural complexes has maintained its distinct nature rather than the rest of the society. But with the breaching of the isolated peripheries of the tribal communities the scope of the inter and intra-tribal relations broadened and the tribal culture took a new turn to modernization. At present a considerable numbers of the tribal communities have constantly been lagging behind their traditional ways of life and are gradually following the path of modernization. In this direction, voluntary organizations, government welfare schemes and the cultural impacts of non-tribal groups on the tribal areas have functionally imparted a significant role. Thus, with an end in view, the Government of India Act 1935, has specified some tribes as backward in the provinces of Assam, Bihar, Orissa, Central provinces, Madras and Bombay. However, the first serious attempt to list 'primitive tribes' in this category was made during the 1931 census. Specifying the Scheduled Tribes, the Article 342 of the Constitution provides that, "President may with respect to any State or Union Territory specify the tribes or tribal communities which shall deemed to be Scheduled Tribes in relation to that State or Union territory. In pursuance of this provision the President made an order in 1950, in relation to the then part 'A' and part 'B' States, called the Constitution Order 1950."

Since then the government has been launching a number of welfare measures for the socio-cultural upliftment of the tribals in India. Besides this, the newly developed mechanical culture, industrial decentralization and the extending influence of the urban culture and education has in turn, resulted in the speed of the media exposure even in tribal areas, which exclusively affected the majority of the tribal communities and their pre-mechanical and unsophisticated culture. The fluxion of tribal culture sometimes seems to be seething in the cauldron of the continuum of tradition and modernity, for on the one hand the traditional moorings of tribal culture have slackened and on the other they (tribals) are unable to assimilate themselves within the main-stream of industrial culture. John H. Bodely (1982) has aptly remarked, "The industrial civilization is now completing its destruction of technologically simple tribal cultures. According to the view point of many authorities within the Industrial Civilization, this disappearance or drastic modification of these cultures is considered necessary for the progress of civilization and is thought to be inevitable, natural and in the long run, beneficial for the people involved."[1]

Since Independence, several plans have been projected for the all round socio-cultural development of tribes, so that the tribal communities, who have persisted in the forests and hills without any causal contacts with the alien cultural groups for thousands of years may share the composite culture of modern India. Under the broad matrix of plans, a number of programmes concerning education, economic development, rehabilitation, health and nutrition, drinking water facilities, protective measures for the interests and the cultures of tribals have been launched by the Government of India. Under the Tribal Sub-plan Approach in 180 Integrated Tribal Development Projects, about sixty six percent of the Scheduled Tribal population in the 18 States and Union territories have been covered for development with a view to bring a larger population of tribals under the tribal development programme and it has been decided during the medium term plan (1978-83), that the pockets with a minimum population of 10,000 having more than 50% tribals, living in contiguous areas should also be taken upto intensive development under a modified area development approach. Moreover, some special programmes have also been taken up for the development of 52 primitive tribes. The major object of almost all the development programmes is to narrow the gap between the tribal areas and the non-tribal areas and to improve the quality of the life of tribals. In this direction many voluntary organizations, particularly, during the seventh decade of twentieth century were given grants-in-aid for undertaking welfare programmes benefiting the scheduled tribes. Thus, the so called aboriginals or primitives, habitating, in almost all the States and Union Territories of Indian sub-continent have gained the empathy of the number of voluntary organisations and also attracted the attention of the policy planners of the Government,who have formulated and executed the welfare policies so that the gap between the tribals and the non-tribals can be abridged and the former may flow with the main-stream of the Indian society. The tribal population have also shown their positive aptitude as well as the receptivity towards these programmes. But the findings of the scholars in regard to the cultural standard of the Scheduled Tribes and the primitive tribes vary from each other. In fact, the efforts taken by the government and voluntary agencies have affected the tribal culture in general but the results of it have got the bilateral consequences. That is to say the tribal culture, on the one hand flourished but on the other hand it has misshapen its originality.

In general, the majority of the tribal population has lost their traditional identity. They have started to make an entry into the modern era with other members of Indian society. In the constitutional frame of reference, they have ascertained their own position in the various spheres of national life. Particularly in the field of education, medical, administrative and allied services, they have got reservations of certain seats. However, in every place of socio-religious life, they seem to be isolated and therefore, disintegrated. Thus, it is imperative to know objectively their socio-religious life, their political and economic organization, their behaviour patterns and their habits and customs, which combinedly form the cultural system of any given community.

Since long, various religious organizations have been playing a vital role in the diversion of tribal religion into the respective ones. Consequently, the tribal communities who have come out of their isolated peripheries are helpless to maintain their native religious beliefs with purity. While a handful tribal population who have still persisted in an isolated habitation are trying to maintain their distinct socio-religious existence yet, the infiltration of the vested interest groups even into the remote tribal areas have influenced the tribal religion on account of which an original tribal religion has become a mirage in the present context.

Today, the majority of the tribal population have followed the Hindu religion in one form or the other while a considerable number of tribals have adhered Christianity and only a nominal numbers of tribals observe Buddhism, Islam, Jainism and others. But the outstanding feature, which must be kept in mind, is that the tribals, inspite of adhering the alien religions have not shed completely their religious beliefs and practices and many of them still observe animism i.e. the tribal religion alongwith the newly adopted religion.

In the same way, the economic and occupational structure of the tribals have also undergone numerous changes. The primitive form of agriculture has transformed into a settled agriculture as well as the service based economy. At present a huge population of tribals is either inclined to the industrial areas for its economic pursuits or engaged in settled cultivation to such extent that they are aware of all the means of agriculture while a considerable number of the tribals are employed in government, semi-government and private concerns. However, a birds eye view observation of all the tribal communities, particularly those who have still confined to their original abodes and are away from the impact of the communication and transportation, exhibit that the esalient features of tribal economy still exist among them.

Thus, it may be asserted that the tribal culture, with the effect of various instinctive and planned processes of change has undergone numerous changes and resultantly the traditional cultural traits of tribals have got their antithetical or discrepant or sophisticated forms. But the degree of the cultural transformation varies in accordance with the variations of the cultural development of the different tribal communities.

As a matter of fact, the Indian tribes, which constitute 8% of the total population of the country present a wide spectrum of racial traits, linguistic affinities, cultural levels, economic gradings, religious beliefs and political awareness. Since long the ethnographers of India and abroad have made significant efforts for the holistic interpretation of the tribal situation in India. Concerning this the tribal population on the basis of the geographical propinquity has been demarcated as the North, North-Eastern, the Central or the Middle and the Southern Zone.[2] The North-North Eastern Zone would lie approximately between 31°.7" N and 35°.0" N at its Western and 23°.30" N and 28°.0" N on its eastern end and between 77° .33" E and 97° .0" E having for its out posts Shimla and Leh in the west and the Lusai Hills and the Mishai Tract in the east. The tribal areas of eastern Kashmir, east Punjab, Himachal Pradesh, Northern U.P., Assam and Sikkim fall in this zone. The central or middle zone would lie approximately between latitudes 20°.0"N and 25°.0" N and longitudes 73°.0" E and 90°.0" E. It would include Bengal, Bihar, Southern U.P., Southern Rajasthan, M.P., Northern Bombay and Orissa. Northern Rajasthan, Southern Bombay and Bastar form the peripheral areas of this zone. In area and numbers it comes first among the three zones.

South-East of the Central zone would lie the southern zone,

approximately between latitudes 8°.0" N and 20°.0" N and longitudes 75°.0" E and 85°.0" E. Hyderabad, Mysore, Coorg, Travancore, Cochin, Andhra and Madras fall within this zone. B.K. Roy Burman[3] has divided the tribal communities living in different regions into five territorial groupings,taking into account their historical ethnic and socio-cultural relations as follows:

(a) North-East India comprising Assam, NEFA, Nagaland, Manipur and Tripura.

(b) The sub-Himalayan region of North and North-West India comprising the Northern and mountain districts of U.P. and Himachal Pradesh as a whole including the areas transferred from Punjab.

(c) Central and East India comprising West Bengal, Bihar, Orissa, Madhya Pradesh and Andhra Pradesh.

(d) South India comprising Madras, Kerala and Mysore.

(e) Western India comprising Rajasthan, Gujarat and Maharashtra.

Dr. B.S. Guha[4] has also classified the Indian tribes into three broad geographical zone: (i) North and North-Eastern zone; comprising Leh, Shimla, Lusai Hills, Eastern Kashmir, Eastern Punjab, Himachal Pradesh, Northern U.P. and the hills of Assam. This zone has been inhabited by Gaddi, Gujjar, Lamba, Khampa, Kanota, Lahaula, Jaunsari, Bhotiya, Tharu, Naga, Kuki, Khasi, Khachati and Rabha tribe. (ii) Centralzone, consists of Bengal, Bihar, South U.P., South Rajasthan, M.P., Northern Bombay and Orissa. The main tribal communities of this region are Santhal, Oraon, Ho, Khariya, Birhor, Bhuyan, Gond, Baiga, Kand, Kota, Chenchu, Vehara, Korawa, Munda and Bhil. (iii) The Southern zone which includes Hyderabad, Mysore, Coorg, Travancore, Cochin, Andhra Pradesh and Madras. The main tribal communities dwelling in this zone are Chenchu, Kota, Kuramba, Baraga, Toda, Kadar Malayan, Wrali, Irula and Pulayam. S.C. Dube[5] has demarcated the Indian map into four major tribal zones; (i) North and North Eastern (ii) Central zone (iii) Western zone and (iv) Southern zone. Further, corresponding to the three geographical regions, D.N. Majumdar has mentioned three broad linguistic zones of tribal India. In the North and North-Eastern region, most of the tribal people speak some form or the other of Sino-Tibetan and Tibeto-Burman. In certain North-Eastern areas there is an admixture of the Mon-Khmer (Austric) speech, as for instance among the Khasi. It has been estimated that in the Naga hills, apart from numerous dialects, sixteen languages are spoken. In the Central zone, the Austric family of language is dominant, although important tribes like the Oraon and the Kolam, the Khond and the Gond speak languages having a Dravidian affinity. The Austric speech family includes the Kol and Munda languages and dialects of the central and the eastern India. Such languages and dialects deal with the Santhal, Mundari, Ho, Kharia, Bhoomij, Garo and Khasi languages and dialects which are mainly spoken in Bihar, Orissa, Bengal and Assam. In the south, the tribal people speak some form or other of some Dravidian languages like Tamil, Telgu, Malayalam, Canarese or Coorgi. The Kadar of Travancore-Cochin speak a Malayalam dialect. There has been Dravidianization of significant south Indian tribes like the Chenchu and the Yenadi. Thus, the geographical regions (denoted by Majumdar) correspond roughly to the three linguistic zones.[6]

The anthropological connotation of linguistic affinities of Indian tribes makes clear the linguistic origin of the tribal communities dwelling in different regions of India, but with the course of time the medley of the different ethnic groups, the culture contacts and the cultural transmission have made the original linguistic features of tribes too obscure to ascertain their linguistic affinity.

The aforesaid delineation of linguistic affinities of the Indian tribes done by the prominent anthropologist, D.N. Majumdar affined the tribal communities of North-North East India to Sino-Tibetan and Tibeto-Burman language family. But today the tribal communities of U.P., viz. Tharu, Buxa, Bhotiya, Raji and Khasa (Jaunsari) have become multilingual. They generally speak their original dialects with their indigenous akins only. However, the dialectical terms of Hindi, Kumauni, Punjabi, and Garhwali which are spoken respectively by the respective neighbouring groups are also spoken by the respective tribal communities. Thus, the Tharu and Buxas have smattering of Hindi, Kumauni and Punjabi whereas Bhotiyas not only understand Hindi and Kumauni but also they frequently speak these dialects. But Rajis apart from their local dialect, can speak Kumauni and broken Hindi, while Jaunsari apart from their own dialect speak Garhwali and Hindi i.e. the language spoken in Western U.P. Thus, the tribal communities have picked up the dialects of their neighbouring groups. But inspite of sharing the alien languages the tribes have maintained their distinctive cultural position in the broad matrix of Indian culture.

So far as the racial affinity of Indian tribes is concerned, there is practically no direct evidence of these ethnic stocks who inhabited in different parts of India in prehistoric times.[7] The available knowledge about the racial composition of India in historic times is equally scanty.[8] The first scientific racial classification of India, based on anthropometric and other data, was attempted by Sir Herbert Hope Risley,[9] who supervised the census operation in 1891. He classified the people of India into seven racial types: Turko-Iranian, Indo-Aryan, Scytho-Dravidian, Aryo-Dravidian, Mongolo-Dravidian, Mongoloid and Dravidian. These seven types can be reduced to three basic types viz. the Dravidian, the Mongolian and Indo-Aryan. The former two types would account for the racial composition of tribal India. A.C. Haddon[10] seeking the evidence for migration of people mainly in their physical characters, artifacts, customs, folk-tales and language, tries to reconstruct the racial background of India. According to him, the oldest inhabitants of India must have been the pre-Dravidian jungle tribes whom he defines merely as an existing stratum. Haddon regards the central Indian tribes as the autochthons of India and the brachycephalic element as post-Mongolian and alpine in origin. Guha[11] lists six main races, with nine sub-types;

1. The Negrito
2. The proto-Australoid
3. The Mongoloid
   - (i) Palaeo Mongoloids
     - (a) long headed
     - (b) broad headed
   - (ii) Tibeto-Mongoloids
4. The Mediterranean
   - (i) Palaeo Mediterranean
   - (ii) Mediterranean
   - (iii) Oriental types

5. The Western Brachycephals (i) Alpinoid
(ii) Dinaric
(iii) Armenoid

6. The Nordic

Guha[12] states that the ancestry of the present tribal population is traced chiefly to the first three types. The Negrito is regarded as the earliest racial element as found among the Kadar. The central Indian tribes are assigned to the Proto-Australoid race and the North-North Eastern to the Mongoloid race. The Palaeo-Mediterranean stock is also held responsible for the ancestry of some tribal communities. Regarding the racial composition of tribal India Guha has summed up his conclusions as follows:

(i) The Kadar, the Irula and the Paniyan of South India with frizzly hair, have an undoubted Negrito strain.

(ii) The tribes of Middle India belong to the proto-Australoid stock.

(iii) The brachycephalic Mongoloids of North-Eastern India with typical features of the face and the eyes.

(iv) A slightly different mongoloid type with medium stature, high head and medium nose, living in the Brahmaputra valley.

Indian tribes belong to the different cultural levels. Some tribal communities have got the cultural position in the composite cultural system of Indian society; some are passing through the transitional period while some are still bind up with the pivot of their traditional moorings. Besides this, some tribal communities have constantly been mobilizing towards the urban and the industrial centres and following the respective cultural complexes; some inclined to move towards the glorified and glamourous world of urbans; while some have still maintained their isolation and seem partly happy and frustrated too in the shelter of the primitivism.

The cultural levels of Indian tribes have been classified by the prominent anthropologists on different bases. Varrier Elwin[13] has described four types of aboriginals viz., those who are most primitive, live a joint communal life and cultivate with axe; those who, though equally attached to their solitude and ancient traditions, are more individualistic, less occupied with axe cultivation, more used to out side life, and generally less simple and honest than the first category; those, the most numerous, probably 20 million, who under external influence are already on the way to the loss of their tribal culture, religion and social organization, and finally he lists tribes like Bhil and Naga who are said to be representatives of the old aristocracy of the country who retain much of their original tribal life and who, he regards, have won the battle of cultural contact.

Elwin's classification of cultural levels of Indian tribes is too old to be appropriate in the present day context, because with the passage of time the tribal culture has undergone tremendous changes and the traditional cultural traits have lost their traditional shape and transformed into the modern ones. In fact, the emergence of industrialization, urbanization, multiple occupational opportunities as well as the modern education system and prevailing means of communication and transportation have speeded up the modernization process in India, which eventually has broken the socio-cultural and psychological isolation of tribals too. At present they are at the cross-road of cultural transformation.

D.N. Majumdar[14] has also classified Indian tribes on the basic idea of 'distance' from rural-urban groups, as follows; firstly, those who are culturally most distant from rural urban groups; that is more or less out of contact; secondly, those who are under the influence of the culture of rural-urban groups and have developed discomforts and problems consequently; and thirdly, those who, though in contact with rural-urban groups have not suffered as they have now got acculturated into rural or urban culture.

In 1952, the Indian Conference of Social Work appointed a 'Tribal Welfare Committee' who has suggested the cultural classification of tribes as follows: (i) Tribal Communities (ii) Semi-tribal Communities (iii) Acculturated Tribal Communities and (iv) Totally assimilated tribes.

Thus, the cultural situation of tribal India present their half baked cultural maturity of tribes. The rapid dissolution of traditional or primitive mode of economic subsistence, the infiltration of out-groups into the tribal areas and penetration of their unavoidable cultural traces into the primitive culture have overloaded and broken the traditional cultural moorings of tribes and coerce them to come under the impact of alien cultural traits. Now, almost all the tribal communities are in the frequent rural-urban contacts and embracing the non-tribal culture patterns, yet they are not in the state of complete abandonment of their tribal cultural traits and retaining them in one form or the other. Thus, tribal culture of India seems to be a nursery where the primitive as well as the modern non-tribal culture is simultaneously growing and flourishing. Today most of the tribal communities and their cultures are in the process of continuum of tradition and modernity.

Economically, the scheduled tribal communities vary from each other. The prominent anthropologist, Dr. D.N. Majumdar[15] has classified the Indian tribes into following economic gradings.

Firstly; the Indian tribes who are dependent upon forests and inhabit forested regions particularly those who have the food gathering type of economy. The Kadar (Cochin), the Malapantaram (Travancore), the Paliyan (Madras) and the Paniyan (Wynand) are some examples of this type.

Secondly; there are tribes in India who have an economy midway between the food gathering and primitive agricultural types. The Kamar, the Baiga and the Reddy of Bison Hills belong to this type.

Thirdly, the tribal population depending upon some form of agriculture, with forest produce as a secondary support. The tribes of North-Eastern India belong mostly to this category and so do many middle Indian tribes.

Finally; a new economic category of tribes-men have come into existence following the growth of industry in India. In certain parts of the country, mainly in Bihar, Bengal and Assam there has been two sided force driving the tribes men away from their traditional occupations on the one hand and there has been an outward 'push' following economic hardships due to land alienation and indebtedness and on the other hand there has been a 'pull' from out side; the demand of labour from industries and forests and from tea plantations in Assam.

In short there are tribes-men who follow industrial pursuits and generally observed to be as the daily wage labourers or contract labourers.

There are some more classifications made by some prominent thinkers. Ernest Gross describes five forms of tribal economy; (a) Collectional economy (b) Cultural nomadic economy; (c) Settled village economy; (d) Town economy; (e) Metropolitan economy.

Forde and Herskovits agree as to a five fold division of economy i.e. collectional hunting, fishing, cultivation and stock raising.

Jacobs and Stern have divided the primitive economy into two major parts and the each part consists of two sub parts; (a) Hunting, Fishing and Food-gathering economy which (i) simple food gathering economy (ii) advanced food gathering economy. (b) Agriculture and pastoral economy which includes (i) simple agriculture and pastoral economy (ii) advanced agricultural and pastoral economy.

A more significant classification of tribal economy has also been made by Nicboer, who divides economic life into seven types; (i) gleaners, (ii) hunters (iii) fishers (iv) settled agriculturists of a lower grade who also hunt or tend cattle (v) agricultural nomads or hunter agriculturists, (vi) superior farmers who have complex implements and (vii) nomad shepherds.

Thurnwald[16] has categorised the primitive economy into seven categories; (i) Homogeneous communities of hunters, trappers and food collectors, (ii) Homogeneous communities of hunters, trappers and agriculturists, (iii) Graded society of hunters, trappers, agriculturists and artisans, (iv) Herds-men, (v) Homogeneous hunters and herds-men, (vi) Ethnically stratified cattle breeders and traders and (vii) Socially graded herds-men with hunting, agricultural and artisan population.

Thus, it may be concluded that a number of thinkers and scholars have made the economic gradation or the classification of the tribal economy in their own way but it seems any of the classifications is not appropriate and complete in itself, and unsuitable particularly in the present day context. Because, the majority of the tribal communities of today cannot be identified with any particular occupation or the source of subsistance, they either follow a marginal economy or more than one occupation as the sources of subsistence. Thus, the classical classification of tribal economy seems inappropriate at present time.

In view of the multifarious occupations and the sources of livelihood in the different regions of the tribal India in which the tribals are generally engaged, the tribal economy may be graded as follows; (i) forestry and food gathering, (ii) shifting cultivation, (iii) settled agriculture, (iv) agricultural labour, (v) animal husbandry, (vi) household industry and (vii) miscellaneous occupations.

Thus, in Indian tribal scenario, we can observe that some tribal communities like; Andamanese, Onges and Somphans etc. of Andaman and Nicobar Islands are engaged in forestry and food gathering. While some tribal communities of NEFA, Nagaland, Manipur, Tripura, Orissa, Assam and Madhya Pradesh practised shifting cultivation as the main source of livelihood, but the overwhelming majority of the tribal population in India follow the settled agriculture as the primary source of livelihood. There are tribal communities in some parts of Kerala, Gujarat, Maharashtra, West Bengal who earn their livelihood as agricultural labourers. Some tribal communities like Gujars of Himachal Pradesh, Bhotiyas of U.P. and Todas of Nilgiri Hills subsist on animal-husbandry. Household industry, as the main source of livelihood is found only among small tribes with scattered population, such as the Mahalis of West Bengal, Turis of Bihar and Agarias of Madhya Pradesh. Besides this, some of the tribal communities such as Santhal, Oraons, Mundas, Bhils and Gonds have been engaged to a great extent in some modern industries as tea plantations, mining industries and other industrial areas. Thus, it is quite difficult to classify the tribal communities into some particular categories as mentioned above by different scholars, because each and every tribal community of the country today follows more than one source of livelihood. D.N. Majumdar has aptly stated, "The grading of the tribes on the basis of their economic life and occupation and in accordance with any approved scheme of classification is indeed difficult as most of the tribes possess either 'Marginal' cultures or follow more than one occupation. The tribal stage does not provide for any specialization of functions and as such a variety of occupations are followed by a tribe."[17]

Indian tribes can also be classified on the basis of their religious beliefs. In fact, the cultural contact and the impact of various religions have brought about a tremendous change in the religious beliefs and practices of tribals. Only these tribal communities who are leading an almost isolated social existence in dense forests have maintained their traditions and religious beliefs more or less with purity. But such tribal communities are negligible in numbers. According to the census data of 1961 and 1971, Indian tribes may be classified into the following religions— (a) Hinduism, (b) Christianity, (c) Buddhism, (d) Islam, (e) Jainism, and (f) Others. About 90 percent of the tribals of India follow Hindu religion in one form or the other, while the remaining 10% tribal population follow Christianity, Buddhism, Islam, Jainism and others. But the remarkable thing which is to be noted is that the tribes who have adhered to any of the religious faiths have still maintained their own traditional beliefs, faiths and rituals which are practised alongwith the newly acquired religious faiths.

Thus, the aforesaid delineation presents that the various tribal communities in Indian sub-continent belong to a variety of linguistic families and racial stocks and also differ from each other in regard of their economic standard, religious faiths and cultural systems.

U.P. like other States and Union territories of the country also possesses some tribal pockets but in a scanty and scattered form. The tribal population of the State is comparatively low in comparison of its total population. There are about 19 tribal communities in the state out of which only five tribal communities i.e. Bhotiyas, Buxas, Tharus, Rajis and Jaunsaries have been declared as Scheduled Tribes in June 1967. The Buxas and Rajis have also been recognized as the primitive tribes. According to the 1981 census,[18] the total population of the Scheduled Tribes in the State was 225678 out of which 173609 live in the hill areas and the rest 52069 live in the plains of the State. The following table depicts the Scheduled Tribe-wise population in U.P.

Table 1

Population of Scheduled Tribes in U.P. (1981 Census)

Name of the Tribe	*Areas Where Lived (District)*	*Population*
Bhotiyas	Almora, Pithoragarh Chamoli, Uttarkashi	26593
Buxas	Dehradun, Pauri Garhwal, Nainital	31037
	Bijnor.	3308
Tharus	Nainital	53406
	Lakhimpur, Khiri, Gonds Beharaich,Gorakhapur	48761
Rajis	Pithoragarh	371
Jaunsari	Dehradun	63210
Total		225678

Besides these Scheduled Tribes, fourteen other tribal communities namely; Kol, Gond, Khairwar, Chero, Sahariya, Panika, Agaria, Ghasia, Bhuiya, Oraon, Pathari, Parahiya, Korawa and Jaunsari types in the State are still awaiting for their turn to be included as 'Scheduled Tribe'. All the tribal communities except Jaunsari type, are the residents of south-east U.P. The majority of the Scheduled Tribal population is concentrated in Kumaon and Garhwal regions which jointly constitute the Uttarakhand zone of the State. The Scheduled Tribal communities of the region present a wide spectrum of cultural varieties. Geographically, the Scheduled Tribal communities of Uttarakhand may be categorised as the tribes of the sub-Himalayan region of the North and North-west India. Ethnological notes of the eminent scholars depicts that the Mongoloid racial characteristics are very common among Bhotiyas, Buxas, Tharus and Rajis while Jaunsaris belong to the Mediterranian racial stock.

In view of the socio-economic standard and cultural patterns, the Scheduled-Tribal communities under reference vary from each other. It is so because of the uneven impact of the various factors of change, which have breached in general the dormancy of socio-cultural isolation of the tribals and caused the socio-economic and cultural transformation among them. Besides this, a tremendous change can also be observed in the sophisticated tribal religion and faiths. Though the cultural impact of the overwhelming majority of non-tribal cultural groups have constantly affected the cultural complexes of the tribals and also paved the way of getting transformed their primitive cultures into the modern and civilized culture. But the process of cultural transformation among Scheduled Tribal communities of Uttarakhand, in particular, speeded up since Independence. In fact, the statutory provisions and reservation policies of Indian government for tribal development, and the means of communication and transportation and the expansion and prevalence of educational facilities in tribal areas have not only awakened the tribal people from their centuries old slumber but also compelled them to come under the influence of the civilized society. It seems that the tribal culture had shrunk within the threshold of their homes and in turn, the emerging new forms of cultural patterns, which have actually been borrowed from the alien cultural groups are taking place even in the cultural life of the Scheduled Ttribal communities of Uttarakhand. Verrier Elwin has rightly said, "Roads are every where urging their way into places which have hitherto been virtually inaccessible. Education, as it spreads, is revolutioning the social and economic conditions of the tribal villages and is creating new demands as it generates new skills.[19]

Thus, in view of the impact of different processes of change, the present study was projected under the following objectives in mind. So that the process of cultural transformation among the scheduled tribal communities in Uttarakhand can be studied and the correlation between the process of cultural transformation and several other processes of cultural change can also be enumerated.

Objectives of the Study

1. To explore and examine the reaction of tribal people for statutory provisions and any other reformatory bodies.
2. To enumerate the correlation between the statutory provisions, reformatory agencies and cultural transformation of

the tribal people of Uttarakhand.

3. To ascertain the criterion of their tribalism as to why they are still remaining in the tribal stage of cultural evolution inspite of being supported by different welfare agencies.

4. To evaluate their present status and conditions in context of the developmental activities and welfare schemes of various agencies and thus to assess the actual stage of their cultural development.

5. To analyse the old customary mode of living and the status and role of traditional tribal organizations such as tribal council and dormitory system in the present day context.

6. To gather the opinions of the tribal people whether they want to retain the tribal existence like other minorities side by side with the majority of Hindus.

7. To measure the desires for absorption of tribal people in the majority and dominant Hindu society.

8. Whether they want to seek the dominance in one way or the other by going beyond the principle of equality.

9. To measure the degree of the abandonment of unclean non-Hindu habits, non-Hindu deities and instead of it the degree of adoption of Hindu habits, Hindu deities and the methods of Hindu rites.

10. To understand the degree of the abandonment of all the major elements of tribal social customs and the traits of pre-Sanskritized stage and instead of it the adoption of great Hindu traditions.

11. To describe the nature of the commensal and connubial relations and to assess their attachment with an Aryan and non-Aryan language.

12. To examine the tribal situation in the context of the very basic concept of tribe and to know if the tribal people of Uttarakhand want to remain in that very tribal status or desire for any change or up-gradation to Hindu caste hierarchy.

13. Whether the tribal people of Uttarakhand share the culture and language of the respective regions they live in.

14. To trace out the forces which have compelled the tribals to come under the influence of the civilised societies and also to point out the forms of their cultural contacts with non-tribal groups.

15. To assess the role of the different planned processes of change in the cultural transformation of tribal people in Uttarakhand.

Ecology of the Region: An Overview

Alongwith the Northern part of Uttar Pradesh in India the region of Uttarakhand is situated. It is predominantly a hilly and border region of India, the main land of which is formed by the rugged mountainous terrain of Himalayas covered with dense forests and shrubs, while the southern part of the region is constituted by the plain belt of Tarai and Bhabhar which has been stretched from the western-most part to the eastern-most part alongwith the foothills of the region.

Geographically, the region of Uttarakhand is located between the latitude of 28°-51′and 31°-9′ North and longitude 78°-0′ and 81°-31′ east. Topographically, the whole of the region can be divided into three parts : first; greater Himalaya, second; lower Himalaya and the third; Sub-Himalaya. The major part of the region is uneven in altitude and inaccessible and abstruse. The height of the different parts of the region ranges from 300 meters to 7800 meters from the sea level. Except some of the valleys and the Tarai and Bhabhar's plain belt of Dehradun and Nainital district, the whole of the region is full of varieties of land structures and flora and fauna. The region comprises eight hill districts namely; Almora, Nainital, Pithoragarh, Chamoli, Pauri, Tehri, Uttarkashi and Deharadun. The former three districts form the Kumaun Commissionery while the rest five districts constitute the Garhwal Commissionery. The region has an area of 51122 sq. kms., with 48.37 lakhs population out of which the Scheduled Tribal population is 173609. Thus, Scheduled Tribal population of the region constitute 3.59% of the total population. The district wise area and the breakup of the population has been given in the following table:

Table 2

District wise Breakup of the Area and the Population of Uttarakhand

Name of Commission-ery	*Name of District*	*Area Sq. Km.*	*Total Population*	*Scheduled Tribal Population*
Kumaun	Almora	7023.00	757373	1452.00
	Nainital	6792.00	1136523	69667.00
	Pithoragarh	7217.00	489267	14531.00
	Total	21032.00	2383163	85650.00
Garhwal	Chamoli	9125.00	364346	9164.00
	Pauri	5440.00	638000	893.00
	Tehri	4421.00	498000	—
	Uttarkashi	8016.00	190948	1817.00
	Dehradun	3088.00	761668	76085.00
	Total	30090.00	2452962	87959.00
Grand Total		51122.00	4836125	173609.00

Uttarakhand is situated on the fringe of the two political communities i.e., Nepal and Tibet in east and north respectively. The eastern-most district of the region i.e. Pithoragarh makes the international boundary with Nepal in east, while the western core of the region is demarcated by Himachal Pradesh. The western most districts of the region i.e. Uttarkashi and Dehradun contiguously form the inter-state boundary with Himachal Pradesh. The northern part of the region forms the international boundary with Tibet (China) which is demarcated contiguously by the northern parts of the Uttarkashi, Chamoli and Pithoragarh districts, while the southern boundary of the region has been constituted by the district boundaries of Saharanpur, Bijnor, Moradabad, Rampur, Bareilly and Pilibhit. The picturesque region of Uttarakhand is famous for its natural beauties of tourist spots, sacred rivers, lakes and snow covered mountain peaks on the one hand and the diversified cultural complexes of various ethnic groups which have been rearing and caring in the varieties of geographical cradles of the region, on the other.

Climate of the Region

Because of the topographical differences, the climate of Uttarakhand differs vastly from one region to another. The extreme northern mountain peaks of the region are always covered with snow and the temperature always remains below the freezing point. Normally, there is heavy rain fall on the hill slopes of the region which stands approximately to 300 cm annualy. In several parts of the region there is snowfall alongwith the falling of hail, which of course stand for a long duration particularly in high altitudes and forest areas and short duration in domiciled areas. But the Tarai-Bhabhar belt of the region is quite different from the hill region in climate. The summer is extremely hot but it is very cold in winter. The annual rainfall in this region ranges between 152 cm. to 229 cms.

Flora and Fauna

The land structure and soil make-up of Uttarakhand differs from region to region resultantly the flora and fauna also vary from one region to another. The high snowy peaks of the region have a dark black soil which is always covered with snow and therefore no vegetation can grow in these areas. There we see the snow fox, snow bear and many other species of deers in majority which are to be observed litting up the snow and the small shrubs grown out of the land during summer when the snow begins to melt. But on the slopes of the hill region the dense forests of pine, teak (sagaun), sal and the varieties of herbs and vegetables can be observed in lower Himalaya. A number of species of wild animals are found in the forest areas of the region. The important wild animals to be found in this region are tigers, elephants, chitals, nilgai, monkeys, apes, foxes, wolves, wild dogs etc. and the varieties of birds like peacock, parrots, hoopes, hawks, eagles, partridges, and red legged partridges are also found in the dense forests of the region.

Thus, the region contains a diverseful ecological features with the varieties of geographical conditions and a number of ethnic groups domiciled with their peculiar cultural traits in the different parts of the region, which form a beautiful aromatic bouquet, the aroma of which can be felt through the cultural activities, life style and many other ways of social-cultural life presented on different occasions by them. In fact, the people from different caste, creeds, class and race form the distinct cultural complex of the region and the tribal culture is one of the manifestations of its distinctiveness.

An Over-view of the Ethnographic Traits of the Scheduled Tribal Communities of Uttarakhand

The Scheduled Tribal Communities of Uttarakhand belong to the sub-Himalayan region of the North and North-West India. The ethnographic notes of various eminent scholars depict that the Mongoloid racial characteristics are very common among the Bhotiyas, Buxas, Tharus and Rajis while the Khasas or the Jaunsaris belong to the Mediterranean racial stock. An overview of the ethnographic traits of the tribal communities under reference are essentially important so that they may be looked upon in their racial and historical perspectives.

The Khasas

In fact, the Sub-Himalayan region from western Kashmir to eastern Nepal has largely been inhabited by a number of ethnic groups, but almost all the groups are referred to by the generic term, 'Paharhi' i.e. the 'Hill-people'. Khasa, an Indo-Aryan speaking group is one of those ethnic groups which is generally believed to have contributed to the present 'Paharhi' population. Khasas are very ancient people. A reference to the Khasas is found in the Vishnu-Puran. In the Karan Parva of the Mahabharata, the Khasas are referred to as the inhabitants of the Punjab.[20] Sanskrit literature contains frequent references to a tribe whose name is usually spelt 'Khasa' with variants such as 'Khasa', Khasha and Khasia.[21]

Majumdar[22] says that despite some intermixture with Mongoloids of the Upper-Himalayas or with the 'Doms' of the lower region, the Khasas are clearly distinguishable from the Proto-Australoid or Mongoloids, who form the bulk of the tribal peoples. He talks about their (Khasas) true Mediterranean 'features'. Grierson[23] has stated that Khasa were one of the tribes who lived in the extreme North-West of India on the Hindukush, the mountainous tracts to the South and in the Western Punjab. They were, however, considered to have lost their claims as 'Aryans' and to have become 'Malechchhas' or barbarians, owing to their non-observance of the rules for eating and drinking observed by the Sanskritic peoples of India. R.N. Saxena[24] has also stated that, "It is possible that there were many waves of Aryan settlers which preceded the Vedic Aryans and one of them, a warrior group, settled in the mountainous tracts adjoining the Hindukush and later moved along the southern slopes of the Himalayas, but did not fully adopt the Vedic cult. But their close contact with the Aryan Kshatriyas was never lost. And it is this close affiliation that provided the latter an asylum during the dark middle period of Indian history, when they had to suffer great privations and persecution at the hands of Muslim rulers. Atkinson[25] writes, "Jaunsar-Bawar" a representative Khasiya tract forms a very important link between the almost Hinduised Khasiyas of Kumaun and their brethren converts to Islam on the ethnic frontier in the mountains of the Hindukush, and apparently gives customs and practices of the Khasiya race in full force at the present day which distinguished them a thousand years ago."Thus, the Khasas which include Brahman and Rajputs are basically of the Aryan origin,which later on converted into 'Malechchhas' due to the non-observance of the Aryan cultural traits.

Besides this, "the Khasa community associates itself with Pandavas of 'Mahabharata'. In the 'Mahabharata' the Khasas are expressly mentioned amongst the northern tribes who brought presents for Yudhisthira."[26] The Mahabharata credits them with great courage and calls them unyielding and obstinate in battle.[27] They are included among those who bring presents to King Yudhishtira on the occasion of his "Rajsuya" sacrifice.[28] The Drona Parva describes them as "arrivals from diverse realms".[29] 'Karna' castigates them for their unorthodox immorality together with the Bahlikas, Mudras and Gandharvas.[30] Briffault [31] remarks that the

Khasas hold festivals in honour of the Pandavas, who are their favourite deities. Many important spots in Jaunsar Bawar are supposed to have associations with the Pandavas. They have temples dedicated to the Pandavas, called Pandavon-ki-Chauri. The courtyard of the temple is called Pandavon-ka-Angana. The central feature of their festivals is the Pandav dance. It has been suggested that 'Satsrings' of the Mahabharata, where Pandu lived in retirement, according to the story, was around the same region. Whatever their origin, it is evident that the Khasas have been in the sub-Himalayan hills for a long time. At present this community dwells in the Jaunsar-Bawar area of the Chakarata and Kalsi blocks of Dehradun district of Uttarakhand. The Khasas, as Majumdar [32] notes, constitute the high caste people of the cis-Himalayan region are either Rajput or Brahmin. But here it is worth noting that 'Khasas' are meant by the scheduled tribal people confined in the Jaunsar-Bawar area of Dehradun district, after which a generic term 'Jaunsaris' is used to denote this territorial group of people.

Virtually, Khasas or the Jaunsaris are well known for their customs, costumes and particularistic socio-cultural values. The social organization of Jaunsaris, as has been noted by Mukherjee (1947), is based on caste hierarchy. Different Hindu castes, namely: Brahman, Rajput, Baddi, Bajki, Nai, Deov, Lohar, Sonar, Kolta and Nat are there. Clear organisation is not at all elaborated and effective, but village exogamy is. Inter-caste marriages and hypergamous and hypogamous unions do take place. Exclusive polyandry has been modified to some extent and bi-polyandry, polygyny and monogamy are practised. Decent, succession, inheritance and residence are reckoned in the male line. Family structure is basically polyandrous. The eldest male member is the authority in the family.[33] Today the Khasas universally define themselves as Hindus who are in some respects culturally distinct from others on their religion and castes.[34] Their unorthodox practice of Hinduism is well known and long recognized. Manu looking at the Khasas from Brahmanical point of view, says that Khasas are the offspring of out-caste Kshatriya and again he says that Khasas are those who became out-caste through having neglected their religious duties.[35] Atkinson has looked on the Khasas as heretical members of great Aryan family than as out-caste and aborigins.[36]

Thus, it may be concluded that 'Khasas' had been affined

with the Aryan origin, who with the passage of time neglected their Aryan character and turned into the heretical and barbarian group with some unorthodox practices of Hinduism.

Bhotiyas

"When we pass to north of the great snowy peaks we get among a different people, the Bhotiyas. 'Bod' the native name for Tibet, corrupted by the people of India into 'Bhot', has given rise to the name 'Bhotiya' for the border tribes between the two countries".[37] Basically, the term 'Bhotiya' indicates to a territorial group dwelling in the 'Bhot' tract. The earliest scholars viz; Shering (1906), Smyth (1930), S.D. Pant (1935) etc. agreed that, "If a straight line is drawn between Askot and Kapkot, the area to the north of this line will constitute the region locally known as the 'Bhot' or the Bhotiya tract which is entirely distinct from the remaining South-Eastern portion of the rest. But this delineation excludes the Mana and Niti groups." In fact, " the term 'Bhotiya' stands for a generic term of several distinct ethnic groups, which share many features in common at the same time each group also exhibits certain sets of distinctive features which may be unique for one or more groups but not shared by the rest."[38] That Bhotiyas themselves are of Tibetan origin is sufficiently shown by the language that they speak, by their Mongolian cast of countenance and those unmistakable peculiarities that belong to the Tibetan race and which are as well marked in them as in the Huniyas themselves.[39] But today, Bhotiyas are least inclined to admit this generic term, Bhotiya as well as their assignment with 'Huniyas', the inhabitants of 'Hundes', the adjacent province of Tibet. Despite it they prefer to be called as 'Sakas'. Atkinson states, "In the traditional account of the colonisation of the Bhotiya Valley ....they disclose themselves as the offsprings of a Rajput, immigration from beyond the snows that succeeded a Soka colony, but they are usually called 'Sokas' themselves".[40] William Crook is also of the same opinion when he remarks, "They (Bhotiyas) usually call themselves Raghubansi Rajputs, and trace their origin to Bhutwal in Nepal. They fix their immigration into Northern Oudh in the region of Nawab Asaf-Uddalua (1775-1797). They now present a curious instance of non-Aryan origin who are now in a short time completely Brahmins."[41]

For a long time Bhotiyas of Uttarakhand have been habitating in seven river valleys after which they have derived their name, viz., Joharis, Darmisa, Vyansis, Chaundasis (in Kumaun), Marchhas, Tolchhas and Joda (in Garhwal). But some scholars are of the opinion that the 'Bhotiyas' of the different valleys are not of the common origin. As Chaterjee has stated that, "........ the fact appears to have been recognised that the Bhotiyas of all the seven valleys have no common origin. That there has been a lot of admixture of different ethnic strains in the past, has also been recognised by most authors..... There are Aryans, Scythians or Shakas, Tibeto-mongols, Nepali and Gorkhalis."[42] According to Ram Rahul, "...... the Jods (the Bhotiyas of Uttarkashi) claim to have come from Kinnaur in Himachal Pradesh. The eastern Bhotiyas used the term "Shokas" to indicate their origin—its phonetic similarity with 'Shakas' (the Scythians a branch of Nordic Aryans) is generally underlined."[43] Thus, it may be concluded that there are different views regarding to the origin of Bhotiyas. It is, however, irrefutable that the Bhotiyas are of the Mongolian origin and belong to the Sino-Tibetan language family. The physical appearance and the dialect they speak, evidently show their racial resemblance with Tibetans, a most representative group of the Mongolian stock in Northern India. Besides this, it is equally true that the adjoining provinces of the Southern Tibet, termed as Bhotanchal and its river valleys have been inhabited by the Bhotiyas, who were attributed a particular nickname after the locality or the valley they live in. Hence, it appears merely a derivation to affine the Bhotiyas of different valleys to the different origins. In fact, the variation of locality and the contact group and its impact would be supposed to develop the varied cultural traits among the respective community which may not be taken into account as the evidence of the racial affinity because the racial traits can only be looked on the physical characteristics of the people. As Majumdar has also stated, "if the people of one race can be distinguished by physical markings, then they constitute a race."[44]

In this way the Bhotiyas, apart from their distinguished racial features, are also looked upon their peculiar socio-cultural system which chiefly consists of the institutions, beliefs, practices, customs, traditions as well as the costumes, means of subsistence, economy and their trans-humance nature. Today, the two phases of the Bhotiya community can be observed: one in the form of traditionality which still exists, without any sophistication within the peripheries of their traditional habitations and the other in the form of modernity, which implied among those people who have come out of their original settlements and engaged in some sort of modern or the non traditional occupations with the non-tribal group in urban or city areas. Consequently, the 'Bhotiya' culture appears to be oscillating in between the tradition and modernity since, a newly emergent group of Bhotiya population, lagging behind in its traditional life style and anxiously looking forward to a clue to be absorbed into the Hindu caste hierarchy while a considerable numbers of the Bhotiya population are still orthodox.

Rajis or the "Ban-Rauts"

In addition to the tribal communities of the sub-Himalayan region, there are Rajis or Rajyas, the modern representatives of the 'Rajy-Kirat.'[45] Rajis, the generic term 'Ban-Raut' is used to denote them are the descents of prehistoric Kiratas, who were comparatively the early settlers of 'Uttaranchal' than the Khasas, Nagas, Aryas and the Tibetans. As stated by Atkinson, ".... there is every reason to suppose that the Nagas, Kiratas and Khasas entered India by the same route as the Aryans and that the Kiratas were the first to arrive than the Khasas and Nagas".[46] Referring to Varaha Samhita, Atkinson further states that, " the Rajya-Kiratas was spread over Amarvans and China or between Jageswar and Tibet.[47] But by the invasion of different ethnic groups the Kiratas gradually vanished from Uttaranchal and their descents remained in Kumaun and Nepal. In Kumaun the descents of Kiratas were called Rajis. But Rajis are not aware with their pre-historic Kirati origin, hence they claim to be descendants of one of the princes of Askot". According to Mr. Traill, the then Commissioner of Kumaun," ...... Rajis represent themselves as descendants of one of the aboriginal princes of Kumaun who with his family fled to the jungle to escape the destruction threatened by an userper......[48] William Crooke has affined them with the non-Aryan affinities.[49] And Atkinson has found the racial mixture of Tibetans and Khasas in their physical features[50] while D.N. Majumdar has related them with Mongolian affinity. Besides this, Dr. Pritchard conjectured that the Rajis would be found to resemble the other numerous aboriginal tribes found along the Himalayan borders, all possessing the physical character of the Bhotiyas in general and very unlike to Domes".[51]

Apart from the numerous scholarly references of the different scholars, a number of legends connote the affinity of Rajis with an ancient king of Askot. But the views of different scholars about the origin of Rajis are not more than the conjectures or surmises which have been expressed merely on the basis of imaginations. For, there is no any particular authentic written records, inscriptions, plates or relics regarding to the origin of Rajis. Though the existence of Raj Kiratas has been referred in Purans, yet no clue of the Kirates origin of Rajis are available any where. Even the countenance and the physical traits in common do not present any clue to look upon their racial affinity. Today, no Mongolian traits can be observed in the physical appearance of Rajis as the earlier scholars Dr. Pritchard and Majumdar had observed. Today by physical appearance and caste countenance Rajis are almost wheatish coloured complexion, are of average height, have straight and scanty hair which are slight brownish in colour, intermidiate headed type with medium nose, round to long face with half or there about ears and small eyes with grey pigment. Thus, Rajis are very much alike of the low Hindu caste of countenance and unlike to that of Bhotiyas. It appears, that the medley of different ethnic elements for ages has caused the disappearance of the original racial elements among Rajis.

Thus it may be concluded that the social scientists are different of opinions about the racial strain of Rajis. It is however incontestable that they, at present, exhibit a mixed racial traits of Aryo-Dravidians and Mongoloids in common.

Socially, Raji or the 'Ban Raut' is one of the most backward tribes, therefore the Government of U.P. has recognised it as the primitive tribal group in 1965. Raji is numerically a small and little known tribal community confined in the forest and hilly areas of Dharchula and Didihat and Champawat Tehsils of Pithoragarh district in Kumaun region. "They call themselves Hindus by religion. They worship Devi...... when any one gets ill, they worship the gods, ghosts and demons of the jungle, but they erect no temples in their honour."[52] According to Atkinson, "The Rajis themselves are of Hindu origin .... The Rajis are said to have their own peculiar Gods, but they also worship those of the Hindus and like the people of Kumaun and indeed of the entire Himalaya, attribute great power to the local deities, spirits, goblins and defined men."[53] According to Crooke,[54] Rajis observe only three rituals pertaining to birth, betrothal and death. The whole of the Raji community has been divided into five Dharas'.[55] A 'Dhara' is an exogamous group which bears the nature of the 'Caste', yet no where is the basis of social stratification. Majumdar states that, "They are divided into exogamous clans and are monogamous." In regard of the economic aspects of Rajis, Atkinson remarks that, "They manufacture wooden bowls for sale and live under huts frequently moving from place to place amidst the jungle. Their principal subsistence being certain edible roots of wild plants and what game they can catch and they occasionally get present of cooked food from the villages."[56] According to William Crooke, "They live almost altogether on the produce of their jungles and their only industry is that of making rude wooden bowls, which they barter with the people of the plains for scraps of coarse clothe and grain".[57] Majumdar has also presented the same views. In his own words, "They are a nomadic people, moving about in search of jungles to clear and virgin soils in which to sow seeds... They also manufacture crude wooden vessels which they exchange with neighbouring people for coarse cloth and grain..... They are known locally as invisible traders."[58]

It may therefore be concluded on the basis of the scholarly notes of some prominent scholars, that about fifty years back Rajis were in the stage of nomadism. They were the food gatherers having not any permanent settlement or residence. They subsisted on the jungle produce. Socially they were isolated from the rest of the non-tribal society. They were far away from literacy and the means of communication and transportation and therefore deprived from all sorts of inter and intra-tribal relations. They had their own peculiar traditions which were quite distinct from the neighbouring Kumaun Hindus and the Bhotiyas. But in the present day context the socio-cultural systems of Raji community has undergone numerous changes. Now they have got their permanent settlement of residence. They are ekeing out their maintenance with crude cultivation, jungle produce and as agricultural labourers. Now they are aware of their tribalism and realize the importance of education, means of transportation and communication for the over all development of their community. The social contacts with out groups have also brought about some structural and organizational changes in their community. It appears that the natural process of change has ultimately overcome the prolonged traditional lethargy of Rajis by dropping a particle of change. Now they have woken-up and anxiously, by rubbing the eyes, trying to join the flowing stream of change and development. Yet they are not in the position of lagging behind their traditional position in full. The forthcoming interpretation of the research based information of the present study would enumerate the process of cultural transformation among Rajis.

Tharus

"In the country lying along the foot of the Kumaun hills from the Kosi eastward we have a tribe known as 'Tharus' which may be traced farther east to the Bagmati river. They are dwellers in swamps, and great rice cultivators and are proof against malaria."[59]

The generic term, 'Tharhuwa' and the 'Tharhuwat' are used respectively to denote the 'Tharus' and their place of habitation. In this way the major part of Nainital Tarai particularly, the Khatima and Sitarganj block area have largely been noticed as the 'Tharhuwat' for the native place of Tharus. The 'Tarai' belt stretches from Nainital in west to Gorakhpur in east and has largely been inhabited by the Tharus. But the Nainital Tarai has been the largest concentration of Tharu population. The scholars are not of the consensus of the opinion about the origin of the Tharus. Majumdar states that, "The Tharu claim Rajput origin on the mother's side and Bhil on the father's; but the Mongoloid features are definite among them and even the skin colour is yellow brown and oblique eyes are numerous."[60] According to a legend 'Tharus' are of the Rajput origin related to the Sisodiya akin of Rana Pratap in Chittaurh. But Majumdar[61] has proved through the racial and serological survey, that there are no traces as to affine the Tharus with Sisodiya Rajputs of Chittaurh. While Crooke has looked upon Tharus, a mixed tribe with some Mongolian and some Dravidian blood, who occupy the malarious Tarai at the foot of the lower Himalayas.[62] Thus, the available references showed the inconsistency of the findings drawn by the different scholars regarding to the origin and the racial affinity of Tharus. The prevalent legends are nothing more than the conjectures concocted by the tribal people themselves. In spite of what have been referred by different scholars, the physical appearance of Tharus, even today utter itself their Mongolian strains. They have got the medium height, round face with yellow-brown complexion, medium to short nose, oblique or slant eyes and straight hair. Thus, there are every possible traces of countenance and physical features as to look upon the Tharus of Mongolian origin.

At present the Tharus under study, have been divided into seven endogamous groups viz., Ranas, Bukhusas, Garhaurha Dhannara, Khunka, Jugiya and Saunra. In a hierarchical order the 'Ranas' are the superior one and have the majority of population, while the Bukhasas, Garhaurha, Dhannara, Khunka, Jugiya and Saunra constitute respectively the second, third, fourth, fifth, sixth and seventh strata of the 'Tharu' community. Almost all the sects of the Tharus claim the Rajput origin and like the Hindu Kshatriyas they also affix the surname 'Singh' and the sect with their name. S.K. Srivastava[63] has termed it as the process of Kshatriyakaran. Tharu is the monogamous tribal community, who follow the rules of patriarchy for lineage and patrilocal to live after marriage. Traditionally, there was joint family system which has now has changed in to nuclear family. The women-folk is a privileged class among Tharus. The women possesses the prestigious position in the community and manage almost all the socio-economic matters of family life. Tharus call themselves Hindu by religion and celebrate the festival of Holi, Diwali and Teej along with their distinguished customary tribal festivals like Charai etc. They observe only two life cycle rituals i.e. the marriage and the death. Yet some educated Tharus have started to celebrate the 'Naming and Chhati' ceremonies. An average Tharu man and woman is very much fond of meat and drink. They all are nonvegetarian. However, it has been observed that a new 'Panth' or the 'religious sect' i.e. 'Radha Swami' has utterly changed the traditional social organization and its values. The Tharu people' who have adopted the Radha Swami sect do not practise any traditional ethos, neither they call themselves Hindus nor they worship the deity named, 'Bhumsen' the ancient 'God' of Tharuwat. The 'Tharus', adhering Radha Swami sect are pure vegetarian. They have least participation with the traditional Tharus particularly when the male and female of the later group eat, drink and make merry by dancing and singing jointly on the occasion of different festivals in general and the 'Holi' in particular. Even the 'Tharus' under the influence of the Radha Swami sect have started to abstain the traditional 'Salutation', rather they utter the venerable term 'Radha Swami' with folded hands as a mark of respect. It appears the 'Radha Swami' sect has been playing a vital role to determine the socio-economic and cultural patterns of Tharus. But the percentage of the Tharu followers of Radha Swami sect is very nominal. Yet, it is a status group psychologically motivating the majority of Tharus to follow the ethical values of the sect.

Besides this, Tharus of today are in frequent contact with out-groups. They are availing the facilities of communication and transportation. Occupationally, they are mobilized to the non-traditional occupations. The literacy percentage among Tharus (man and woman) is increasing day by day. They may be seen as a labourer, as an artisan and as the Government personnels. At present a wave of change can apparently be viewed in every aspects of the tribal community.

Bhukhasa or the Buxas

"The Bhukasas, a tribe some what similar to the Tharus are found in the Tarai and Bhabar from the Pilibhit district on the east to Chandpur on the Ganges on the west and few scattered colonies also occur in Deharadun."[64] At present the total population of Buxas is 34345 out of which only 31037 is spread in Dehradun, Paurhi Garhwal and Nainital, the hill districts of Uttarakhand and the rest 3308 population live in Bijnor. Alike of the other tribal communities under reference, the origin of the Buxa community is based on some legends concocted by different people in different manners. Even the etymon of the name Bhukasas or Buxas leads to a number of stories as to prove the exactness of the appelation used for this tribal community. For instance, some Buxas of Bijnor are of the opinion that their ancestors had the long beard quite resembling the 'Bok', a 'he-goat' found in the adjoining hill provinces of their settlement and thus called the Bokasas or Buxas or Bhuksas.

While some Buxas relate the etymon of their name with the English word 'bogus'. Amir Hasan has stated that," ...... the word Buxa is a corrupted form of the Persian word 'eksa' which means uniform. Such a name might have been given by the Mughals, who were struck by the fact that as unlike most of other Indian communities, this tribe had no caste or sub-caste differences among its members."[65] But the etymological explanation of the name Bhukasas or the Buxas is not more than a surmise presented as a derivation by the Buxas' themselves and the scholars in general.

The etymological explanation of the appelation Bhukasas or the Buxas can not be considered as such. It is rather a corrupted form of the Hindi term. "Sarva-Bhaksi" or the "Bhakosane Wala" means the 'omnivorous' as has been supported by a number of aged Buxa people of the Nainital Tarai, who as early as their settlement in the Tarai used to devour every thing to keep their body and soul together and thus called to be a 'Bhaksi' and gradually as 'Bhukasa' by the neighbouring communities. With the passage of time this nomadic community had also adhered the appelation 'Bhukasa' under the pretension of their Rajput origin.

The available references, in regard of the origin of the 'Bhuksas' have referred to an irrefutable contradiction and thus made it too vague to look on the Bhuksa community in its original convas. In the district gazetteer of Nainital we look upon the Bhukasas and their neighbourers *i.e.* the Tharus, as the kindred races. Both of them claim royal blood from the female side. While Henry Eliot has said, "They claim to be Panwar Rajputs and assert that their chief Udyajit, was driven from home because of a quarrel that he had with his brother Jagat Deo, the Raja of Dharanagar. Udayjit had come with a few dependants at Banbasa on the Sarda. Udayjit had not been there long, before his aid was solicited by the Raja of Kumaun whose territories required defence against some of the neighbouring powers. Success attended the efforts of the Panwar and the gratitude of the Raja induced him to offer his defenders an asylum in his territories. Upon this, they left Banbasa and have taken up their residence in their present abodes.[66]

Thus some Buxas, even today claim that they belong to Panwar clan of Dhara nagar. In this regard another story goes to prove that 'Bhuksas' had a descent from Raja Jagat Deo, a great warrior of Rajasthan. According to Crooke, Jagat Deo was a worshipper of Goddess Durga and offered his head to her. The Buxas claim to have brought the deity Durga (now known as Kashipur Devi) to Tarai. The 'Narial' (Palmnut) was offered to the deity as symbolic of his head. Some Bhuksas say that Raja Jagat Deo had two sons, Chittaur and Nandhaur, while Tharus are the descendants of the former Bhuksas are stated to have descended from the latter.[67] Crooke further mentions that, many Bhuksas say that they came from the Dakkhin, others from Delhi, but they were expelled from the Dakkhin by the Marathas.[68] Thus, it is observed that the historical facts presented by earlier scholars depict a frequent contradiction in regard of the origin of the Bhukasas. In fact, the Bhukasas are not of the Rajput origin but the absence of any historical clue has resulted in a number of legends to prove their Rajput ancestry. Even today the aged Bhukasas admit that at the time of their migration to Tarai and Bhabar area, everyone was not the descendant of the Rajput, for there were the people belonging to different castes who managed into one community due to some adverse geo-social circumstances and dispensed all the previous caste and class barriers which later on emerged as the Bhuksa community.

It is however, more authentic to mention that the so called Bhukasas are of the non-Aryan family, who at the end of their nomadism got settled in the isolated and quitely uninhabited provinces of Tarai-Bhabar of Nainital and Dehradun districts. And with the passage of time the medley of different ethnic groups in Uttaranchal and the frequent contact of Hindus have inspired them to concocted the legends as to prove their ancestry with Rajput origin, so that they may have a social position in the broad spectrum of Hindu caste hierarchy. This fact is self evident by the countenance, physical traits of the Bhukasas and the mores, beliefs and rituals they observe since long.

By appearance an average Bhukasa possesses an average height with stout built. Both the male and female are of wheatish or dark complexion with broad face, oblique eyes, flat nose, thick lips and black hair. The beard and the moustaches of a Bhukasa is very scanty. Such a countenance and the physique eventually pave no clue of the particular racial origin of Bhukasas. It is rather a canvas of a mixed racial traits which came into existence as an outcome of the mixture of different racial elements occurred due to the enterance of the different ethnic groups in Uttaranchal during remote past. However, some prominent anthropologists have affined them with Mongolian racial stock.

Apart from the racial origin, the Bhukasas at present have more resemblances with the low caste Hindus particularly in their habits and customs. They also claim to be Hindus by religion and have had a number of castes and sub-castes groups, like Hindus, in ancient time, who under some special circumstances merged into one single casteless class. Amir Hasan has also stated that, "The Bhukasas are one of the most Hinduised tribes of India. They themselves claim to be Hindus and to prove that they are authentic Hindus, they point out that they originally belonged to various Hindu castes and sub-castes from Kshatriyas to Sudras, who decided to merge into one class under the special circumstances in the hoary past."[69] At present the whole of the Bhukasa community has been divided into a number of exogamous 'Gotras' or 'Kheras'. Almost all the 'Gotras' are identical with Hindu sub-castes and theoretically stratified into two major groupings. The 'Gotras', associated with 'Kshatriya' or higher Hindu caste origin do have a feeling of superiority; while the 'Gotras' synonymic to low caste Hindus are looked on as inferior. However, almost all the 'Gotras' are equal and do not observe any bar or social taboos in the determination of the connubial and commensal relations. At present the Bhukasas on the one hand, observe some Hindu beliefs, worship Hindu Gods, speak broken Hindi language with some admixture of Kumauni and Garhwali dialect, on the other hand they still observe their traditional customs, speak their own dialect, adhere the concept of animism and follow their traditional way of life. Thus, it may be concluded that Bhukasas have hitherto been adhering their tribal character in its original form side by side of the adoption of the Hindu way of life and some cultural patterns of modern society. However, the most striking fact which came into light during my investigation was that the Bhukasas have comparatively more emotional attachment with their own traditional cultural patterns to whom they not only follow with great enthusiasm and reverence but also wish to preserve and transmit to the coming generations. While the Hindu style of life and the religious practices are observed in a partial and superficial manner only by nodding acquaintance of the neighbouring Hindus as to show their pseudo canvas of Hinduism.

References

1. Bodley, John H., Victims of Progress, California, The Benjamin Cumings Publishing Company, 1982.

2. Majumdar, D.N., An Introduction to Social Anthropology, Asia Publishing House, Bombay, 1963, p. 253.

3. Burman, B.K. Roy, Tribal Demography, in, Tribal Situation in India, ed. by K. Suresh Singh, Indian Institute of Advanced Study, Simla-5, 1972.

4. Guha. B.S., Racial Elements in Indian Population, Oxford Pamphlet on Indian Affairs, Oxford University Press, Bombay, 1944.

5. Dube, S.C., Manava Aur Sanskriti, Raj Kamal Prakashan, Delhi.

6. Majumdar, D.N., An Introduction to Social Anthropology, Asia Publishing House, Bombay, pp. 255-256.

7. *Ibid.*, p. 256.

8. *Ibid.*, p. 257.

9. Risely, H.H., People of India (1915).

10. Haddon, A.C., The Wandering of Peoples 1919, Quoted by D.N. Majumdar and T.N. Madan, in Social Anthropology, Asia Publishing House, Bombay, 1963, pp. 257-258.

11. Guha, B.S., Racial Elements in Indian Population, Oxford Pamphlet on Indian Affairs, No. 22, Oxford University Press, Bombay, 1955.

12. *Ibid.*

13. Elwin, Varrier., Quoted by D.N. Majumdar and T.N. Madan in Social Anthropology, Asia Publishing House, Bombay, 1963, p. 263.

14. Majumdar, D.N. and T.N. Madan, Social Anthropology, Asia Publishing House, Bombay, 1963, pp. 265-266.

15. *Ibid.*, pp. 267-268.

16. Thurnwald R., Nomads, Encyclopaedia of Social Sciences, 1933.

17. Majumdar, D.N., Races and Cultures of India, p. 138.

18. Census-1981.

19. Elwin Varrier, quoted by Nadeem, Hasnain, in Tribal India Today, Harnam Publications, New Delhi, 1983, p. 6

20. Majumdar, D.N., Races and Cultures of India, Asia Publishing House, Bombay, 1955, p. 154.

21. Grierson, George A., Linguistic Survey of India, Vol. IX, Part IV Calcutta Superintendent of Govt. Printing 1966, p. 373.

22. Majumdar, D.N., Some Aspects of the Cultural Life of the Cis-Himalayan

Region, Journal and Proceeding of the Royal Asiatic Society of Bengal IIIrd Series, Vol. VI, 1940.

23. Grierson, George., A Linguistic Survey of India, Vol. IX, Part IV, Calcutta Superintendent of Govt. Printing, 1916, p. 373.
24. Saxena, R.N., Social Economy of Polyandrous People, Agra University Stud ies Series No. 1, Agra, 1956, p. 12.
25. Atkinson, E.T., Gazetteer of Himalayan Districts of the North Western Provinces, Vol. II, p. 353.
26. Majumdar, D.N., Races and Cultures of India, Asia Publishing House, Bombay, 1955, p. 155.
27. Mahabharata, VII, 20. 10-11, Calcutta.
28. *Ibid.*, II, 48, 3-5, Critical Edu.
29. *Ibid.*, VII, 11, 17-18, Calcutta Edn; VII, 18, n.18 on p. 59 Critical Edn.
30. *Ibid.*, VIII, 44-45, Calcutta Edn. VII, 30-47, n.47 on pp. 264-265 the Critical Edn.
31. Briffault, R., The Mothers, I Vol., London, 1927, p. 671.
32. Majumdar, D.N., The Fortunes of the Primitive Tribes, Lucknow; Universal Publishers, 1944, p. 110.
33. Mukherjee, P., Comparative Study of the Kinship System of Two Polyandrous Communities in Eastern Anthropologist, Vol. V-16, No. 2, 1963, p. 75.
34. Berreman, Gerald D., Hindus of the Himalayas, University of California Press 1972, p. 19.
35. Grierson, George, A., Linguistic Survey of India, Vol. IX, Part IV, Calcutta Superintendent of Govt. Printing, 1916, p. 5.
36. Atkinson, E.T., The Himalayan Districts of the North-Eastern Provinces of India, Vol. II, North Western Provinces and Oudh Press, Allahabad 1884, p. 283.
37. Atkinson, E.T., Himalayan Gazetteer, Vol. II Part I, Cosmo Publications 1882, p. 366.
38. Chatterjee, B.B., Bhotiyas of Indo-Tibetan Border of Uttarakhand, Typed project Report, 1975, p. 138.
39. Atkinson, E.T., Himalayan Gazetteer, Vol. I Part II, Cosmo Publications 1882, p. 393.
40. *Ibid.*, p. 369.
41. Crooke, William, Tribes and Castes of North-West Provinces and Oudh Region, Vol. II.
42. Ram Rahul, The Himalayan Border Land, Delhi, Vikas Publications 1970, p. 140.

43. *Ibid.*, p. 151.
44. Majumdar, D.N., Races and Cultures of India, Asia Publishing House, Bombay 1958, p. 31.
45. Atkinson, E.T., The Himalayan Gazetteer, Vol. II Pt. I, Cosmo Publications, New Delhi, 1982, p. 365.
46. *Ibid.*, p. 365.
47. *Ibid.*, p. 365.
48. *Ibid.*, p. 366.
49. *Ibid.*, p. 366.
50. *Ibid.*, p. 366.
51. *Ibid.*, p. 366.
52. Crooke, W., Tribes and Castes of the North-West Provinces of Oudh. Vol. II, Calcutta, 1896.
53. Atkinson, E.T., Himalayan Gazetteer, Vol. I Part II Cosmo Publications, 1882, p. 367.
54. Bisht, B.S., Social Structure and Organization of Raji tribe of Kumaun, Typed Research Thesis, Kumaun University Nainital, 1982, p. 85.
55. Majumdar, D.N., Races and Cultures of India, Asia Publishing House, Bombay, 1944, p. 148.
56. Atkinson, E.T., Himalayan Gazetteer, Vol. I, Part II, Cosmo Publications, 1982, p. 366.
57. Crooke, W., Races of Northern India, Cosmo Publications, New Delhi, 1973, p. 119.
58. Majumdar, D.N., Races and Cultures of India, Asia Publishing House, Bombay, 1944, p. 150.
59. Atkinson, E.T., Himalayan Gazetteer, Vol. I Part II, Cosmo Publications, 1982, p. 371.
60. Majumdar, D.N., Races and Cultures of India, Asia Publishing House, Bombay, 1944, p. 70.
61. Majumdar, D.N., The Tharus and their Blood Group, in Journal of Royal Asiatic Society of Bengal, Vol-VIII, Part I, 1942, p. 33.
62. Crooke, William., Races of Northern India, Cosmo Publications, New Delhi 1973, p. 118.
63. Srivastava, S.K., Tharus: A Study in Cultural Dynamics, University Press, 1958.
64. Atkinson, E.T., The Himalayan Gazetteer, Vol. I, Part II, Cosmo Publications, New Delhi, 1882, p. 371.

65. Hasan Amir, The Buxas of the Tarai, B.R. Publishing Corporation, Delhi, 1979, p. 23.

66. Henry Elliott, Referred by, Atkinson in the "Himalayan Gazetteer", Vol. I, Part II, Cosmo Publication, 1982, pp.371-372.

67. Crooke, William., The Tribes and Castes of North West Provinces and Oudh, Vol. II.

68. *Ibid.*

69. Hasan, Amir, The Buxas of the Tarai, B.R. Publishing Corporation, 1970, p. 25.

2

CONCEPTUAL ANALYSIS AND REVIEW OF THE LITERATURE

In order to make the scientific analysis more and more intelligible and in view of the applicability and utility, the conceptual analysis of the concepts used in the present study have scientifically been explained. And to have the expertise on the description and the conclusions drawn through the scientific investigation, the concepts must be looked upon in the name frame of reference as has been explained as follows—

'Tribe' and 'Scheduled-Tribe'

The term 'Tribe' possesses an indispensable position in the wide spectrum of the Indian social organisation. However, the anthropologists, sociologists, social workers and administrators are still not on the same wave length about the definition of the term 'Tribe'. The eminent ethnologists viz.; Risley, Grigson, Shoobert, Tallents, Sedwick, Martin and others have described them as 'aborigines' or 'aboriginals'[1] while Hutton,[2] Verrier Elwin[3] and Bens[4] have called them respectively as the 'Primitive Tribes';

'Original Owners' and 'Jungle People' or 'Forest Tribes' or 'Folk'. G.S. Ghurye has indicated them as the so-called-aboriginals; or the Backward Hindus'.[5] Some other scholars have called them as 'Adivasis'. Arthur Wilke[6] puts the problem in proper perspective by stating that for years ambiguity has stalked Indian official portrait of tribal people. From 1971, for instance, the nomenclature referring to tribes underwent successive modifications, involving primary changes in descriptive adjectives such as "aboriginals' or 'depressed classes'. It is pertinent to note that the different 'designations' or the nomenclatures' used by different scholars to describe the term 'Tribe' bear different meanings based on different criterion which seem to be contradictory from one another. But in its simplest sense, the 'Tribe' is a name referred to the group of people or the collection of families professing the primitive religion known as 'Animism', dwell comparatively in some inaccessible territory, ekeing out their livelihood with some sort of primitive occupations and generally bear a common name and dialect and affined with one another by a common ancestry and yet follow the rules of endogamy.

According to Oxford Dictionary, "A tribe is a group of people in a primitive or barbarous stage of development acknowledging the authority of achief and usually regarding themselves as having a common ancestor.[7] Gillin and Gillin has stated that, "Any collection pre-literate local groups which occupies a common general territory, speaks a common language and practise a common culture is a tribe."[8] Prominent anthropologist D.N. Majumdar has said, "A tribe is a collection of families or group of families bearing a common name, members of which occupy the same territory, speak the same language and observe certain taboos regarding marriage, profession or occupation and have developed a well assessed system of reciprocity and mutuality of obligations."[9] Many other scholars have also defined the term 'tribe' in different manner.

But with the passage of time almost all the definitions regarding to the concept 'Tribe' or 'Tribal Community' have lost their literary meaning and seem to become void and therefore inadequate. The successive modifications of the nomenclature referring to the tribes are cause of the conceptual changes, occurred due to socio-cultural changes among the tribal communities. Hence, 'tribe' or a 'tribal community' may neither be looked upon as the collection of families which have a common name, common dialect, common territory, as has been explained in the Imperial Gazetteer of India nor as an independent political division, as has been observed by Lucy Mair. Even D.N. Majumdar's concept of 'Tribe' does not stand a test in the present day context. In fact, a group of people having a common name, common dialect, common territory and who observe some common taboos regarding to the marriage, profession etc. should not be considered a 'tribe' or 'tribal community'. Because every territorial group particularly in Indian sub-continent, possesses all these characteristics in common, yet are not called upon as the 'tribes' or the tribal communities. Besides the common characteristics as almost all the scholars have mentioned to denote the 'tribals', some basic differences pertaining to the socio-economic and cultural standard, which virtually distinguish the tribals from non-tribals have not been indicated by any social scientists so far.

Thus, in view of the basic difference of tribals from non-tribals the term 'tribe' in its broadest sense may be used to denote a territorial homogeneous group of families which is backward in respect of socio-economic and cultural development and lives in the semi-nomadic stage and still confined to their traditional abodes quite away from the civilized world and other tribals any sorts of socio-occupational mobility.

However, there are some common characteristics which as most of the anthropologists, sociologists and others agree to constitute a tribe; for example a group of people affined with some kinship affines, have common territory, common dialect, a distinct cultural system, comparatively backward economy, customary laws and community panchayat as an influential institution to maintain social order within the community and comparatively geographical as well as social isolation from the rest of the civilized society can be referred as a tribe. Though some anthropologists do not agree with some of the above mentioned characteristics, yet in perspective of the Indian tribes, the characteristics as outlined above seem more appropriate. Moreover, a prevalent deprivation, constant socio-economic backwardness, psychological adherence with conservatism are some outstanding features observed in Indian tribes.

In view of the over all development of some of the tribal groups the Constitution of India has specified some tribes as the 'Scheduled Tribes'. "The specification of tribes or tribal communities as 'Scheduled Tribes' arose only after the Constitution of India came into force........ In the list of 'Scheduled Tribes', prepared in 1950, the primitiveness and backwardness were the tests applied for specifying a scheduled tribe. The main characteristics which are common to all the scheduled tribes are : (1) tribal origin (2) primitive way of life (3) habitation in remote and less easily accessible areas and (4) general backwardness in all respects."[10]

Since Independence a number of lists of the 'Scheduled Tribes' were notified by the President in accordance with the provisions of article 342 of the Constitution. The lists are contained in the schedules appeared in the following orders issued by the President; (1) The Constitution (Scheduled Tribes) Order, 1950, (2) The Constitution (Scheduled Tribes part 'C' States Order 1951 (3) The Constitution (Andaman Nicobar Islands) Scheduled Tribes Order 1959 (4) The Constitution (Dadar and Nagar Haveli) Scheduled Tribes Order 1962, (5) The Constitution (Scheduled Tribes) U.P. Order 1967 and (6) The Constitution (Goa, Daman and Diu) Scheduled Tribes Order 1968"[11] Under the Constitution (Scheduled Tribes, U.P.) Order 1967 the tribal communities i.e. the Bhotiyas, Buxas, Tharus, Rajis and Jaunsaris of Uttarakhand in U.P. were specified as the 'Scheduled Tribes'. In fact, under the Article 342 of the Constitution, "The President may with respect to any State or Union Territory and where it is a State, after consultation with the Governor thereof, by public notification, specify the tribes or tribal communities or part of or groups within tribes or tribal communities which shall for the purposes of this Constitution be deemed to be 'Scheduled Tribes' in relation to that State or Union Territory."[12] The Constitution of India provides a number of safeguards for the 'Scheduled Caste and Scheduled Tribes......... All these safeguards have apparently been provided to facilitate the implementation of the Directive Principles contained in article 46 of the Constitution."[13]

Thus, it may be concluded that, if the President of India, under the article 342 of the Constitution notify any tribal group for the purpose of the safety of its socio-economic interests and also to protect it from social injustice and all sorts of exploitations, then it (the tribal group) may be regarded as the 'Scheduled Tribe"

In the present study the researcher has selected five tribal communities of Uttarakhand in U.P. which has been notified as the Scheduled Tribes' by the Constitution Order 1967.

Culture and Cultural Transformation

Systématic investigation of the problem of cultural transmission or cultural borrowing dates from about the beginning of the twentieth century."[14] In fact, the process of cultural transmission or cultural borrowing has caused, in one form or the other, the process of acculturation and culture-dynamics which in turn have reproduced the process of cultural transformation by virtue of which the cultural patterns change their forms and functions. Thus, in the study of cultural transformation, the conceptual analysis of the term 'culture' is essentially important as to know how the cultural system develops and changes with the change of cultural patterns.

Numerous thoughts pertaining to the concept 'Culture' apparently proves the lack of unanimity of the scholars, philosophers, literatures, social scientists and the anthropologists. Hence, "Kroeber and Klukhon reviewing the definitions and conceptions of culture associated with them, list over one hundred and sixty different formal delimitations of the term."[15] However, there is a general agreement that culture is a learned behaviour, "that allows man to adapt himself to his natural and social setting; that it is greatly variable, that it is manifested in institutions, thought patterns and material objects."[16] K.B. Tylor, the first anthropologist to define the term 'Culture', has stated, "Culture is that complex whole which includes knowledge, belief, art, morals, law, customs and any other capabilities and habits acquired by man as a member of the society."[17] Tylor defines the culture as a social heritage which is a gift to an individual from society. As he emphasized culture as the capabilities acquired by man as a member of society. Thus 'Culture', as Tylor defines, is far more than material culture.[18] Many other thinkers, including Malinowaski have paraphrased this definition to point out that the social heritage may be said to consist of a material part and non-material, intangible imponderable part..... culture is a total way of life and the instruments, mental, social and material of which this way is constituted.[19] And, the similar views regarding the concept, 'Culture' has been propounded by Bidney. David Bidney the prominent philosopher-anthropologist has defined culture as 'the product of agro-facts (products of cultivation), artifacts (products of industry), socio-facts (social organizations) and menti-facts (language, religion, art and so on).[20] Bidney has broadly defined the concept, 'culture' which may be summed up as the two major segments i.e. material and non-material culture.

Ruth Benedict has presented the formalistic, aesthetic views regarding the concept of culture and stated that, "A culture like an individual, is a more or less consistent pattern of thought and action within each culture there come into being characteristics and purposes not necessarily shared by other types of society."[21] Benedict has conceived culture only in its formal ordering and organization of cultural traits or the culture patterns. According to him, culture deals only with its forms or patterns but not with its contents. Benedict emphasises that the culture of a given society includes the thoughts and activities of the social life of the given society thus we only can understand the term culture, as an integrated pattern of social activities and mental products which alone give birth to a particular type of cultural patterns.

Malinowaski and Radcliffe Brown, the prominent anthropologists take this instrumental, humanistic view of culture.[22] Malinowaski delineated culture as a total way of life which secures for an individual the satisfaction of his bio-psychic derives and the fulfilment of other wants and cravings and ultimately, invests him with freedom while Radcliffe Brown regards culture as cultivation, the process of handing down and acquiring traditions, as a result of which society is perpetuated.

Kluckhohn has espoused some different view points rather than of the previous ones which have been quoted as, "Culture may be defined as, all those historically created designs for living, explicit and implicit, relational and non-relational which exist at any given time as potential guides for the behaviour of men."[24] Kluckhohn has described the culture as a way of thinking, acting and feeling of a man in a given time. This view point indicates to the dynamic nature of culture that eventually change or modify its own nature by itself with the change of time and place. Kluckhohn has also talked about the explicit and implicit elements of culture.

He says not every thing in a people's life may be yielded to us and added to our knowledge, merely through sensory observations. Such elements as may be perceived with the aid of the eye and the ear are the explicit items of culture, while other items which can be perceived by human beings after being specially trained for looking for all that is not obvious, the motivations and impulses underlying human action of which the actions themselves may not be conscious, these would be the implicit items of culture. Thus, culture is a integrated whole of various elements whether explicit or implicit and which can be comprehend by its dynamic nature rather than static.

Kroeber has termed the culture as, "the mass of learned and transmitted motor reactions, habits techniques, ideas, values and the behaviour they induce.[25] "He also talked about the base of its receptivity and existence. It is (culture) always something adopted, used believed, practised or possessed by more than one person. It depends upon group life for its existence.[26] Kroeber has told about two major aspects of culture which he calls 'eidos' and 'ethos'. By Kroeber, eidos means formal appearance of a culture derived from its constituents and contrasted with the aggregate of constituents is ethos, the desposition of a culture which determines its quality, its main themes and interests. He logically delineated the nature of culture treating it, both super-individual and super-organic.[27] Infact, culture is more than the organism which can be maintained by the process of heredity while the culture can not be transmitted or maintained by heredity. For instance, "heredity saves for all that she has from generation to generation. But heredity does not maintain and has not maintained because it cannot maintain one particle of the civilization which is the one specifically human being."[28] Thus, culture is super-organic, super organic for Krober does not mean non-organic or free from organic influence nor is it beyond the organic life. Super organic means something more than organic.

Herskovits has delineated that, 'Culture is the man made part of environment........ culture includes all the elements in man's nature endowment that he has acquired from his group by conscious learning or by a conditioning process techniques of various kinds, social and other institutions, beliefs and patterned modes of conduct.[29] Herskovits says that culture is more than a biological phenomena. He has also presented various series of paradoxes to comprehend the essential nature of culture, these are as follows.[30]

1. Culture is universal in man's experience, yet each local or regional manifestation of it is unique.
2. Culture is stable, yet is also dynamic and manifests continuous and constant change.
3. Culture fills and largely determines the course of our lives, yet rarely intrudes into conscious thought.

The above mentioned paradoxes in regard to the nature of culture denote its essential attributes that the culture is a universal, stable concept which largely determines the course of human living yet there is a particular culture-area of every culture, culture is dynamic in nature and it never intrudes into the conscious thought of man.

Besides the views enumerated as above, many other scholars have largely presented their views in regard of the concept of the culture, yet it is found that there is no unanimity among them. But inspite of the different views of various social scientists the term culture may be delineated as "the super-organic phenomena which consists of all learned behaviours of a social being which are internalized through the process of socialization and acquired by the new generations in the form of cultural heritage and symbolically transmitted generation to generation and therefore treated as the accumulative efforts of generations and the accepted modes of life for group living."

Thus, the term culture is not absolute in itself, but it is a segmental division of numerous constituent units, the systematic arrangement of which constitute the cultural integration or the cultural organization. Culture is a complex whole which is incomprehensible unless the constituent units of it are not looked upon in the structural functional frame of reference which eventually make possible the existence and continuity of culture. These constituent units or the components of culture may be termed as the culture traits, culture complex and the culture patterns. Culture trait is the basic and minutest unit of the cultural system which may be in the form of material, non-material and, undividable for the use of a given culture. Herskovits has termed it as the smallest identifiable in a given culture.[31] Kroeber has defined it as a minimal definable element of culture.[32] Hoebel has stated that a culture element is a pattern of behaviour (or the material product of such behaviour) that may be treated as the smallest unit of its order."[33] And these culture elements, while closely get together or interrelated with each other constitute the culture complex, which satisfies the need of human beings in a given culture. Sutherland and Wood Ward has explained the term culture complex as a whole set of culture traits that 'cluster' together in a meaningful interrelationship."[34] Infact, culture complex is a segment of culture that is the inevitable consequence of the interaction of different culture element and hence meaningfully capable to satisfy the human needs in a given society. D.N. Majumdar and T.N. Madan have explained that, "If a number of culture traits combine together to produce a meaningful congery, a segment within the total culture then the same is called a culture complex.[35] Thus, it may be concluded that culture complex is a great combination of culture traits which may be termed as a pattern of the interaction of culture traits.

Besides this, a very much similar term culture pattern also exhibit the essential feature of a culture. In fact, the systematic arrangement of culture complexes within the cultural structure which presents the characteristics of a culture, as a whole is culture pattern. Sutherland and Wood-Ward state that "the culture pattern is a grouping of traits, complexes into a sort of generalized picture of the culture as a whole."[36] Herskovits has delineated culture which as consensus of the individual behaviour patterns manifest by the members of a society, give to this way of life coherence, continuity and distinctive form.[37]

A more component of 'cultural organization' is 'culture area' which is used to denote the geographical region that consists of the sufficiently homogeneous culture. Systematically, the concept of the culture area was first used by Wissler' when he employed it to orient his work on American Indian Culture. Wissler says, "the natives of the new world could be grouped according to culture traits, "this would give us food areas, textile areas, ceramic areas, etc.......... If however, we take all traits into simultaneous consideration and shift our point of view to the social or tribal units, we are also able to form fairly definite groups. This will give us culture areas or a classification of social groups according to their culture traits."[38]

Wissler says, 'culture area is a geographical region in which reside a considerable number of relatively independent tribes with similar cultures.[39] But in the present day time due to the introduction of various means of transportation and communication the geographical limit of any culture area has loosend its nature and the usefulness of 'culture area' concept can be extended only to the analysis of the tribal culture which is cut-off from the main stream of the culture contact with civilized, non-tribal cultures and this occurred due to the lack of the means of transportation and communication, inseperable geographical hinderances for culture contacts and other ecological conditions which make culture transmission if not impossible but difficult.

In fact, the cultures of those groups who live close to one another tend to have greater similarities than those groups who live farther apart. Thus, the area, as defined by Herskovits, in which similar cultures are found, is called a culture area.[49]

Thus, it may be concluded that, "culture is a integrated whole of various cultural traits, cultural complexes and culture patterns out of which every culture component is functionally inter-related with each other and jointly fulfill the needs of human being and perpetuated symbolically through the process of transmission from generation to generation and acquired through learning process by a man as a member of society."

The historical account of the cultural evolution shows that the culture right from the beginning has constantly transformed its nature and functions and acquired the present state of cultural existence. Yet there are questions to be answered; as to how the culture and culture-components came into existence and how they expanded through the ages and how they have modified their forms and functions with the change of time and needs of the people? The earliest anthropologists have tried to answer these questions through different, prevalent approaches of culture growth. In this regard the first and foremost approach was the evolutionary approach based on 'Darvinism', which later on followed by Herbert Spencer, who states that "Evolution is the integration of matter and concommitent dissipation of motion during which matter passes from an indefinite incoherent homogeneity to a definite coherent heterogeneity."[41] He is of the opinion that the same law of evolution may be applied to comprehend the culture and its evolution. Herbert Spencer was preceded by the prominent anthropologists E.B. Tylor, L.H. Morgan, Haddon and Levy Brunt.

Alike of the evolutionists, some German thinkers viz., Graebner, Ankermann and Schmidt have propounded the theory of "Diffusion". According to the German diffusionists various culture complexes develop at various times in different parts of the world and later on diffuse over the corresponding portions of the earth. The three different schools viz., the 'Pan Egyptian',[42] the German Austrian Culture-Historical by Graebner, F. and Foy, and the American[43] have based the study of culture history or cultural mobility or the both on the theory of cultural diffusion. In fact, during the process of cultural diffusion the cultural patterns some times assimilate some new traits as to enable themselves according to the ecological and socio-cultural demand of the corresponding communities and some times lose their original character or get some sorts of modifications as to the variations of the time, place and the needs of the people living there in. This process virtually gives birth to the process of cultural transformation.

Alike of the preceding theories, the "Social Science Research Council Committee" (1935) applied the term, "Acculturation" and stated that, "Acculturation comprehends those phenomena which result when groups of individuals having different cultures come into continuous first hand contact with subsequent changes in the original cultural patterns of either or both groups."[44] Thus, the process of acculturation ultimately accelerate the process of cultural transformation by changing the forms of the original cultural patterns of a given social group due to the cultural contact with another cultural group. In this process the two different cultural groups, in the state of culture contact follow the cultural traits of one another either by imitation or by the pressure. But in every respect the cultural patterns of the either cultural group or the both transmit from one to another vice-versa and consequently develops the process of cultural transformation.

Barnett[45] has looked on the cultural transformation or cultural change with the help of innovation, which occurred particularly when the new invention, discoveries and the introduction of new culture-traits replace the older culture traits or modified their customary forms as to make them more useful and fit for the socio-cultural background of a given society. This process accepts the ways of doing old things as well as the modifications of the old ways of social life. Herskovits has stated that, "indeed, it is here that inventions, discoveries, and diffused elements meet and can be grouped under the category of innovations for whether discovered, invented or introduced, each innovation responds to the propensity for conscious human experimentation and the play of human experimentation and the play of human ingenuity. Small changes being immediately on the introduction of an innovation and the process of alteration never ceases."[46]

Thus, it may be concluded that the culture patterns ceaselessly change their forms and functions through the processes of evolution, diffusion, acculturation and the innovation. These processes add some new changes, great or small, in the contemporary cultural patterns and thus give birth to the new cultural system. Besides these well established processes some newly emerged concepts viz. sanskritization, westernization, modernization, parochialization and democratization have also played an important role in the transformation of the cultural system of the society.

Thus, the cultural transformation in its broadest sense may be defined as a multi-dimensional process of cultural change which characterise changes brought about in the cultural patterns of a given community as a result of various processes or the factors of change. The concept subsumes any alteration occurring in the material and non-materials aspects of the cultural system of a given community.

Review of the Literature

In the former half of the twentieth century the study of races and cultures in India by Sir Herbert Risley was considered as an outstanding contribution in the field of social anthropology. Since then a number of eminent scholars have made various studies on races, tribes, castes and cultures. In the field of tribal culture the work of D.N. Majumdar is of great importance. He studied the racial types of the tribals, their beliefs, customs, traditions, religion and faith and also the economic transition and cultural mal-adaptation. The systematic investigation of cultural dynamics process was started from the beginning of the twentieth century. Different schools were founded to make scientific study on the cultural history of the various tribal groups in India and abroad. In India G.S. Ghurye, A. Aiyappan, M.N. Srinivas, S.C. Roy, and B.K. Roy Burman have made a significant contribution in the field of cultural anthropology. Majumdar (1972)[47] in the study of tribe-caste continuum and the process of sanskritization among the Bodo speaking tribes of Garo Hills has observed that the process of sanskritization has intimately linked with the process of trans-formation of a tribe into caste. Besides this the anthropological studies of A.R. Desai, Martin Orans, N.N. Vyas, Surjit Sinha, N.K. Bose and S.K. Srivastava in the field of tribal culture have also presented a wide understanding about the cultural dynamics of the different tribal communities in India.

M.N. Srinivas (1966)[48] in the analysis of social change in India has developed the concepts of sanskritization, westernization and secularization and also emphasized the increasing dominance of politicization in Indian social and cultural life. In the book, "Religion and society among the Coorgs of South India", Srinivas has used the model of sanskritization to denote the process of caste mobility and stated that the low castes took over, as far as possible, the customs, rites and beliefs of the Brahmins and the adoption of the Brahminic way of life by the low castes seems to have been frequent, though theoretically forbidden. This process has been called 'Sanskritization' in this book."[49] He further stated that the mobility associated with sanskritization results only in positional changes in the system and does not lead by structural change.[50] He is of the opinion that the process of 'Sanskritization' is not confined to Hindu caste only but occurs in the tribal and semi-tribal groups. Such as the Bhils of Western India, the Gonds and Oraons of Central India and the Pahadis of Himalayas who are in the process of Sanskritization and claiming to be a caste and therefore, Hindu.

K.L. Sharma (1973)[51] has considered the economic progress as an important variable for the upgradation in the caste hierarchy. He also states that the cultural change is impossible without economic progress.

R.P. Srivastava (1962)[52] has made a study on the tribe caste mobility. This study deals with the Bhotiya Tirbe of Kumaun in Uttar Pradesh.

K.L. Kothari (1978)[53] has also studied the tribal change and observed that the tribals who lived in happy isolation with their own mythology, customs, rituals and life style for centuries are now confronting the various problems of massive social change resulting from the opening of their isolated country through the introduction of development plans, education new technology and modernization.

B.D. Ray (1979)[54] has completed a research project on the occupational mobility among the Khasis of Shillong and concluded that the occupational mobility is greatly motivated by the availability of occupational opportunity in urban areas.

Hari Mohan (1969)[55] has conducted a study on the Parhaiya tribe in the Palamu district of Bihar in perspective of culture change. The monograph follows the usual ethnographic model and contains details about the style of living, the means of subsistence, trade, market and indebtedness, family and kinship, the lifecycle, crime and punishment, religion and magic etc.

Anita Horsey (1974)[56] has find out the impacts of modernization on the socio-cultural life of the Warli tribe, and observed that Warlis are politically backward and are not aware with the meaning of citizenship, rights and duties and still possess the 'Ma-Bap' mentality towards government. The researcher has selected eight different variables i.e. literacy, mass media exposure, cosmopolitaness, empathy, opinion-leadership, achievement motivations, fatalism and innovativeness as they observe their comparative impact on the different villages.

In the study, "The missionary among the Khasis" Nalini Natrajan (1977)[57] has regarded the missionary as an important factor of social change. The study deals in a historical perspective with the arrival of the missionaries and discusses their impact on various aspects of Khasi life.

S.M. Dubey (1972)[58] has made a study to assess the role of modern education in bringing about the social change and political awareness among the tribals of North-East India and concluded thus though education is not the only but it is an important variable for social change and political consciousness.

N. Sahay (1976)[59] has studied the impact of Christianity on the different aspects of the tribal life and discerned five cultural processes of change which began with the introduction of Christianity. These stages are characterized by the processes viz. oscillation, scrutinization, combination, indigenization and retroversion. The processes are consecutive. However, different areas may reveal different processes.

L.P. Vidyarthi[60] conducted a study on the Hatia industrial complex to understand the form and process of cultural change and its consequences upon industrialization. This study highlights the impact of industrialization on the tribals, since it deals with the socio-cultural implications of industrialization not only for the tribals but for the vast numbers of non-tribals who are also part of the industrial scene. Besides this, L.P. Vidyarthi (1977)[61] has surveyed the conditions of the primitive and vanishing tribes of Bihar such as the Birhor, Hill Kharia, Parahiya, Korwa and Waler, and concluded that these tribes have remained relatively isolated and less developed for ecological, historical and political reasons while some are declining in numbers.

N.N. Vyas (1980)[62] made a study of the Kathodi tribe in Rajasthan and concluded that Kathodis have different stages of cultural development according to their occupations. In the study, N.N. Vyas observed how the programme of colonization and the provision for houses, subsidy, maintenance allowance etc. have changed the socio-economic life of Kathodi tribe.

R.N. Pareek (1977)[63] published a book, entitled, "Tribal culture in Flux" in which the different aspects of the community life of Jatapu have extensively been described. The study also deals with the transition of the Jatpus and their aspirations as well as the general problems and their solutions.

S.L. Doshi (1971)[64] has made a study on the Bhils of Banswara in Rajasthan with special reference to their self awareness and cultural synthesis which they are building up with neighbouring communities. The study deals with the delineation of the tribal organization occupational patterns, family and kinship, religious beliefs and practices and the trends of change resulting in the process of cultural integration.

J.K. Doshi (1974)[65] has conducted a full length study of a 'Bhil' village while describing the social structure and cultural change, the author deals with the means of subsistence, the life cycle, religion and witchcraft, political organization and changes noticeable in various aspects of their life and culture. He has concluded that the process of change has accelerated with the improvement in communication channels and state intervention on account of welfare programmes.

S. Topno (1970)[66] presented a research article on "Changing pattern of Munda personal names." In this paper he has made an attempt to study the impact of Hinduism and Christianity on the choice of names for children. It is observed that the religion appears to be largest single factor in the choice of names.

G.S. Aurora (1972)[67] has discussed the life and culture of the Bhilala of Alirajpur in the Jhabua district of Madhya Pradesh. He describes the regional community, its territorial and the kinship axis and the extension of the political, economic, and cultural frontiers. The study points out how tribe, caste and class encounters have led to changes among the Bhilala.

Besides the aforesaid account of the different scholarly studies many other scholars have also made studies on the changing patterns of socio-cultural system of the tribal communities in India. Particularly in post-Independence era the rate of socio-cultural change has been accelerated due to the impact of planned processes of tribal development. Viewing to this, I.S. Chauhan[68] has examined the important trends of culture change in the tribal life. D.N. Majumdar (1972)[69] made a study on the process of acculturation among the Hajong of Meghalaya, B.H. Mehta (1965)[70] studied the dynamics of Gond society with special reference to its habitate, socio-economic conditions, religion and culture, R.K. Kar (1974)[71] has observed how the Adis community is flowing in the stream of social change. D.L. Narayana (1976)[72] has surveyed the socio-economic conditions of the tribal village in Chittor district. In this study the author has enumerated the socio-economic changes taking place through the implementation of government welfare programmes. R.K. Gulati (1970)[73] describes social change among the Bhils of the west Khandesh district. R.S. Mann (1972)[74] examines the relationship between the leadership and planned change in tribal Rajasthan.

P.K. Mishra (1977)[75] discusses the process of transformation that has taken place among the food gathering Jenu Kurubas in Mysore. In this study the author reveals how the Jenu Kurubas in Mysore failed to adjust themselves to the changes in their environment which led to their sources of food supply drying up or when there were impediments to their food gathering activities. In contrast to the Jenu Kurubas, however, the Soligas who inhabit a similar environment made a successful adjustment. Mishra attributes this difference to the presence of certain institutional devices of health, of school and other development schemes sponsored by Government agencies among Soligas who accepted and benefited from such schemes.

Rizvi (1982)[76] made a study of the factors influencing health in a tribal community. The study in particular deals with socio-cultural analysis of the Jaunsari community in U.P. In this work he has tried to examine the state of health and the effect of different factors on health among a primary agricultural people in hills of district Dehradun in U.P. It is concluded that climate and geography, beliefs, isolation and poverty influence attitudes with regard to health and states of illness, to a very great extent.

D.L. Prasad Rao (1970)[77] has made a full length study on Jatpu society. In this study he has presented an analytical picture of the Jatpu community. Particularly the pattern of kinship, economy of Jatpu, religious institutions and their functioning in Jatpu life and the problems the Jatpus are encountering in their contact with the non-tribals.

W.G. Archer (1984)[78] has presented a report on tribal law and justice. The report consists of three volumes. The first volume deals with the civil law in Santhal society, the rights of men and women and the law of marriage and divorce. The second volume deals with the Santhal criminals, criminal justice and the Santhals and the Indian Penal Code. While the third volume deals with the structure of the judicial system in tribal regions and show the erasion of tribal customary laws and their supersession by statutory laws.

Basudev Sarmah (1978)[79] studied the economic organization of the tribal communities of North-East India and concluded that, the economy of the tribals is predominantly agricultural. As per 1971 census 57.57 percent of tribal workers were cultivators, 33.64 percent were agricultural labourers and another 2.53 percent were engaged in live stock, forestry, hunting, fishing and plantation, 0.16 percent of tribal workers were engaged in mining and quarrying.

N.N. Vyas and N.D. Chaudhary (1968)[80] in their study, Tribals: Past and Present, have presented a cross section of the tribal development in Rajasthan. The study consists of the historical background of the tribes, perspective of tribal development and area development—its history, pre-requisites, limitations and an outline of the proposed area development plan to be implemented in Dungarpur Tribal Development area as a pilot project are objectively dealt with the study. The study sums up that in tribal development, the funds are not the only requirement but organization and method of working with the people need to be reoriented to suit the situation prevailing in tribal area of Rajasthan.

In an article Ajit K. Pandy (1987)[81] has made an attempt to understand the life of Oraons of Chotanagpur region of Bihar in the context of kinship and power structure. It describes the tribal societies not only from the point of view of the principles that govern their organization but also in terms of the practices, strategies and manipulations that they involve. The paper concludes that the traditional 'patrimonialism' of the Oraons and their heads has certainly been weakened. It has gradually been replaced by modern political machinery.

Jakka Parthasarthy (1988)[82] made a case study of the Malayali of the Jawadhi Hills in the context of language, culture and tribe. In this study an attempt has been made to delineate the role of language and culture among the Malayali. The study reveals that Malayali are backward Hindus who follow their own traditions and beliefs within the frame of the Hindu concepts.

V. Rama Rao (1988)[83] concludes that the education is one of the instruments to unlock the doors of modernization. It is the education that exposes the tribes men to the outside world, widening their mental horizon and providing them with information about many matters relevant to the modern life. It is widely recognized that the spread of education plays a vital role in the socio-economic and cultural modernization of the country in general and social mobility of weaker sections in particular.

Besides this, some more studies have also been completed on the tribal communities of Uttarakhand in U.P. some of those can briefly be described as follows:

S.K. Srivastava (1958)[84] deals with the study of cultural dynamics among Tharus. B.S. Bisht (1982)[85] has described the different components of the social structure and organization of Raji tribe of Kumaun. Amir Hasan (1979)[86] has studied the process of change occurring in the Buxa community of Nainital 'Tarai.. Gerald D. Berreman (1972)[87] has made a full length study on the Hindus of Himalaya and presented a vivid picture of ethnography and change. P.N. Sharma (1976)[88] in course of a study in micro-level planning observed the development of the tribal region in the hill districts of Uttar Pradesh. Saroj Mathur (1967)[89] in course of a short paper describes how the marriage ceremony among Tharus of Chandanchoki is performed. B. Mukherjee (1963)[90] deals with the comparative study of the kinship system of two polyandrous communities i.e., the Jaunsaris and the Todas. B.B. Chatterjee (1975)[91] has completed a project on the Bhotiyas of Indo-Tibetan border of Uttarakhand. This report consists of a sociological survey of ideological convictions, customs, modes of social behaviour and attitudes of the tribal people. Ram Rahul (1970)[92] has presented his views regarding the religious patterns among Bhotiyas. S.P. Dabral (1965)[93] has also made a study on the Bhotiyas of Uttarakhand. The study deals with the religious beliefs and practices of the Bhotiya community. S.D. Pant (1935)[94] has studied the social economy of the Bhotiyas. Besides this C.A. Sherring (1907)[95], P.K. Chattopadhyay (1934)[96] and Panna Lal (1942)[97] have also presented their views in regard of the different aspects of the Bhotiya community.

Thus the review of the literature shows that a considerable number of tribal studies have come into being. Some of these, generate basic data pertaining to the demographic and ethnographic sketch of the tribals, some analyse the social, cultural, economic and political processes while some assess the impact of the various factors of planned change. There are studies which enumerate the alteration occurred on the tribal life from past to present. All these studies irrespective of nature, present a clue to the researchers of the respective discipline. Even in the present study some extracts, notes and conclusions of some of the relevant studies have taken into account as the baseline references as to enumerate the process of cultural transformation among the scheduled tribal communities under study.

References

1. Desai, A.R., Tribes in Transition, in Rural Sociology in India, ed. by A.R. Desai, Popular Prakashan, Bombay, 1969, p. 223.
2. Hutton, J.H., Census of India, Vol. I Part I, 1931, p. 391.
3. Elwin, V., The Begas., p. 519.
4. Census of India, 1981, Vol., I Part I, p. 158.
5. Desai, A.R., Tribes in Transition, in Rural Sociology in India, ed. by A.R. Desai, Popular Prakashan, Bombay, 1969, p. 223.
6. Wilke, Arthur S., Fran French and Raj P. Mohan, Tribal India: Unintentional Acculturation, Bulletin of International Committee on Urgent Anthropological and Ethnological Research No. 21, 1979, p. 31.
7. Oxford Dictionary; Quoted by Nadeem Hasan in Tribal India Today. Harnam Publications, New Delhi, 1983, p. 13.
8. Gillin and Gillin, Cultural Sociology, The Mac Millian Co., New York, 1950. p. 282.
9. Majumdar, D. N., Races and cultures of India., Asia Publishing House Bombay, 1944.
10. Chandra, Bimal, Hand Book on Scheduled Castes and Scheduled Tribes, Office of the Commissioner for Scheduled Castes and Scheduled Tribes - Govt. of India. New Delhi 1968, pp. 27-28.
11. *Ibid* . p. 28.
12. *Ibid* . p. 10.
13. *Ibid.* p. 1.
14. Herskovits, Melville J., Cultural Anthropology, Oxford and IBH Publishing Co., New Delhi, 1958, p. 581.
15. A.L. Kroeber and C. Kluckhon., Passion, Quoted by Herskovits, in Cultural Anthropology, Oxford and IBH Publication Co., New Delhi, 1958, p. 305.
16. Hersokovits, M.J., Cultural Anthropology, Oxford and IBH Publishing Co., New Delhi, 1958.
17. Tylor, E.B., Primitive Culture, New York, 1874, p. 1.

18. Ogburn, W.F., M.F. Nimkoff., A Hand Book of Sociology Eurasia Publishing House Pvt. Ltd., Ramnagar New Delhi, 1979, p. 29.

19. Majumdar, D.N. and Madan, T.N., Social Anthropology, Asia Publishing House, New Delhi, 1956, p. 14.

20. Bidney, D., Theoretical Anthropology (Columbia U.P. 1953) Quoted by D.N. Majumdar and T.N. Madan in Social Anthropology p. 14.

21. Benedict, Ruth, Patterns of Culture, Routledge and Kegan Paul Ltd., London, 1904, p. 16.

22. Quoted by Majumdar and Madan in Social Anthropology, Asia Publishing House, New Delhi, 1956, p. 15.

23. Kluckhon, Cylde and Kolly, William., The Concept of Culture; The Science of Man in World Crisis ed. Ralph Linton, Columbia University Press, New York 1945, p. 97.

24. Kluckhon, Clyde and Kolly, William., The Concept of Culture; The Science of Man in World Crisis (ed). Ralph Linton, Columbia University Press, New York, 1945, p. 97.

25. Kroeber, A.L., Anthropology, Harcourt, Brace and Co. New York, 1948, p. 13.

26. Kroeber, A.L. and Klukhon, Culture; A Critical Review of Concepts and Definitions, p. 133.

27. Kroeber, A.L. The Nature of Culture, The University of Chicago Press, Chicago 1952, Chapter 3, on 'The Super Organic'.

28. Kroeber, A.L., The Super Organic; American Anthropologist, Vol. 19, p. 178.

29. Herskovits, M.J., Cultural Anthropology, Oxford and IBH Publishing Co., Delhi, 1955, pp. 305-306.

30. *Ibid.* p. 306.

31. Herskovits, M.J. Man and His works, Alfred knopt; New York 1956, p. 17.

32. Krocber, A.L. Culture element distributories, University of California Publications in American Publications in AmericanEthnology 1936, p. 101.

33. Hoebel, E.A., Man in the Primitve World. Mc-Graw Hill Book Co. New York, 1958 p. 167.

34. Sutherland and Wood Ward, Introductory Sociology, J.B. Lippin Cott. Co. New York, 1748, p. 34.

35. Majumdar, D.N. and Madan T.N., Social Anthropology, Asian Publishing House, New Delhi 1956 p. 18.

36. Sutherland and Wood Ward, Introductory Sociology, J.B. Lippin Cott. Co., New York, 1948 p. 36.

37. Herskovits, M.J., Cultural Anthropology, Oxford and IBH Publishing Co. New Delhi, 1958 pp. 411-412.

38. Wissler, C., The American Indian, New York, 1922, p. 218.

39. Wissler, C., An Introduction to Social Anthropology, Henry Holt and Co. New York, 1929, p. 345.

40. Herskovits, M.J., Cultural Anthropology, Oxford and IBH Publishing Co., New Delhi, 1955, p. 396.

41. Spencer, Herbert; First Principles, D. Applation and Co. New York, 1906, p. 396.

42. Perry, W.J., Children of the Sun, London 1923.

43. Boas, Franz., The Mind of Primitive Man, The Macmillan Co. 1911 and Wissler, Clark, Man and Culture, New York. Thomas Y. Crowell 1923.

44. Radfield, R., Linton R. and Herskovits M.J., Memorandom on the Study of Acculturation, American Anthropologists, XXXVIII-1936 pp. 149-150.

45. Barnett, H.G., Innovation: The Basis of Cultural Change, New York, 1953.

46. Herskovits, M.J., Cultural Anthropology, Oxford and IBH Publishing Co. New Delhi 1955, p. 460.

47. Majumdar, D.N., A Study of Tribe Caste Continuum and the Process of Sanskritization among the Bodo-Speaking Tribes of the Garo Hills, in Tribal Situation in India, by K. Suresh Singh, Indian Institute of Advanced Study Simla, 1972, pp. 263-270.

48. Srinivas, M.N., Social Change in Modern India, Orient Longman Ltd., New Delhi, 1966.

49. Srinivas, M.N., Religion and Society among the Coorgs of South India, Asia Publishing House, New Delhi, p. 30, 1952.

50. Srinivas, M.N., Social Change in Modern India, Orient Longman Ltd., New Delhi, 1966 p. 7.

51. Sharma, K.L., "Downward Social Mobility" Some Observations, Sociological Bulletin, 22, 1973.

52. Srivastava, R.P., Tribe Caste Mobility in India and Case of Kumaun Bhotiya, School of Oriental and African Studies, University of London, 1962.

53. Kothari, K.L., Tribal Social Change in Rajasthan.

54. Ray, B.D., Occupational Mobility among the Khasis of Shillong. Three Urban Centres of Meghalaya, Research Project sponsored by ICSSR, New Delhi, 1979.

55. Mohan, Hari, The Parhaiya; A Study in Culture Change, Patna, Bihar Tribal Welfare Research Institute, Mimeographed, 1969.

56. Horsey, Anita, The Impact of Modernization on the Social Cultural Life of the Warli Tribe. Typed thesis, University of Bombay 1972.

57. Natrajan, Nalini, The Missionary among the Khasis, Sterling Publishers, New Delhi 1977.

58. Dubey, S.M., Education, Social Change and Political Consciousness among the tribes of the North-East India, in, Tribal Situation in India (ed) by K. Suresh Singh, Indian Institute of Advanced Study Simla, 1972.

59. Sahay, K.N., Under the Shadow of the Cross, Calcutta, Institute of Social Research and Applied Anthropology 1976.

60. Vidyarthi, L.P., Socio-Cultural Implications of Industrialization in India, New Delhi, Planning Commission 1970.

61. Vidyarthi, L.P., Primitive and Vanishing Tribes of Bihar, Journal of Social Research, 1977.

62. Vyas, N.N., Kathodi-A Tribe in Transition, in, Indian Tribes in Transition, (ed) R.S. Mann and N.N. Vyas, Rawat Publication Jaipur, Delhi, 1980.

63. Pareek, R.N., Tribal Culture in Flux, B.R. Publishing Corporation, Delhi 1977.

64. Doshi, S.L., Bhils Between Social Self Awareness and Cultural Synthesis, New Delhi, Sterling Publications 1971.

65. Doshi, J.K., Social Structure and Cultural Change in Bhil Village, New Hights, Delhi 1974.

66. Topno, S., Changing Pattern of Munda Personal Names, Eastern Anthropologist, 1970, 22(2).

67. Aurora, G.S., Tribe-Caste-Class Encounters: Some Aspects of Folk Urban Relations in Alirajpur Tehsil. Hyderabad Aministrative Staff College of India, 1972, p. 293.

68. Chauhan, I.S., "Culture Change in Tribal Life", Economic and Political Weekly, 1970.

69. Majumdar, D.N., Acculturation among the Hajong of Meghalaya, Man in India, 1972.

70. Mehta, B.H., Gonds of the Central India. High Lands, Research Project (1965).

71. Kar, R.K., "Social Change among the Adis"-Tribe 1969.

72. Narayan, D.L., An Appraisal of the Economic Conditions of Scheduled Tribes in Rayala Seema, 1976.

73. Gulati, R.K., A Profile of Social Change Among the Bhils of West Khandesh, Tribe, 1970.

74. Mann, R.S. Leadership and Planned Change in Tribal Rajasthan, Bulletin of Cultural Research Institute, 1972.

75. Mishra, P.K., Social Transformation among Food Gatherers in Dimensions of Social Change in India (ed). M.N. Srinivas, Allied Publishers Private Ltd., Bombay, 1977.

76. Rizvi, Syed Nazar Haider, Factors Influencing Health in a Tribal Community. A Socio-Cultural Analysis of Jaunsar in R. Thesis Deptt. of Anthropology, Lucknow University, Lucknow 1982.

77. Rao, D.L. Prasad, An Analysis of Kinship, Economy and Religion of the Jatpus— A Scheduled Tribe in Andhra Pradesh, Research Thesis, Andhra University, 1970.

78. Archer, W.G., Tribal Law and Justice.

79. Sarmah, Basudev, Economic Organization of Tribal Agriculture (With special reference to North-East India) Typed thesis, University of Bombay, 1978.

80. Vyas, N.N., and Chaudhary N.D., Tribals: Past and Present (Research Project) Tribal Research Institute, Department of Social Welfare Rajasthan, Udaipur, 1968.

81. Pandey, Ajit K., Kinship and Power Structure among the Oraons of Bihar; A Study in Continuity and Change in Relevant Sociology; A Journal of Contemporary Sociology Vol. IV No. I April, 1987.

82. Parthasarthy, Jakka., Language, Culture and Tribe; A Case Study of the Malayali of the Jawadhi Hills; in Man and Life; A Journal of the Institute of Social Research and Applied Anthropology (ed). P.K. Bhomik, R.K. Gupta and M.K. Gautam, Vol. 14, Nos. 1 and 2, 1988.

83. Rao, V. Rama; Tribal Education and the Role of the Teacher in Man and Life. A Journal of the Institute of Social Research and Applied Anthropology (ed), P.K. Gupta and M.K. Gautam, Vol. 14, Nos. 1 and 2, 1988.

84. Srivastava, S.K., Tharus: A Study in Cultural Dynamics, Agra University Press 1958.

85. Bisht, B.S., Social Structure and Organization of Raji Tribe of Kumaun. Research Thesis, Kumaun University, Nainital, 1982.

86. Hasan, Amir., The Buxas of Tarai, B.R. Publishing Corpn, New Delhi, 1979.

87. Berreman, Gerald D., Hindus of the Himalayas; Enthnography and Change, University of California Press, 1972.

88. Sharma, P.N., Development of Tribal Region in Hill Districts of Uttar Pradesh (A Study in Micro-Level Planning) Deptt. of Social Work, Kashi Vidhyapith, Varanasi, 1976.

89. Mathur, Saroj, Marriage Among Tharus of Chandan Choki, Eastern Anthropologists, Vol. 20, No. 1, 1977.

90. Mukherjee, B., Comparative Study of the Kinship System of Two Polyandrous Communities; Eastern Anthropologist, Vol. 16 No. 1, 1963.

91. Chatterjee, B.B., Bhotiyas of Indo-Tibetan Border of Uttara Khand, Project Report, Deptt. of Psychology and Education, Gandhian Institute of Studies, Raj Ghat, Varanasi 1975.

92. Rahul, Ram., The Himalayan Broder Land, Vikas Publication, Delhi, 1970.

93. Dabra, S.P., Uttarakhand Ki Bhotantik, Dogadda Veer Gatha Prakashan, 1965.

94. Pant, S.D., The Social Economy of Himalayas, London, George Allen and Unwin, 1935.

95. Sherring, C.A., Notes on the Bhotiyas of Almora and British Garhwal, Calcutta; Asiatic Society, Bengal, 1907.

96. Chattopadhyay, P.K., Himalaya Pare Kailash Mansarovar, Orient Book Co. Calcutta 1934.

97. Lal, Panna, Hindu Customary Law in Kumaun, Allahabad Govt. Press, 1942.

3

RESEARCH DESIGN AND METHODOLOGY

Research design is a plan of study, worked out before the commencement of the research work by a researcher to gain new knowledge or to solve a problem scientifically. P.V. Young has aptly remarked that, "the consideration which enter into making the decisions regarding the what, where, when, how much, by what means, constitute a plan of study or a study design.[1] Young further states that, "a study design includes at least the following component parts which are interdependent and not exclusive: (1) sources of information to be tapped, (2) nature of study, (3) objectives of study, (4) socio-cultural context of study, (5) geographical area to be covered by the study, (6) periods of time to be encompassed, (7) dimensions of the study, (8) the bases for selecting the data and (9) techniques to be used in gathering data."[2] In working out the plan of the present research work the component parts as suggested by P.V. Young have been taken into account as the bases of the study in general. However, in view of the nature of the study, problem and the objectives outlined, the descriptive and experimental research designs have simultaneously been applied in particular. The first hand information have been collected through observation and interview schedule method and presented in a descriptive manner while the impact of the different variables viz., education, transportation, communication, modernization, westernization, sanskritisation, on the cultural patterns of the scheduled tribal communities have been observed on the basis of the ex-post-facts experiment. Besides the first hand information, some relevant facts obtained through secondary sources are also used to substantiate the hypothesis formulated for more accurate investigation.

Universe of the Study

The total scheduled tribe population of Uttarakhand constitute the universe of the present study. The tribe-wise break up of the universe is as follows :

Table 3

Scheduled Tribe-wise Break up of the Universe

Scheduled Tribe	*Population*	*Percentage*
Bhotiya	24406	14.86
Buxa	22375	13.62
Tharu	53406	32.51
Raji	371	0.23
Jaunsari	63710	38.78
Total	164268	100.00

Out of the total tribal population the Jaunsaris constitute the highest percentage, i.e., 38.78 percent of the total Scheduled Tribe population in Uttarakhand. Which is followed by Tharus, Bhotiyas and Buxas with as much as 32.51 percent, 14.86 percent and 13.62 percent of the total Scheduled Tribe population respectively. While Raji is the smallest tribal group with 0.23 percent population of the total scheduled tribes population in Uttarakhand. The Scheduled Tribes population under reference has been spread over in seven districts of Uttarakhand.

The district and block wise distribution of the Scheduled Tribe population is as follows :

Table 4

District and Block-wise Distribution of Scheduled Tribes Population

(Based on 1981 census)

District	*Block*	*Bhotiya*	*Buxa*	*Tharu*	*Raji*	*Jaunsari*
Pithoragarh	1. Dharchula	7004	--	--	173	--
	2. Munsyari	7192	--	--	--	--
	3. Didihat	279	--	--	87	--
	4. Berinag	342	--	--	--	--
	5. Kanalichhna	--	--	--	67	--
	6. Champawat	--	--	--	44	--
	7. Bina	405	--	--	--	--
Total		15222	--	--	371	--
		(62.37%)			(100%)	
Almora	1. Kapkot	1179	--	--	--	--
	2. Garurh Baijnath	73	--	--	--	--
	3. Bageswar	197	--	--	--	--
	4. Takula	11	--	--	--	--
Total		1460	--	--	--	--
		(5.98%)				
Nainital	1. Kathaghariya	205	--	--	--	--
	2. Kashipur	--	121	--	--	--
	3. Bajpur	--	7307	--	--	--
	4. Gadarpur	--	7867	--	--	--
	5. Ramnagar	--	969	--	--	--
	6. Sitarganj	--	--	20924	--	--
	7. Nainital	171	--	--	--	--
	8. Khatima	--	--	32482	--	--
Total		376	16264	53406	--	--
		(1.54%)	(72.68%)	(100)	--	--
Uttarkashi	1. Bhatwarhi	940	--	--	--	--
	2. Rajgarhi	78	--	--	--	--
Total		1018	--	--	--	--
		(4.18%)				

District	Block	Bhotiya	Buxa	Tharu	Raji	Jaunsari
Chamoli	1. Joshimath/ Badrinath	6329	--	--	--	--
Total		6329	--	--	--	--
		(25.93%)	--	--	--	--
Paurhi-Garhwal	1. Dugdda	--	893	--	--	--
Total			893	--	--	--
			(3.99%)	--	--	--
Dehradun	1. Chokrata	--	--	--	--	33513
	2. Kalso	--	--	--	--	30197
	3. Doiwala	--	1053	--	--	--
	4. Sahaspur	--	4168	--	--	--
Total			5221	--	--	63710
Grand Total of the Population		24406	22378	53406	371	63710

The highest percentage of the Bhotiya population i.e. 15222 (63.35%) is concentrated in Pithoragarh district, which is followed by Chamoli with as much as 6329 (26.34%), Almora 1460 (6.08%) and Uttar Kashi 1018 (4.24%), respectively. The majority of Buxa population i.e. 16264 (72.68%) reside in Nainital district which is preceded by Deharadun and Paurhi Garhwal with as much as 5221 (23.33%) and 893 (3.99%), respectively. The rest of the tribal communities i.e., the Tharus, Rajis and Jaunsaris dwell, respectively in Nainital, Pithoragarh and Dehradun districts. Thus, it may be concluded that the total Scheduled Tribe population under study is spread over in 26 blocks of seven districts of Uttarakhand in U.P.

Besides this, the area wise break up of the scheduled tribes population shows that the majority of the population reside in rural areas, while a small portion of the tribal population live in towns. Table No. 3 presents an account of the area-wise distribution of the Scheduled Tribes population in Uttarakhand.

Table 5

Area-wise Distribution of the Scheduled Tribe Population

District	*Area-wise Scheduled Tribes Population*									
	Bhotiya		*Buxa*		*Tharu*		*Raji*		*Jaunsari*	
	Rur.	*Urb.*	*Rur.*	*Urb.*	*Rur.*	*Urb.*	*Rur.*	*Urb.*	*Rur.*	*Urb.*
Pithoragarh	12545	2677	--	--	--	--	371	--	--	--
Almora	1085	375	--	--	--	--	--	--	--	--
Nainital	--	376	14704	1560	51501	1905	--	--	--	--
Uttarakashi	843	175	--	--	--	--	--	--	--	--
Chamoli	4765	1565	--	--	--	--	--	--	--	--
Dehradun	--	--	4816	405	--	--	--		61583	2127
Paurhi Garhwal	--	--	795	98	--	--	--	--	--	--
Total	19238	5168	20315	2063	51501	1905	371	--	61583	2127
Per cent	78.82	21.18	90.8	9.2	96.43	3.57	100	--	96.66	3.34

It is observed that the majority of the Scheduled Tribes population is confined within their traditional abodes located in the interior villages of Uttarakhand. For instance 78.82 percent Bhotiyas, 90.78 percent Buxas, 96.43 percent Tharus, 100 percent Rajis and 96.66 percent Jaunsarias still live in rural areas while the rest of the population of every Scheduled Tribes has mobilized to town areas. It is also observed that there is comparatively more mobility among Bhotiyas, for 21.18 percent of the Bhotiya population have got their settlement in towns which is largest in comparison to the rest of the Scheduled Tribes population under study. On the contrary, Rajis have the least mobility as the total Raji population still live within the periphery of their villages. In order to make more comprehensive the distribution of rural population of Scheduled Tribes, the district and block-wise numbers of villages inhabited by the Scheduled Tribes population may be presented as follows:

Table 6

(Based on 1981 census)

District and Block-Wise Numbers of Villages and the Distribution of the Tribal Population

District	*Block*	*Nos. of Villages and the Distribution of the Tribal Population.*									
		Bhotiya		*Buxa*		*Tharu*		*Raji*		*Jaunsari*	
		Nos. of Vil	*Total pop*	*Nos. of Vil*	*Total pop*	*Nos. of Vil*	*Total pop*	*Nos. of Vil*	*Total pop*	*Nos. of Vil*	*Total pop*
1	2	3	4	5	6	7	8	9	10	11	12
Pithoragarh	Dharchula	64	5068	–	–	–	–	4	173	–	–
	Munsyari	97	6990	–	–	–	–	–	–	–	–
	Berinag	14	342	–	–	–	–	–	–	–	–
	Didihat	16	145	–	–	–	–	2	87	–	–
	Kanalichhina	-	–	–	–	–	–	2	67	–	–
	Champawat		–	–	–	–	–	1	44	–	–
Almora	Kapkot	28	895	–	–	–	–	–	–	–	–
	Bageswar	07	130	–	–	–	–	–	–	–	–
	Garurhbaij-Nath	04	49	–	–	–	–	–	–	–	–
	Takula	02	11	–	–	–	–	–	–	–	–
Nainital	Khatima	–	–	–	–	75	31361	–	–	–	–
	Sitarganj	–	–	–	–	66	20140	–	–	–	–
	Bajpur	–	–	38	6741	–	–	–	–	–	–
	Kashipur	–	–	05	102	–	–	–	–	–	–
	Gadarpur	–	–	23	7133	–	–	–	–	–	–
	Ramnagar	–	–	20	728	–	–	–	–	–	–
Uttarkashi	Bhatwarhi	10	775	–	–	–	–	–	–	–	–
	Rajgarhi	02	68	–	–	–	–	–	–	–	–
Chamoli	Joshimath/ and Badrinath	49	4765	–	–	–	–	–	–	–	–
Dehradun	Sahaspur	–	–	45	3873	–	–	–	–	–	–
	Doiwal	–	–	26	943	–	–	–	–	–	–
	Kalsi	–	–	–	–	–	–	–	–	204	29687
	Chokrata		–	–	–	–	–	–	–	152	31896
Paurhi Garhwal	Dogadda	–	–	16	795	–	–	–	–	–	–
Total	24	291	19238	173	20315	141	51501	09	371	356	61583

The rural Scheduled Tribes population i.e. 153008 live in 970 villages spread over in 24 blocks of seven districts of Uttarakhand. Numerically, Jaunsaris have the maximum strength i.e. 61583, dispersed in 356 villages of Kalsi and Chokrata blocks in Dehradun. While the rural population of Bhotiyas is scattered in 291 villages and 173 villages are inhabited by Buxas, 141 by Tharus and only 09 small villages with as much as 371 population are inhabited by Rajis. But the percentage range of tribal population to total population in each village vary from one another. The following table shows the percentage range of Scheduled Tribe pupulation and the Nos. of tribal villages in each Range.

Table 7

Nos. of Scheduled Tribe Villages in Each Range

Percentage Range	*Nos. of Bhotiya Villages*	*Nos. of Buxa Villages*	*Nos. of Tharu Villages*	*Nos. of Raji Villages*	*Nos. of Jaunsari Villages*	*Total*	*%*
00-20	151	104	28	05	03	291	30.00
20-40	36	23	31	--	14	104	10.72
40-60	28	25	33	02	31	119	12.77
60-80	25	12	35	--	73	145	14.95
80-100	51	09	14	02	235	311	32.06
Total	291	173	141	09	356	970	100.00
	(30.00%)	(17.83%)	(14.54%)	(0.93%)	(36.70%)	(100%)	

There is however, Scheduled Tribe population living in town areas of Uttarakhand and engaged in different occupations which are mostly non-traditional. The Pithoragarh district has the maximum percentage of Scheduled Tribe population living in its different towns. While district Paurhi Garhwal has the least scheduled tribe population dwelling in town areas. Out of the total five Scheduled Tribes, Bhotiyas have the maximum urban population which stands 4993 in numbers and is followed respectively by Jaunsaris, Buxas, Tharus with as much as 2127, 2063 and 1905 population. While none of the Rajis reside in any town area, it is observed that the Scheduled Tribe population living in different towns are engaged either in business pursuits or in some sort of services.

Thus, the Scheduled Tribes population under study has been spread over 970 villages and 45 town areas of Kumaun and Garhwal regions of Uttarakhand. But in view of the nature and objectives of the study only few villages and the town areas having maximum percentage of the Scheduled Tribes population have been selected for the study.

Selection of the Study Units

Since the universe of the present study is vast, complicated, heterogeneous and spread over in a large geographical area of Kumaun and Garhwal region, hence, the whole of the universe has been divided and sub-divided into different homogeneous groups as to bring about the homogeneity in the universe. For, the homogeneity of the universe is essentially important for the scientific selection of the most representative samples. If the data are highly homogeneous, that is, if the difference between the various items composing the whole body of data are negligible then any item or group of items is representative of the whole.[3] Thus, the universe of the study under reference is stratified into different homogeneous categories and the sub-samples have been taken on the basis of the purposive sampling method. Thereafter, the study units have been selected out of the sub-samples on the basis of the random sampling method.

At the first step the whole of the universe has been stratified into five major groupings viz., the Bhotiyas population, the Buxa population the Tharu population, the Rajis population and the Jaunsari population, for every tribal group constitute a homogeneous part of the universe on the basis of the origin and the racial traits.

On the second step every major group i.e. the tribal group has been sub-divided into three occupational categories which are as follows :

(i) First Category

The first category deals with that part of the total population of the universe who follow agriculture as the main source of subsistence and reside in rural communities. The total numbers of the villages consisting the tribal population constitute this category.

(ii) Second Category

The second category consists of the tribal population engaged in some sorts of business in the town areas. The shopkeepers, traders, transporters and the peddlers have been included under this category. The total number of the towns (Municipal area, Notified area, Cant. area) and the scheduled tribes population engaged in business pursuits constitute this category.

(iii) Third Category

The third category of the universe deals with that part of the Scheduled Tribe population which is engaged in government services and posted in different towns of Uttarakhand.

The first category comprises 291 villages with 19238 population of Bhotiyas, 173 villages with 20315 population of Buxas, 141 villages with 51501 population of Tharus, 09 villages with 371 population of Rajis and 356 villages of Jaunsaris with as much as 61583 population. The second category consists of 21 towns with 800 population of Bhotiyas, 7 towns with 120 population of Buxas, 3 towns with 130 population of Tharus, 13 towns with 200 population of Jaunsaris. While none of the Rajis dwells in any town area nor follow any sort of business pursuits. In third category total 1200 employees from Bhotiya community, 200 employees from Buxa community, 300 employees from Tharu community and 350 employees from Jaunsari community have been included out of which the sample is drawn. But Rajis have no representation in the third category too.

At the third step the total number of the units of the three categories within the different scheduled tribal groups have been analysed separately as to make possible the selection of an approximate representative samples respectively from every category.

At the last step the sample have been drawn from every category on the basis of random sampling method. Since, the numbers of the units in every category differ largely from one another and it is impossible to weigh the equal proportion to every category of every scheduled tribe. However, in the case of first category, almost all the villages having more than 80 percent tribal population have been selected as sub-samples through purposive sampling method out of which a single village from every block has been selected on the basis of random sampling method (lottery method). Thus, almost all the villages selected through purposive sampling method are given equal chance of being drawn as the representative study unit. In this way total 5 Bhotiya villages namely Go, Suring, Tarthal, Bangari and Niti, respectively from Dharchula, Munsyari, Berinag, Joshimath and Bhatwari blocks, 4 villages of Buxas namely; Dhaki, Majara Hasan, Rajpur and Maherkagaon each from Gadarpur, Ramnagar, Bajpur and Shaspur blocks, 2 villages of Tharu namely Bigarabagh and Karghata each from Khatima and Sitarganj blocks, 2 villages of Rajis i.e Ganagaon and Chaurani each from Dharchula and Didihat blocks and 2 villages of Jaunsaris (Khasa) i.e. Masarar and Bangpur each from Kalsi and Chokarata blocks have been selected for the study.

In regard of the relevance against the selection of the equal number of the sample unit from each block, the researcher argues that there is great variation among the units of the sub-samples of different blocks and it is not possible scientifically to give proportionately equal representation to every block, hence, an equal number has been sampled on the basis of the random sampling method from each block. It is also scientific in the sense that every tribal community, irrespective of the variations of the location of the villages constitute an approximate homogeneous group particularly on the basis of the same ethnic traits. Yet in order to observe the impact of the different topographical and agro-climatic conditions as well as the alien cultural groups the different blocks located in different districts of Uttarakhand have been taken into account to select the sample units. Hence, almost all the 15 sampled villages have been chosen from different blocks located in different part of Uttarakhand.

Though every sampled village constitute a study unit for observation, yet approximately 72 to 75 percent families from each sampled village have been selected for focussed interview and every family head has been treated as the respondent unit. Thus, total 370 families are sampled for study.

Since the units of the second and third category includes respectively the business class and the service class Scheduled-Tribes population dwelling in the different towns of Uttarakhand. Hence, for the selection of the most representative sample units and also to give the equal representation to every Scheduled Tribe community, the sub-samples out of the units of the second and third category have been selected on the basis of purposive sampling method. Thus, almost all the district headquarters and the town area having the maximum Scheduled Tribe population in every district have been included in the sub-samples out of which the sample units have been selected through random sampling method (lottery method).

Thus, only 125 samples units have been selected out of the total 1250 units of the sub-sample of the second category, while 205 samples have been taken out of the total 2050 units of the sub-samples of third category. In this way the total numbers of the sampled units for second and third category stand at 330. Every tribal community, except Raji, has proportionately equal representation in the total numbers of samples because the total Raji population has been spread over in rural areas and none of them found neither in any business pursuit nor in any government service.

Method and Approach of the Study

Keeping in view the nature and the objectives of the study the scientific method have been applied in the present research work.

Both the primary and secondary sources have been used for the collection of the information related to the different aspects of the problem. The observation method consisting of all sorts of sense perceptions has been used as the main source of field data while an interview-schedule was used for the attainment of the general information regarding to the socio-economic profile of the respondents and also to measure their attitudes particularly in reference of the Government Welfare Schemes and the constitutional provisions made for the upliftment and the betterment of the tribal communities under study. An interview guide was structured and has to be got by heart. The interview-guide has been prepared for researcher's own sake, for, it included all sorts of extremely sensitive questions which cannot be put forward the informants. These questions were arranged in a special manner and asked only after the establishment of the good rapport with the respondents concern. Besides this, a short village schedule was also prepared which chiefly includes the questions regarding to the ecological and demographical aspects of the village.

The ethnographic and comparative approaches are simultaneously used in the study. The ethnographic approach has been used in order to analyse the ethnic traits found among the scheduled tribes under reference. The process of cultural transformation and the standard of cultural development has been conceived through comparative approach. The earlier studies and their findings have been treated as the base line information for the comparative interpretation of the existing cultural system.

Moreover, the views of the aged persons, their attitudes towards newly emergent processes of social change, behaviour patterns and the ethos and morales of socio-cultural life as they still preserve are also present as the clue to make the comparative delineation between the old and the new generations. Besides this, the study of the different tribal groups and the cultural traits they possess, have been based on the comparative approach. Lastly, the structural-functional approach has also been used to define the contribution of every component units of the tribal cultural system which they impart by working together with a sufficient degree of harmony for the integration of the cultural system.

Techniques of Data Collection

Every scientific research aims to present the most reliable, factual, authentic and exact findings, in order to make objective delineation of the problem under study. The exact and factual conclusion of any of the scientific researches basically depend on the data gathered through various sources.

In view of the present study the researcher has used the observation technique to collect the first hand information through field or primary sources. Observation is one of the most important technique of obtaining the objective data particularly at the time of their occurrences. This technique is also used for the final validation of the scientific conclusions drawn through the scientific methods by the scientists. Goode and Hatt have therefore, made a comment that "Science begins with observation and must ultimately return to observation for its final validation."[4] In this technique a researcher attentively, carefully and consciously collects the data with the deliberate use of the senses, attention and perception, which can be considered as the most distinguished components of the observation technique. Young has rightly said, "Observation a deliberate study through the eye may be used as one of the methods for scrutinising collective behaviours and complex social institutions as well as the separate units composing a totality".[5]

The validity of observation technique is greatly commended in all scientific researches whether natural or social. It is so because the scientist applying observation technique not only observe the study units from every direction directly and fully but also uses many other techniques such as interview, interview guide/schedule, retrospective reports and records as its supplementary techniques for the attainment of the valid, reliable, intensive and exact information regarding the study units. Moreover, the researcher has the sufficient time to test the validity of the data collected through observation. In the field of cultural study, the use of observation technique seems more appropriate and useful for the most complicated, recondite and versatile aspects of any cultural groups which need a penetrating sight to bring them in light which is effectual merely when a view finder directly using one's all human-senses observe with an analytical view. Some times, the cultural group to be studied may vary with the cultural background of the researcher, the communication gap, illiteracy prevailing among the given cultural group, conservatism, reserved and shy nature of the respondent units and some sorts of topographical inaccessibility and the problem of cultural contact make insuperable the process of the attainment of objective data, which can eventually be faciliated only by the use of the observation technique.

Ensuring the accuracy of observation and its scientific significance, Lindman states, "........... if you wish to know what he is really doing, watch him don't ask him."[6] But observation procedure vary according to the variation of the nature and the types of the study group. The observer may participate actively, deliberately and consciously or he may be an observer or his status may be as an outsider whose purpose of presence may be unknown to the people he is observing. Moreover, in viewing, the observer may use precision instruments, mechanical aids, standardised procedure or may not use them. Thus, the various observational procedures applied in different natural and social life settings may broadly be categorised into two major divisions viz., the controlled and the uncontrolled observation. The uncontrolled observations could be either of the non-participant or of the participant in type. But the use of any of the types depends on the nature of the socio-cultural system and the respondent units as well as the nature of the study. By all means, observation is one of the most reliable techniques for obtaining measurable data of socio-cultural phenomenon through various measuring devices such as one way screens, mirrors, monument recorders, sound recorders, motion pictures and observation guide etc.[7] Stuart Chapin also appreciates the importance of the precision tools of observation and states, "Observation instruments are important and accurate just as truely as are the thermometer or the stethoscope of the physician."[8]

In the study, the uncontrolled quasi-participant observation technique, particularly to achieve rapprochement and the opportunities for following the problem in hand more closely, correctly and comprehensively is used. Moreover, the use of precision instruments, *viz.*, Camera, Schedule and Observation Guide have deliberately been applied to study the problem intensively. Actually, the degree of participation depends largely on the nature of the study and the practical demands of the situation. Many investigators must have necessity to identify themselves closely with groups studied, because the subject matter is so novel that it needs intensive study under close proximity.

Conversely, if the subject matter is familiar with the investigator may perceive it primarily in terms of his own previous life unless he deliberately takes another role to enable him to experience in himself the more subtle differences.[9] Following the observation technique the researcher with the status of a participant observer had to set up a rapport with the study group and took part in all of their general most activities. He had to develop several sorts of informal but pseudo kinship relations with the members of the study units being observed. At the first stage of the social intercourse with the members of the different tribal communities in hand, the researcher had to face many adverse situations, sarcastic comments, suspecious, penetrating and searching looks of each and every person, always revolving around him. But as an efficient and professional spy, the researcher had to reciprocate them in a very meaningful, cohesive, brotherly and in every possible treatment which always made them realize the research as to be their own member of the respective community.

In fact, the success of this procedure basically depend on the degree of the assimilation of the researcher within the study group and to what extent he becomes the part of the members of the group. Goode and Hatt has rightly said, "This procedure is used when the investigator can so disguise himself as to be accepted as a member of the group."[10] Hence, to be considered as the bona-fide member of the tribal communities under study and to extend the interpersonal relations with their members, the researcher had to have the acquaintance of the basic social norms, habits, values and ideologies of the communities and also to take part in their day to day activities from hearth to herd, birth to funeral and exorcism to herb by sharing their feelings and taking the account of their aspirations, attitudes towards the traditions and the newly emergent social values. As stated by Young, "This participant observer is an outsider who temporarily becomes an insider. He thereby secures a better in-sight into the situation he is investigating as he is not personally involved and can remain detached, while at the same time taking part in the group activities and sharing their feelings and prejudices."[11] Thus, in view of the nature and the objectives of the present study, the researcher had to become as much a part of the cultural world of the tribal communities of Uttarakhand as was ethically possible and essential to achieve the subtle most facts. To maintain the reliability of the facts the researcher had to make their causal analysis with the help of what, why, how, where and who.

In this way the intensive first hand information are gathered through participant observation and to maintain their reliability, the facts have been noted within the minimum span of time to escape from oblivion. Moreover, to achieve the most reliable facts and to maintain the reliability in observation the field work has scientifically been projected and completed with the help of pre-planned techniques and tools viz; observation guide, camera etc. and inspite of being the participant observer, the researcher has always maintained objectivity by not completely assimilating himself with the tribal communities in study and kept himself free from bias, excitement, hurry and evaluative judgments and has conscience to remove the errors of non-observation and mal-observation and systematically observed the pre-planned and clarified situation as well as their dimensions.

Besides the quasi-participant observation method, an interview-schedule has also been prepared to collect the first hand information in a sequential manner. This schedule comprises the definite, concrete and pre-ordained questions to clarify the inadequate answer and to elicit more detailed responses. Mostly the open-ended, dichotomous, and the multiple choice questions have been designed and included within the schedule. Through open ended questions, the researcher has tried to obtain the attitudes of the respondents as it permits them for free response against the questions. While dichotomous and multiple choice questions present the fixed alternative answer to questions so that the respondent may choose the appropriate one.

Besides this various records, manuscripts, gazetteers and many other related studies and their findings have been used as the source of the secondary information to substantiate the hypotheses and also to measure the process of cultural transformation among the Scheduled Tribal communities in Uttarakhand.

Hypothesis

A tentative solution or explanation or generalisation formulated in regard of the study problem in any scientific investigation is a hypothesis the validity of which is tested on the basis of the facts gathered through the scientific techniques during research. Before the commencement of any scientific research, a researcher proposes to acquire the fruitful, accurate, exact and appropriate facts for which the researcher not only develops some point of views or propositions pertaining to the problem in hand but also bases the whole of the study on such speculative and imaginative propositions which are formulated generally on the basis of the personal and idiosyncratic experiences of the researcher, findings of the related studies drawn by other scholars, analogies and theories promulgated by different scholars. Thus, the view points or propositions formulated as such may be termed as the hypothesis.

In fact, hypothesis suggests the researcher what facts are to be collected and what are not. It indicates the essential points for enquiry and thus avoids the collection of non-essential and useless data and thus helps the researcher in collecting the most significant and useful data. Professor Northrop has reasonably remarked; "The function of the hypothesis is to direct our research for order among facts. The suggestions formulated in any hypothesis may be solutions to the problem. What ever they are, in the task of enquiry."[12]

In view of the research questions of the problem in hand, the researcher has specified the main variables pertaining to which the essential data have to be collected and a comprehensive pilot survey of the universe has performed to gain the personal and idiosyncratic experiences about the problem. Besides this, an overview of the literature concern and of the related studies, the different cultural theories propounded so far for the scientific analysis of the process of cultural transformation and the socio-cultural analogies pertaining to the tribal communities under study have consciously and deliberately been taken into account to develop the hypothesis so that the essential and accurate facts can be gathered for the final validation of the hypothesis and also to draw the scientific inferences about the problem. The hypothesis thus formulated for the present study are as follows :

1. The cultural impact of non-tribal communities has accelerated the process of cultural transformation among the scheduled tribal communities in Uttarakhand.

2. The statutory provisions and reformatory agencies are positively correlated with the process of cultural transformation of the scheduled tribal communities of Uttarakhand.

3. The process of cultural transformation among the scheduled

tribal communities of Uttarakhand varies as according to the socio-cultural standard of the tribal people and the degree of their emotional attachment with the traditional style of life.

4. Inspite of the impact of the various reformatory agencies and of different cultural groups the tribal people of Uttarakhand to maintain their own identity and self respect are not in the state of complete abandonment of the traits of pre-sanskritized religious rituals, beliefs and practices.
5. Education, means of transport and communication and the socio-economic planning for development, have paved the way for inter-tribal relations and extended the sphere of cultural contacts.
6. Because of the prolonged constant contact with non-tribals, the scheduled tribal communities of Uttarakhand have begun to share the cultural traits of the respective residents of the respective regions they live in.
7. Traditional taboos which play an important role in the determination of the nature of the commensal and connubial relations of the tribal people are the main inhibitions in the way of the cultural transformation among the scheduled tribal communities in Uttarakhand.

Analysis and Interpretation of Data

The scientific analysis and interpretation of the compiled data is the creative aspect of research which make possible the attainment of the scientific inferences and yield the answers of the research questions and also verify the validity of the working hypothesis. The bewildering heap of collected data do not lead to any scientific conclusions unless they are not generalized in a systematic manner. Actually, science is built with facts as a house is built with stones, but a collection of facts is no more science then a heap of stones is a house.[13] The function of systematic analysis is to built an intellectual edifice in which properly sorted and sifted facts and figures are placed in their appropriate setting and consistent relationship, so that general inferences can be drawn from them.[14]

Viewing the objectives of the study, the researcher has classified the data compiled through primary and secondary sources. The classified data of the present study which are related with the demographic sphere are tabulated orderly in columns by manual method, i.e. the hand tabulation. The tabulated data have been analysed to draw a causal inference of different variables.

The research findings drawn through the analysis of the data, have thoroughly been interpreted conjoining them with the results of the related studies conducted by many other scholars as well as the theories promulgated earlier to understand the process of cultural transformation. Moreover, the interpretation of the inferences of the present study also substantiate the hypotheses already formulated to direct the research work and also given birth to some more dimensions for further studies which the scholars can follow as the guidelines or the model.

Lastly the research findings or the results of the study have been presented through the research report. The research report has been prepared in view of the communicability to the readers as well as the need of the social scientists or scholars. A systematic delineation of the study problem, the research procedure, the study design, the universe and the samples, techniques of data collection, sources of data, analysis of data, the results or the findings of the study and the interpretation of the research findings, has been presented through the research report. The report starts with the statement of the problem and ends with its findings.

References

1. Young, P.V., Scientific Social Surveys and Research, Prentice Hall of India Private Limited, New Delhi, 1982, p.p. 12-13.
2. *Ibid.*, p. 13.
3. Lundberg, G.A., Social Research, Longmans Green & Co., New York, p. 135.
4. Goode, W.J. and P.K. Hatt., Methods in Social Research, Mc Graw Hill Book Co., New York, 1952, p. 119.
5. Young, P.V., Scientific Social Surveys and Research, Asia Publishing House. London, 1954, p. 199.
6. Lindman, Social Discovery, Republic Publishing Co., 1952, pp. 182-193.

7. Morris, Richard T., The Two Way Mirror; Natural status in Foreign Student. Adjustment, University of Minnesota Press, 1960.

8. Chapin, S., New Trends in Social Research. Journal of Educational Sociology, XI, 565-566. Quoted by P.V. Young, Scientific Social Surveys and Research, Asia Publishing House, London, 1954, p. 169.

9. Johoda, M., Research Methods in Social Relations, The Dryden Press 1951, p. 142.

10. Goode, W.J. and P.K. Hatt, Methods in Social Research, Mc Graw Hill Book Co. Inc., New York, 1952, p. 2.

11. Yang, H.P., Fact Finding with Rural People, p. 30.

12. Northrop, F.S.C., The Logic of Science and Humanities; Macmillan; London; 1947, p. 12.

13. Young, P.V., Scientific Social Surveys and Research, Asia Publishing House Bombay, 1960, p. 509.

14. *Ibid.*, p. 473.

4

SAMPLE STRUCTURE

The present chapter is mainly concerned with the factual interpretation of the various dimensions of bio-social profiles of the sampled units as to make more comprehensible the discussion of the results acquired through the extensive as well as the intensive study. Moreover, an account of the ecological settings of the study area and the socio-cultural background of the respondent units also reserve a sense of relevance and therefore presented in brief so that the contemporaneity of the various non-contemporaneous patterns of tribal culture can be studied scientifically.

Frame-work of Observe Group and the Categories with Respondent Units

In the present study only 15 villages, out of which five Bhotiya villages namely, Go, Suring, Torthal, Bhatwari Niti respectively from Dharchula, Munsyari, Berinag. Bhatwari and Joshimath blocks, four Buxa villages namely; Dhaki, Majara Hasan, Rajpur, Maharakagaun, respectively from Bajpur, Gadarpur, Ramnagar and Shaspur, two Tharu villages namely, Bigarabagh and Karghata from Khatima and Sitarganj block, two Raji villages namely Ganagaunand Chaurani respectively from Dharchula and Didihat block and two Jaunsari villages namely Masarar and Banpur respectively from Kalsi and Chokrata block, as well as almost all the district headquarters and a town having maximum Scheduled Tribe population from each district has been selected as the sample areas of the study. Almost all the families and their population spread over in different sampled areas on the whole constitute the observed-group of the study. The respondent units which are included into the observed group are also selected as primary sources of getting more intensive information. Out of total 700 respondent units, 370 belong to first category and 125 and 205 belong respectively to second and third category. In the first category, only the heads of the agriculturist families which are confined within the different sampled villages have been included for study. In the second category, only a single member from each family who is engaged directly with any of the business pursuits have been considered as the respondent units, while the third category consists of the earning members, employed in any government services, within the sampled area. While selecting the respondent units this fact has been kept in mind that each and every tribal community might have given proportionately equal representation so that the scientific generalization of the information gathered from the respondent units may be brought out. The following table presents the category-wise numbers of the respondent units.

Table 8

Category-wise Break up of the Respondent Units

Category	*Scheduled Tribe*					
	Bhotiya	*Buxa*	*Tharu*	*Raji*	*Jaunsari*	*Total*
Ist	132 (35.68)	103 (27.83)	82 (22.17)	23 (6.21)	30 (8.11)	370 (100)
Iind	80 (64.00)	12 (9.60)	13 (10.40)	-- --	20 (6.00)	125 (100)
IIIrd	120 (58.52)	20 (9.76)	30 (14.63)	-- --	35 (17.08)	205 (100)
Total	332 (47.42)	135 (19.29)	125 (17.85)	23 (3.29)	85 (12.14)	700 (100)

Socio-cultural Profile of the Respondents

Like the several backward and low caste Hindus, the tribal communities of Uttarakhand, beyond the impact of the transportation and communications have been compelled to be confined within the inaccessible, hilly and forest areas of the region. Socially, they were also deprived from all sorts of sacred and beneficial occupations and the equal opportunities of the education as well as the self respect. Consequently, they had to roam in the pitch dark of ignorance, conservatism and backwardness for hundreds of years. It was the state of absolute socio-cultural backwardness of the tribal communities. In real sense, they were the frog in the wells. However, with the confinement of the socio-cultural peripheries, the tribals were happy with the observance of their own mode of living, own economy, own cultural ethos, morals, beliefs and practices, even the law and the Government which were quite distinct from the rest of the civilized societies. They had neither any aspiration for better future nor any one worked for their socio-cultural development for centuries. In fact, who cared for the well being of the forest dwellers or the cave dwellers. They were mere curio and the wonder for a common civilized spectator.

Eventually, the graph of the socio-cultural development of the tribal communities remained at the same point from where it was started, particularly in pre-Independence India. But after independence the welfare Government of India has paved the multifarious ways for socio-cultural development of the tribal communities by providing them an equal opportunities before Constitution like other citizens of free India and also formulated a number of special provisions for the overall development of the tribals declaring them as the Scheduled Tribes. As the article 46 of the Constitution declares that "The State shall promote, with special care, the educational and economic interests of the weaker sections of the people, and in particular, of Scheduled Castes and the Scheduled Tribes and shall protect them from social injustice and all forms of exploitation."[1] But with the passage of time, the traditional form of tribalism seems to have undergone a numerous structural and systemic change. The new dimensions of the tribal cultural change have emerged, resultantly the different spheres of the tribal social life for instance; the familial, the educational, the occupational, the religious as well as the aspirations of the tribal people for future and their attitude towards the various factors of modernization have also blown altogether in the wave of the change. Today the tribal people appear not in favour of doing old things in the way it has already been done, for the potentialities of the multiple techniques have extended even in the tribal areas.

Hence, in the light of the various factors of change and the constitutional frame of reference particularly since 1967 when the tribal communities of Uttarakhand were declared as the Scheduled-Tribes, the cultural transformation occurring in the various spheres of the tribal culture pave the way for the completion of this dissertation.

Age and Sex Composition of Respondent Units

Since ever, sex and age have been the biological bases of social stratification. The cultural history of mankind also witnesses that the statuses and the roles of an individual have ever been determined on the basis of the sex dichotomy and the age difference. Particularly, in primitive societies the status and role of the male and the female have largely determined on the basis of the sex and the age. Even in some civilized societies the female is treated as inferior than male only due to sex differentiation and therefore assigned lower status in the respective societies she lives in and is also supposed to live under the protection of father, husband and son, respectively during her childhood, youth and old age. It is only the biological base that the female was reckoned as the personal property for the male, who not only satisfies the lust of the male but also lends her hand in economic pursuits. Moreover, it is also a sex-based biological base that the female in some societies is kept in a *'purdha'* within the boundary walls of the house where she bears the children and rears and cares them. Thus, her position in society was like a child bearing machine. Being female she had no any participation in public life, her best and ideal position and engagements were in the family.

It was rather a biological base as to deprive the female from all sorts of socio-religious rights and privileges as well as the property ownership. While the male was over all incharge of all sorts of socio-religious rights and privileges as well as the property ownership, hence his position was higher than the female, as is observed among the 'Todas' of Nilgiri. On the contrary in some communities the position of female is comparatively higher than the male, and the female therefore enjoys some special socio-religious privileges and also possesses the key position in regard of the property ownership, as is observed among the 'Khasas' of Meghalaya. Even the difference between the matriarchal and patriarchal type of societies is almost sex-based.

However, there are still some communities where both the male and female enjoy equal socio-religious status. For instance, the tribes of Nicobar Island have no clear-cut sex-based stratification. Besides this the earliest social division of labour was also based on sex-dichotomy. Emile Durkheim[2] has stated that the earliest division of labour was essentially on the basis of sex. In the hunting and food gathering stage the male members of the family used to go out for hunting or in search of other means of subsistence, while the females were left behind to look after the family and for rearing and caring the children. In brief it may be concluded that the sex has been the biological base for the determination of the status and role of the male and the female in every stage of cultural development of mankind.

The age as the biological factor, also plays an important role in determining the status and role of an individual in society. Even the status of the head of the family both in matriarchal and patriarchal type of families is also based on the seniority of the age of the person concerned. In general, the senior most male and female member of the family respectively holds the status of the head of the family in patriarchal and matriarchal type of families and also privileged to take decisions in all familial as well as the socio-economic matters. For, it is supposed that the aged person retains comparatively more knowledge and the experience in respect of the different aspects of social life, and therefore a sense of respect and honour as well as the privileges always centered around him or her. Mostly in primitive societies the aged persons only have monopoly to handle the economic organizations, political institutions and magico-religious practices because all these subjects are serious by nature and therefore need special care to perform and kept away from the participation of the youths as they are supposed to have superficial knowledge and the experience about the matters of collective interests, the faulty operations of which may cause the dangers for the community as well as the unhappiness of the supernatural power which in return may cause the harm of the community. The 'Gonds' of Bastar are the best example of this sort. Besides this the chieftain of the clan and the council of the elders to advise him, as is observed in several tribal communities in the world, is an evidence of the higher status of the aged persons in tribal communities. Moreover, the inherent biological stages, occurred during the growth of an individual, namely; the infancy, the adolescence, the adulthood and the old age, respectively implied a certain degree of the expectations and the liabilities and thus ultimately determine the status and role of the individual in society, are also the indications towards the prevalent age-based stratification of the statuses and roles in society.

The following table presents respectively the sex and age composition of the respondent units of the present study.

Table 9

Sex Composition of the Respondent Units

Sex	*Respondent Units*					
	Bhotiya	*Buxa*	*Tharu*	*Raji*	*Jaunsari*	*Total*
Male	249	121	110	17	71	568
Female	83	14	15	06	14	132
Total	332	135	125	23	85	700

It has been observed that the representation of the male respondents is almost higher than the females in respect of all the five scheduled tribal communities. It is so because :

1. In the first category only the heads of the sampled families have been selected as the respondent units, virtually, the male members, on account of the patriarchal form of family are taken in maximum numbers. Yet the women who look after their families due to their widowhood or separation from the husband or in the absence of their husbands have been given the chance to be included in the samples.

2. While in the second and third category all the males and females have been given equal chance to be included in sample, yet the dominance of the male members even in the business pursuits and Government services has caused the sexual variation in the sample structure of the present study. However, this facet may be considered as an outcome of the comparative dominance of the tribal male persons in the socio-occupational sphere of the tribal life.

Table 10

Age Composition of the Respondent Units

Age	*Bhotiya*		*Buxa*		*Tharu*		*Raji*		*Jaunsari*		*Total*
Group	*Ma.*	*Fe.*	*Ma.*	*Fe.*	*Ma.*	*Fe.*	*Ma.*	*Fe.*	*Ma.*	*Fe.*	
First Category											
0-20	--	--	--	--	--	--	--	--	--	--	--
20-40	17	--	07	02	20	02	04	01	--	--	53
40-60	42	10	43	03	39	04	08	04	04	02	159
60-80	55	20	37	04	13	02	04	01	15	06	139
80-100	05	01	07	--	02	--	01	--	02	01	19
Total	119	13	94	09	74	08	17	06	21	09	370
Second Category											
0-20	02	03	--	--	01	--	--	--	02	--	08
20-40	18	15	08	--	07	--	--	--	12	--	06
40-60	26	11	04	--	05	--	--	--	06	--	52
60-80	04	01	--	--	--	--	--	--	--	--	05
80-100	--	--	--	--	--	--	--	--	--	--	--
Total	50	30	12	--	13	--	--	--	20	--	125
Third Category											
0-20	--	--	--	--	--	--	--	--	--	--	--
20-40	60	32	12	05	18	07	--	--	25	05	164
40-60	20	08	03	--	05	--	--	--	05	--	41

Contd..

60-80	--	--	--	--	--	--	--	--	--	--	--
80-100	--	--	--	--	--	--	--	--	--	--	--
Total	80	40	15	05	23	07	--	--	30	05	205

Thus, the sample structure of the present study includes the respondent units from different age groups which will ultimately enable to evaluate the attitudes and the aspirations of the respondent units belonging to the new as well as the old generations. Particularly, in regard of the various patterns (traditional and the newly emerged) of the cultural system.

Marital Status of the Respondent Units

Every society, whether primitive or civilized comprises some established forms of institutional procedures which basically regulate the sexual alliances between the male and the female and also help in the fulfilment of some biological pre-requisites essentially important for the maintenance and the continuity of the society. Such an institution is to be known as marriage. It is an universal institution which exists in every cultural group and also observed in every stage of cultural evolution as an essential component of the cultural system. But the nature of the marriage institution differ from one society to another. For instance, the Hindu marriage is a sacrament while it is a social contract for Muslims, but in some other communities it is merely a socially approved way of sexual intercourse. Even in tribal communities marriage is considered to be an integral part of the tribal culture, the importance of which is commended for the socio-economic gains the parties achieved after marriage. Thus, marriage not only helps in the fulfilment of the biological instinct of an individual but also it makes up the mentality, view point, as well as the behaviour patterns of the individual in society and also determines the social status he holds and the role he performs as a member of society. Thus, marriage implies multifarious functions as to make possible the existence of a cultural system and its continuity.

Table 11

Marital Status of the Respondent Units

Marital Status	*Bhotiya*		*Buxa*		*Tharu*		*Raji*		*Jaunsari*		*Total*
	Ma.	*Fe.*	*Ma.*	*Fe.*	*Ma.*	*Fe.*	*Ma.*	*Fe.*	*Ma.*	*Fe.*	
First Category											
Unmarried	--	--	--	--	--	--	--	--	--	--	--
Married	101	04	78	03	66	02	15	--	19	09	297
Widow/ Widower	17	08	05	04	08	06	02	06	02	--	68
Separated	01	01	01	02	--	--	--	--	--	--	05
Divorced	--	--	--	--	--	--	--	--	--	--	--
Total	119	13	94	09	74	08	17	06	21	09	370
Second Category											
Unmarried	12	08	01	--	--	--	--	--	--	--	24
Married	29	17	10	--	08	--	--	--	20	--	84
Widow/ Widower	05	05	01	--	02	--	--	--	--	--	13
Separated	04	--	--	--	-	--	--	--	--	--	04
Divorced	--	--	--	--	--	--	--	--	--	--	--
Total	50	30	12	--	13	--	--	--	20	--	125
Third Category											
Unmarried	23	10	04	02	02	--	--	--	--	--	41
Married	57	30	11	03	21	07	--	--	30	05	164
Widow/ Widower	--	--	--	--	--	--	--	--	--	--	--
Separated	--	--	--	--	--	--	--	--	--	--	--
Divorced	--	--	--	--	--	--	--	--	--	--	--
Total	80	40	15	05	23	07	--	--	30	05	205

Table 11 exhibits that the majority of the respondents i.e. 545 (77.85%) out of the total 700 are married and 81 (11.58%) are widows/widowers, 65 (9.29%) are unmarried and only 9 (1.28%) respondents are separated. The tabulated data also makes it clear that none of the respondents is unmarried in first category, while out of the total 65 unmarried respondents the maximum 41 respondents belong to the third category and the remaining 24 belong to the second category. This fact is a natural manifestation of the diminishing trend of child marriages among the tribal communities. Besides this, none of the respondents was found divorced. Though the divorce may take place in some particular situations but it has been noted that in general, the tribals try to avoid any such situation that may cause the divorce between husband and the wife. Because the divorce not only separates both the parties but also creates a problem for economic subsistence. However, few exceptional cases of divorce particularly among Khasas and Tharus have come in light.

Educational Standard

Education is just like a luminary as to make luminous the pitch dark of ignorance. On the individual level it implies a process of self-purification and removes all sorts of narrow and selfish desires, motives and retrograde ego and stimulates all the dormant senses of the personality for their best functioning. It is potent agent of the socialization of a child and also helps in the development of human personality, social mobility, occupational changes and the rise of the professions.[3] It also helps in the development of the human resources as a part of the social milieu and acts as an instrument of socio-economic development. As pointed out by Strumilin, Young, Schultz and Denison,[4] that the education may increase productivity and economic development. Emile Durkheim has considered education as a social institution that functionally promotes consensus and social integration in new generation through cultivation of those personal qualities that can further it as a social process.[5] It is education which imparts a significant contribution in moulding the personality either towards the modernity or the traditionality.

Moreover, education is also helpful in bringing about the socio-cultural transformation by accelerating the modernization and its subsidiary processes. Here the education is one of the variable elements, the impact of which is to be observed in the cultural transformation of the tribal communities under reference. Thus, with an end in view, the educational standard of the respondent units have been presented in Table 12.

Table 12

Educational Standard of the Respondent Units

Education	*Bhotiya*		*Buxa*		*Tharu*		*Raji*		*Jaunsari*		*Total*
Standard	*Ma.*	*Fe.*	*Ma.*	*Fe.*	*Ma.*	*fe.*	*Ma.*	*Fe.*	*Ma.*	*Fe.*	
First Category											
Illiterate	102	13	85	07	60	02	13	06	17	09	314
Primary	12	--	08	02	13	06	04	--	04	--	49
Junior High School	05	--	01	--	01	--	--	--	--	--	07
High School	--	--	--	--	--	--	--	--	--	--	--
Intermediate	--	--	--	--	--	--	--	--	--	--	--
Graduation	--	--	--	--	--	--	--	--	--	--	--
P. Graduation	--	--	--	--	--	--	--	--	--	--	--
Total	119	13	94	09	74	08	17	06	21	09	370
Second Category											
Illiterate	12	12	03	--	04	--	--	--	02	--	33
Primary	23	10	09	--	09	--	--	--	12	--	63
Junior High School	06	08	--	--	--	--	--	--	03	--	17
High School	05	--	--	--	--	--	--	--	02	--	07
Intermediate	03	--	--	--	--	--	--	--	01	--	04
Graduation	01	--	--	--	--	--	--	--	--	--	01
P. Graduation	--	--	--	--	--	--	--	--	--	--	--
Total	50	30	12	--	13	--	--	--	20	--	125

Contd..

Education Standard	*Bhotiya* *Ma.*	*Fe.*	*Buxa* *Ma.*	*Fe.*	*Tharu* *Ma.*	*fe.*	*Raji* *Ma.*	*Fe.*	*Jaunsari* *Ma.*	*Fe*	*Total*
Third Category											
Illiterate	--	--	--	--	--	--	--	--	--	--	
Primary	--	--	--	--	--	--	--	--	--	--	--
Junior High School	--	--	--	--	--	--	--	--	--	02	02
High School	05	03	03	02	01	05	--	--	--	02	21
Intermediate	04	01	10	03	03	02	--	--	08	01	32
Graduation	50	21	02	--	14	--	--	--	18	--	105
Post Graduation	21	15	--	--	05	--	--	--	04	--	45
Total	80	40	15	05	23	07	--	--	30	05	205

Table 12 exhibits that the majority of the respondents i.e. 347 (49.58%) are illiterate out of which 314 (90.49%) belong to the first category and the rest 33 (9.51%) respondents belong to second category. The respondents who are educated upto primary standard are 112 (16.00%) in number, out of which maximum 63 (56.25%) have been engaged in some business pursuits and the remaining 49 (43.75%) are the cultivators. The least number of the respondents i.e. 26 (3.76%) are educated upto Junior High School standard, out of which 17 (65.39%) belong to the second category and the 7 (26.92%) are of the first category. 28 (4.00%) respondents are educated upto High School standard, out of which 21 (75.00%) belong to the third category and the remaining 7 (25.00%) belong to second category. Besides this 36 (5.14%) respondents are intermediate pass, out of which the maximum 32 (88.89%) have been included in third category and the rest 4 (11.11%) are related with the second category. But the maximum 106 (15.14%) respondents are graduates out of which 105 (99.06%) have been engaged in different government salaried jobs and the rest 01 (0.94%) respondents belong to the second category. Moreover, 45 (6.42%) respondents are post-graduate and employed in different government services. Besides this table 12 also depicts the educational standard of the tribal women who are coming out of their traditional peripheries and wish to participate in every sphere of the life. The correlation between the educational standard and the professions will be more useful in mapping out the real canvas of the respondent units.

Social Ecology and the Religion

In general, ecology is the sum total of the geographical, cultural, economic and the demographic factors which keep on interacting with each other to maintain an approximate balance as to give a particular shape to the cultural system of a given community. Alike the social institutions, religious beliefs and practices, folk-ways, customs, traditions, ideology and the patterns of human behaviour and the discoveries, inventions, means of communications and transportations constitute on the whole the social ecology of the spatial group. In fact, there is close relation between the community life and the social ecology of a given community, which ascertain not only the statuses and the roles of the members of the community but also define the nature of the relationship which they develop in reference of the members of other communities. Thus, it is evident that the social ecology of the different communities, that is rural, urban, tribal and so on, will be different from each other which can obviously be observed in the forms of the prevalent patterns of behaviour, attitudes and the ways of the community life. The respondent units and the cultural patterns of the community they live in, have been designed to be observed intensively within two different socio-ecological settings, that is the rural and the urban and it has also been tried to observe that the socio-ecological variation leads to the variations of the cultural system. Since the social ecology subsumes broadly the rural and urban communities as the two important aspects of the social life therefore in view of the study of the impact of the different ecological settings, the respondent units of the first category have been taken from the rural background which represent the rural social-ecology, while the respondents of the second and third categories are from the urban/town areas which eventually represent the urban social-ecology. The following Table 13 will represent the rural and urban-wise distribution of the respondent units.

Table 13

Domicile of the Respondent Units

Domicile	*Botiya*		*Buxa*		*Tharu*		*Raji*		*Jaunsari*		*Total*
	Ma.	*Fe.*	*Ma.*	*Fe.*	*Ma.*	*Fe.*	*Ma.*	*Fe.*	*Ma.*	*Fe.*	
First Category											
Rural	119	13	94	09	74	08	17	06	21	09	370 (100%)
Urban	--	--	--	--	--	--	--	--	--	--	--
Rural and Urban	--	--	--	--	--	--	--	--	--	--	--
Total	119	13	94	09	74	08	17	06	21	09	370 (100%)
Second Category											
Rural	--	--	--	--	--	--	--	--	--	--	--
Urban	40	25	07	--	09	--	--	--	13	--	94 (75.20%)
Rural and Urban	10	05	05	--	04	--	--	--	07	--	31 (24.80%)
Total	50	30	12	--	13	--	--	--	20	--	125 (100%)
Third Category											
Rural	--	--	--	--	--	--	--	--	--	--	-- --
Urban	32	11	02	--	08	02	--	--	07	01	63 (30.73%)
Rural and Urban	48	29	13	05	15	05	--	--	23	04	142 (69.27%)
Total	80	30	15	05	23	07	--	--	30	05	205 700 (100%)

Thus, it is clear from Table 13 that almost 370 (52.86%) respondents belonging to the first category are from the rural background, while out of the total 125 (17.85%) respondents of the second category, 94 (75.20%) belong to the urban areas and the rest 31 (24.80%) are those who belong both in the rural and urban areas. In the same way, out of the total 205 (29.29%) respondents belonging to the third category, the maximum 142 (69.27%) are from both the rural and urban background, while the remaining 63 (30.73%) belong to the urban background. During the investigation, a fact also came in light that some respondents who are engaged either in business pursuits (second category) or in government services (third category) do not accommodate their families with them because of the housing problem and over economic burden in urban areas and therefore, they earn their livelihood by staying in the urban areas and constantly visit their families in villages during holidays, vacation or on some particular occasions.

There is, however, another fact that the respondents frequently in rural-urban continuum have got functionally the motivational significance for those who are absolutely from the rural background. Such a group of respondents refers to the sources of values in shaping the behaviour patterns, evaluations and the aspirations of the rest of the people who are not actually the member of the former one and thus the group virtually ascertains its own prestigious status in the society and also in the mind of the people. Thus, it may be concluded that the socio-ecological background also helps in determining the socio-economic status of the tribal people in the community concerned.

Religious Description of the Respondent Units

Religion has since ever been an integral component of every cultural group. But the philosophers, anthropologists and the sociologists are not consensus about the concept of religion. However, from the etymological point of view Bouquet has stated; religion is derived form the Latin word rel(I)igio, which itself is derived from either the root leg-, which means 'together, count or observe', or from the root lig-, which means 'to bind'. In the former sense the implication is belief in and observation of, signs of Divine communication. In the latter sense the implication is the performance of necessary actions which may bind together man and the supernatural powers.........[6] In fact, religion is a system of beliefs, rituals, emotional attitudes as well as the practices by which a sense of fear, reverence, devotion and also a feeling of sacredness is expressed for the supernatural power which is abstract in nature and differ from society to society and even people to people for its conceptual meaning. As Majumdar has stated that "For some, the supernatural may be constituted of ghosts and spirits; for others it may be an impersonal power which pervades everything in this world; for still others it may be manifested through a pantheon of anthropomorphic gods and goddesses or a single high God and so on."[7]

Thus, in view of the complexity of the nature, the concept religion has been studied by many scholars from various disciplines and also defined in different manners. For instance, Durkheim states the religion as a product of society and an unified system of beliefs and practices relative to sacred things. Maxmuller says, religion is a faculty of the mind which enables a man to grasp the infinite independently of senses and reasons. Feuerbach states religion as a desire which manifests itself in prayers, sacrifices and faith. E.B. Tylor defines, religion is a belief in spiritual being. Marie-Jean Guyan has said, "Religion is a universal socio-morphism." Thus, there are numerous conceptions of religion but in general it can be stated that the religion is the term used to describe the relation between the social being and the supernatural power and also the numerous systems of beliefs and practices in which these relations are manifested.

But since long the tribal religions in India, were termed as animism in various census reports and books, which carries a belief in benevolent and malevolent spirits which are supposed to influence the destiny of man.[8]

But irrespective of the existence of various forms of religion in different times and different societies it is irrefutable that the religion as an essential and potent constituent unit of the cultural system, provides its followers an identity, a set of values and the socio-economic ethics which profoundly influence their attitudes, behaviour patterns and ultimately the socio-economic system.

In the present study almost all the respondent units are from the Hindu religion as they claim to be and therefore supposed to believe in the super-natural power implied in various gods and goddesses and propitiated by the people in different manners in different occasions. But, however, they have still faith in the existence of ghosts, spirits, souls and different such powers which are impersonal by nature and supposed to preside over various departments of man's social life. They still have faith in the magic which they practise for the solution of the different problems in day to day life. Thus, it may be essential that the tribal communities under reference still follow animism, the crude and the earliest form of the religion. The Scheduled Tribe-wise rituals and the systems of beliefs and practices will be presented in a separate chapter.

Occupational Groupings

Occupational groupings, which succeed in defining themselves as professions, occupy a special class in the family of occupations.[9] Professions have risen to prominence and occupy a position of importance in modern urbanized society on a scale unprecedented in history.[10] But they are not new among the occupations, the recorded history of mankind bears testimony to the fact that they have existed since ancient times. As Carr-Saunders and Wilson[11] and Lewis and Maude[12] have also expressed the same views in regard of the history of professions. Since industrial revolution the newly develcped professionalism have become more and more persuasive and pervasive for those people who are engaged in various types of commercial jobs. As R. Pandey has stated that, "Professions as a distinct social group grew to be prominent as a concomitant of the prodigious socio-economic changes that took place since the renaissance through the industrial revolution on the post-second world war era."[13]

During post Independence India, the various dimensions of professionalism have come into existence and subsequently exceeded the various opportunities of multiple professions for the workers. Moreover, the introduction of the process of industrialization, urbanization and the modernization have still more accelerated the prominence of the professions and also motivated, even the traditional most professionals to embrace the newly emerged and pragmatically more useful professions. In fact, the prototypical agriculture based economy of India has undergone a tremendous structural as well as the positional changes during last decades, consequently a new-view point of the people has developed towards the life and the livelihood. Even the tribals are also lagging behind their traditional patterns of livelihood and in view of it professing the newly emerged professions. This tendency of embracing the newly developed professions has practically enabled the tribals to ascribe high social status and also provide them every opportunity for vertical mobility in the socio-economic sphere of life. Thus, it seems to be implicit that the professionalism has imparted an important role in the determination of the psychology and the socio-economic status of the professional group as well as in the socio-cultural change of the group concerned.

Thus, the professionalism, as an inevitable consequence of the modernization process, has been considered as the variable element and its cultural impact have been observed on the different cultural patterns of the tribal communities, so that the process of cultural transformation may be studied even in respect of the various professions. Viewing this the distribution of the respondent units have been made on the basis of the professions. The following Table 14 shows the profession-wise distribution of the respondents.

Table 14

Profession-wise Distribution of Respondent Units

Professi-onal Grp.	*Botiya*		*Buxa*		*Tharu*		*Raji*		*Jaunsari*		*Total*	*G.T.*
	Ma.	*Fe.*	*Ma.*	*Fe.*	*Ma.*	*fe.*	*Ma.*	*Fe.*	*Ma.*	*Fe.*		
First Category												
Land Less Labour	--	--	02	--	04	--	01	--	--	--	07 (1.90%)	
Cultivators	119	13	92	09	70	08	16	06	21	09	363 (98.10%)	
Total	119	13	94	09	74	08	17	06	21	09	370	
Percentage	32.17	3.51	25.4	2.43	20.0	2.17	4.59	1.62	5.68		100.00	

Contd..

Professi-onal Grp.	*Botiya*		*Buxa*		*Tharu*		*Raji*		*Jaunsari*		*Total*
	Ma.	*Fe.*	*Ma.*	*Fe.*	*Ma.*	*fe.*	*Ma.*	*Fe.*	*Ma.*	*Fe.*	
Second Category											
Transporter	02	--	--	--	--	--	--	--	--	--	02 (1.60%)
Wholesale dealer	03	--	--	--	--	--	--	--	--	--	03 (2.40%)
Cloth Merchant	07	--	--	--	--	--	--	--	--	--	07 (5.60%)
Provision Storekeeper	05	01	01	--	02	--	--	--	06	--	15 (12.0%)
Readymade Cloth Merchant	13	09	--	--	--	--	--	--	--	--	22 (17.60%)
Peddler	15	15	--	--	04	--	--	--	--	--	34 (27.20%)
Inn-keeper Restaurant and Tea Stall	05	05	11	--	07	--		--	14	--	42 (33.60%)
Total	50	30	12	--	13	--	--	--	20	--	125
Percentage	40	24	9.6	--	10.4	--	--	--	16	--	100
Third Category											
First Class Officer	01	--	--	--	--	--	--	--	--	--	01 (0.49%)
Second Class Officer	04	03	--	--	--	--	--	--	03	--	10 (4.88%)
Third Class Employees	70	30	04	01	07	02	--	--	15	01	130 (63.41%)
Fourth Class Employees	05	07	11	04	16	05	--	--	12	04	64 (31.22%)
Total	80	40	15	05	23	07	--	--	30	05	205
Percentage	39.03	19.5	7.31	2.4	11.2	3.41	--	--	14.64	2.44	100.00
Grand T.	294	83	121	14	110	15	17	06	71	14	700

It is clear from Table 14 that, in the first category almost all the Bhotiya respondents are cultivators. Besides this, the majority of the respondents of the rest of the tribal communities, belonging to the first category are also cultivators. Yet there are 7 respondents out of which 4 belong to Tharu community, 2 belong to the Buxa community and the remaining one belongs to Raji community, are landless labourers who subsist on the daily wage earnings. This fact came in light that the land of the landless Buxas and the Tharus has been trespassed by the local money lenders and land grabbers by trick and the power display. Even today they are the actual land owners in government records but practically they possess not even a single piece of land. In fact, the land around the Tharu and Buxa villages has either been purchased irregularly or trespassed by the more aggressive outsiders, subsequently, the timid tribals have left their land without any protest. But in order to stop the transfer of land a ban was enforced by an ordinance 1981 of the State Government on the sale of the tribal land, consequently, the land already transgressed by the outsiders could not be transferred legally in their name, nor the timid type of tribal people could get it back from them. Lastly, such type of tribal people have to be deprived from the land ownership and now they are appeared merely as the landless labourers. But in the case of Rajis the cause of landlessness is some what different than the Buxa and the Tharus. As a matter of fact, few families of Rajis, even now, are in the semi-nomadic stage. Because of the unfavourable agro-climatic conditions, they have not settled down permanently in any place and therefore, they have no land in their possession so far, thus, subsequently with the change of the weather they also move from one place to another. Another cause amenable for the landlessness of some Rajis, is their superstitious nature which psychologically scares them for some abstract natural calamities and ultimately compell them to abscond in search of such a new place that can provide them the peace of mind and the better opportunities for subsistence. But the percentage of such Rajis is very nominal.

In the second category out of the total 125 respondents, 50 (40.00%) and 30 (24.00%) Bhotiya male and female respectively are engaged in different business pursuits out of which 15 males and 15 females are engaged in peddler jobs. In this job the females have comparatively more participation than the males. Besides this, 13 Bhotiya males and 9 Bhotiya females are the readymade cloth merchants. While 5 Bhotiya males and 5 females run the restaurants, tea stall and the hotels. Moreover, 5 males and 1 female run the provision stores. While 7, 3 and 2 Bhotiya males are respectively the mercers, whole sellers and the transporters. The rest of the tribal communities i.e. the Buxas the Tharus, the Jaunsaris have respectively 12 (9.60%), 13 (10.4%), 20 (16.00%) respondents who are engaged in different business pursuits. There is no any representation of Rajis in business professions.

The outstanding difference which came in light is that except the Bhotiya females none of the tribal woman was found engaged in any business profession. While both the Bhotiya males and females equally participate in the business pursuits, the most popular job for Bhotiya is the peddlerjob which is operated by both males and the females. Besides this, the Bhotiyas are also the transporters, whole-sale dealers, provision storekeepers, mercers, as well as the inn-keepers. In almost all the business pursuits the Bhotiya female equally participate. It is so because the Bhotiyas have predominantly been a trader tribal community and even today they profess their traditional professions. But the rest of the tribal communities have traditionally been either the food gatherers or the crude cultivators. But today they are a settled cultivators and gradually stepping on some alien profitable jobs too. As the information presented through the Table 14 make it clear that 9.6 percent Buxas, 10.4 percent Tharus and 16.00 percent Jaunsari-Khasas are running the tea stall, restaurants and the provision stores in small scale investments. This emerging tendency of tribals towards the business pursuits is an indication of the occupational mobility of the tribals concerned. However, the Rajis are still particular in regard of the occupation mobility.

In the third category, out of the total 205 respondents, the maximum 120 (58.55%) Bhotiyas are employed in different central and provincial government services. The percentage of Bhotiya male and female employees are respectively 39.03 percent and 19.51 percent to the total respondent employees, which is followed by Jaunsari-Khasas with as much as 14.64 percent male and 2.44 percent female, Tharus 11.21 percent male and 3.41 percent females and Buxa 7.31 percent male and 2.43 percent females. But even in the government services the Raji respondents have no representation.

Thus, it may be concluded that the tribal communities of Uttarakhand are in the process of occupational mobility. Out of the total five scheduled tribes the Bhotiyas are occupationally the more mobilized tribal groups in comparison to the rest of the tribal groups. Bhotiyas are not only the commercial cultivators but also the tradesmen of high status. Besides this, they have also a greater representation in government services of all grades in comparison to the rest of the tribal groups. On the contrary, the Rajis are backward-most tribal group, having nil representation in business professions and the Government services. It is a backward primitive group who even today subsists on a crude type of cultivation. Besides, the Bhotiya and the Rajis, professionally, other than cultivation the representation of Jaunsari-Khasas is much more than the Tharus and the Buxas, while the Tharus and Buxas are comparatively the advanced cultivators than the rest of the tribal communities. It is so because of the favourable agro-climatic conditions of the Tarai-Bhabar domicile of the Tharus and the Buxas.

Occupational Groupings and the Education Standard of the Respondent Units

In order to enumerate the correlation between the education standard and the occupational groupings, the facts have been analysed and presented in Table 15.

Table 15

Educational Standard of the Respondent Units

Professional Groups	*Illiterate*	*Primary*	*Junior High School*	*High Sch.*	*Intermediate*	*Graduate*	*Post-Graduate*	*%*
First Category								
Landless	07 (2.01%)	--	--	--	--	--	--	07 (1.00%)
Cultivators	307 (88.48%)	49 (43.74%)	07 (26.92%)	--	--	--	--	363 (51.86%)

Contd..

Professional Groups	*Illite- rate*	*Primary*	*Junior High School*	*High Sch.*	*Inter- mediate*	*Grad- uate*	*Post- Grad- uate*	*%*
Second Category								
Transporter	--	--	--	--	01 (2.77%)	01 (0.95%)	-- --	02 (0.29%)
Wholesale dealer	--	--	--	--	03 (8.33%)	--	--	03 (0.42%)
Cloth Merchant	--	--	03 (11.53%)	04 (14.29%)	--	--	--	07 (1.00)
Provision Store Keeper	01 (0.29%)	05 (4.46%)	06 (23.08%)	03 (10.71%)	--	--	--	15 (2.14%)
Readymade Cloth Merchant	06 (1.72%)	16 (14.29%)	--	--	--	--	--	22 (3.14%)
Peddler	22 (6.34%)	12 (10.72%)	--	--	--	--	--	34 (4.86%)
Inn keeper/ Restaurant Tea stall/Hotel	04 (1.16%)	30 (26.79%)	08 (30.77%)	--	--	--	--	42 (6.00%)
Third Category								
Ist Class Officer	--	--	--	--	--	--	01 (2.22%)	01 (0.14%)
IInd Class Officer	--	--	--	--	--	--	10 (22.22%)	10 (1.42%)
IIIrd Class Employees	--	--	--	-- (44.45%)	16 (75.48)%)	80 (75.56%)	34	130 (18.58%)
IVth Class Employees	--	--	02 (7.70%)	21 (75.00%)	16 (44.43%)	25 (23.59%)	--	64 (9.15%)
Total	347	·112	26	28	36	106	45	700
Percentage	100%	100%	100%	100%	100%	100%	100%	100%

It is clear form Table 15 that, out of the total 347 illiterate respondents, 88.48 percent are engaged in agricultural activities, 2.01% are landless labourers and 6.34 percent, 1.72 percent, 1.16 percent and 0.29 percent are respectively the peddlers, ready made cloth merchants, innkeepers and the provision store keeper. The respondents who are educated upto primary standard are 112 in numbers, out of which the maximum percentage i.e. 43.74 percent are engaged in cultivation, 29.79 percent run the restaurants, tea stall and the hotels, while 14.29 percent sell ready made clothes, 10.72 percent run the peddlers job and 4.46 percent run the provision stores. There are 26 respondents who are educated upto Junior High School standard, out of them the maximum 30.77 percent run the hotels, restaurants and the tea stalls, 23.08 percent have the provision stores, 26.92 percent are the cultivators and only 11.53 percent are the mercers. Out of the total 28 High School pass respondents, the maximum i.e. 75.00 percent are the fourth class employees, 14.29 percent are mercers and 10.71 percent run the provision stores. Besides this, 36 respondents are educated upto intermediate standard, out of which the maximum 44.45 percent are the third class employees, and the same percentage i.e. 44.45 percent is also employed in the fourth class grade while 8.33 percent and 2.77 percent respondents are respectively the whole-sale dealers and the transporters. The total number of graduate respondents are 106, out of which the majority of the respondents i.e. 75.48 percent are the third class employees, 23.59 percent are fourth class employees and only 0.95 percent is a transporter. In the case of Post-Graduate respondents the maximum 34 (75.56%) out of the total 45 are the third class employees, 10 (22.22%) are the second class officers and remaining 01(2.22%) is first class officers.

Thus, the data analysed as above concluded that the high percentage of literacy and the growing standard of education have brought about the occupational changes among the scheduled tribal communities of Uttarakhand. It is evident from this fact that the illiterate tribal respondents are still engaged with their traditional occupation i.e. agriculture, while the educated tribals have moulded themselves towards the salaried jobs and to some non-traditional but the more profitable jobs. In other words, it may be asserted that the respondents who have been engaged in some salaried jobs, are highly educated while the respondents who have been engaged in some traditional professions are either illiterate or less-educated than that of the respondents belonging to the salaried jobs and the business of high standard.

As it is evident that the literacy percentage among Bhotiyas is comparatively higher than the rest of the tribal communities, hence a considerable numbers of the Bhotiya educated respondents are either engaged in some large scale business pursuits such as the transportation and wholesale dealings of the goods for daily needs, or in some high government posts, like the Indian Administrative Services, Provincial Civil Services, Medical Services, Bank Services etc. On the contrary, Rajis, because of the pervaded illiteracy, have no representation in the field of business and government services,consequently they are still clinging to the traditional crude type of cultivation and similar other subsidiary traditional pursuits.

Thus, finally it may be concluded that, though education is not the only but a potent variable for occupational change. In fact, education has been proved to be an agent of scattering the centuries old clouds of illiteracy and the occupational rigidity prevalent among the so-called aborigines of the Uttarakhand particularly, since Independence when the education was introduced in tribal areas for their socio-cultural development. Today the new generation of the tribals, inspite of the reluctance and even the protest of the old aged persons of the concerned communities appeared to be inclined and advanced towards the education. However, the wide spread poverty, inherited backwardness, motivational vacuum, apathy of the Government officials and the misoperation of the government policies in inaccessible tribal areas, have ever been the inhibitions in the path of their expected educational as well as the cultural development. The Raji community is the burning example of this fact.

References

1. Hasnain, N., Tribal India Today, Harnam Publications, New Delhi, 1983, p. 151.

2. Durkheim, E., The Division of Labour in Society, translated by George Simpson, Free Press, Glencoe, 1947.

3. Dubey, S.M., "Education, Occupational Mobility and the Rise of Professions in a Developing City" (paper for the seminar on Sociology of Development organized by UNESCO in Delhi from Nov. 25 to December 4, 1968).

4. Strumilin, S.G., The Economic Significance of the People's Education, Leningrad, 1924 ; Robert C. Young, "Educational Planning and Economic Criteria" in India's context, in Education as Investment., Ed., by Baljit Singh, Meerut, 1967, p. 79, T.W. Schultz, The Source of Economic Growth in the United State and the Alternatives before U.S. Paris, 1964, p. 63.

5. Durkheim, E., Education and Sociology, Translated by S.D. Fox, The Free Press, 1965, pp. 70-71.

6. Bouquet, A.C., Comparative Religion, Quoted by D.N. Majumdar and T.N. Madan, Social Anthropology, Asian Publishing House, Bombay, 1963, pp. 151-152.

7. *Ibid.*, p. 152.

8. *Ibid.*, p. 165.

9. Ginsberg, Eli, The Professionalization of the U.S. Labour Force, Scientific American, Vol. 240, No. 3, 1979.

10. Parsons, T., The Professions and Social Structure, Social Forces, Vol. 17, May 1939.

11. Carr, Saunders, Morris, A., and Wilson, P.A., The Professions, London; Oxford University Press, 1933.

12. Lewis, R. and Maude Angus, Professional People, London; Phoenix House Ltd., 1952.

13. Pandey, R., Whither Professionalism, in Sociological Bulletin, The Journal of the Indian Sociological Society., Vol. 34, Nos. 142, 1985.

5

TRIBAL SOCIAL ORGANIZATION: STATUS AND ROLE IN TRIBAL LIFE

The inter-functional integration of different components of any structure, constitutes invariably its organization. In this context, "Social organization is a state of being, a condition in which the various institutions, in a society are functioning in accordance with their recognized or implied purposes."[1] Majumdar[2] contends that "Social organization of a great association is the pattern of inter-group relations within it." In regard to the tribal social organization Majumdar further states that, "Tribal social organization is different in so far as there is not much inter-tribal contacts and communication in India except where geographical contiguity has forced it upon some tribes."[3] But so far as the component parts of tribal social organization are concerned, Majumdar has expressed his views as, "Social organization would consists of the inter-relations between a particular type of groups, viz., those groups which make social life possible. The family, school (if any) dormitory, clan and men's club are examples of such groups. Groups of people engaged in economic pursuits comprise the economic organization of a tribe; and groups like panchayats constitute its political organization... The inter-relation between the three would present the total pattern of tribal organization."[4] Ralph Piddington[5] has suggested ten factors i.e. the sex dichotomy, age difference, kinship, locality, social status, political power, occupation, religion, totem, magic and voluntary agencies, as the basic postulations of the tribal social organization. While Herskovits[6] has looked on social organization as the combination of different institutions which are mainly of two types; firstly those institutions which are related with the kinship system and secondly, the institutions which are beyond the kinship frame of reference. Thus, the component parts of the social organization, as mentioned respectively by Majumdar, Piddington and Herskovits are commonly observed among most of the tribal communities in India. However, the scholarly conclusions of the various tribal studies incontestably assert that the nature, statuses and the roles of the tribal institutions differ from one community to another because of the variation of the socio-ecological background of the tribal communities.

The present chapter deals with the scientific delineation of the social organization of the Scheduled Tribal communities in Uttarakhand. The description of the tribal social organization is based on the study of some major tribal institutions in terms of their forms, functions and statuses. This attempt towards framing the canvas of the tribal social organization aims to interpret analytically and synthetically the socio-cultural patterns of the tribal communities in perspective of change, so that the correlation between the transformation of different cultural patterns and the factors amenable for it, can be enumerated and the scientific conclusions based on cause-effect relationship can be drawn. The findings, thus drawn through the scientific approach will be an unprecedented contribution in the field of cultural anthropology and also be useful for the social scientists and scholars in future. Thus, the major social institutions i.e. the family, marriage, youth club, kinship system, occupation, religious beliefs and practices and political organizations of the tribal communities under reference have intensively been studied in the structural-functional frame of reference.

Family: Forms and Functions

Family is the basic and universal social structure of human society. It fulfils needs and performs functions which are indispensible for the continuity, integration and change in the social system. The forms and functions of family have undergone an adaptive change with changes in technological and economic super-structure of society. Historically, it is consistent to assert that the family in one form or the other has been existent in every stage of the cultural evolution. But with the passage of time the family has undergone numerous changes particularly in its structural and organizational frame of reference. The transition from extended family based society to nuclear-family based society is thus, in essence, an example of structural change, since this involves systematic changes in role-structures through the processes of differentiation.[7]

However, the basic functions of the family which are centered around the primary bio-psycho-social needs of man have not been altered so far. In fact, family in its earliest origin was reproductive association consisting of male and female and gradually transformed into a basic social unit of greatest significance for mankind. Mac-Iver and Page also observed that, "Of all the organisations, large or small, which the society unfold, none transcends the family in the intensity of its sociological significance. It influences the whole society in innumerable ways, and its changes....... reverberate through the whole social structure. It is capable of endless variation and yet reveals a remarkable continuity and persistence through change."[8] But, if we turn over the pages of history, there we find only an obscure canvas of the association called family. As for evidence, the anthropologists and the social scientists are different of opinion about the historical origin of the family, subsequently they propounded various theories based on different doctrines, speculations, premises and deductions.

An earliest anthropologist, Lewis Morgan[9] has concluded that the family was unknown among the simplest and the rudest of people and postulated a sequential growth of the institution of family. Morgan has suggested five different and successive forms of family i.e. the consanguine, the punaluan, the syndyasmian, the patriarchal and the monogamous family. Almost all the successive forms of family have been associated with a corresponding and distinctive type of marriage and seem to be resultant of the evolutionary process. Morgan also dated the origin of the family only after man's role in begetting children became known and right of passing property to his own, rather than to his sister's or mother's children had been recognized and accepted.

Westermark propounded the theory of monogamy for the factual analysis of the origin of the family, the comprehensive account of which is found in his book, "The History of Human Marriage."

Malinowaski also considered the monogamy as an earliest form of marriage which apparently originated the monogamous type of family. Later on the Westermark's theory of monogamy was criticised by Briffault, who subsequently founded the theory of 'Matriarchy' and accepted the supreme authority of the 'Mother', while the classical thinkers i.e. Plato, Aristotle have traced out the 'Patriarachal' form of family as the earliest one. Thus, a number of theories regarding to the origin of the family have been abundantly propounded.

Whatsoever been the origin of the family, but it is an established fact that there are sufficient evidences to prove the existence of the family at all stages of the cultural evolution. As Mac-Iver and Page has stated that, "The family has no origin in the sense that there ever existed a stage of human life from which the family was absent or another stage in which it emerged."[10] It is also consistent to contend that the family would have been developed in different cultural contexts and therefore found in varied forms. As a matter of fact the variation of space, time and the stages of cultural evolution have caused the variation even in the forms of the families of different communities. Majumdar aptly remarks, "That is why family is still what it was and at the same time it was not what it is."[11]

Even today a number of tribal communities present a diversified canvas of the varieties of the family types. Some tribal communities, like Kharia of Orissa observe patriarchal and patrilineal form of family while some tribal communities like Khasi of Assam follow matriarchy. Thus, the composition and the organizational frame work of the family in different tribal communities not only vary from each other but also present historically a particularistic cultural patterns which ultimately brought about a particular family system into existence. The anthropologists and sociologists have distinguished the variety of families on different bases for instance; on the basis of numbers of the family members and the generation depth the families have been divided as the nuclear and the joint or extended family. I.P. Desai, defining jointness, "with reference to residence, property and mutual obligations among the kin, "offers four categories of family types:

I-a husband and wife only;

I-b unimember house holds;

II-a husband, wife and married sons without children and other unmarried children;

II-b the above group with other relatives who do not add to generation depth;

III three generation groups of lineal descendants and

IV four or more than four generations of lineal descendants.[12]

Under the category of nuclear family he included the family types I-a to II-b, while III and IV types, he defines as joint family. I.P. Desai has made the distinction between the nuclearity and jointness of families on the basis of lineal collateral depth.

Moreover, one more attempt has also been made by P.M. Kolenda, who has classified family types into twelve categories for a comparative evaluation;

first, single person house hold;

second, sub-nuclear family (a fragment of a former nuclear family as a widowed or divorced parent with unmarried children, or unmarried, widowed or divorced siblings living together);

third, supplemented sub-nuclear family (a sub nuclear family plus some other married, widowed, or divorced relative(s) who were not part of the original nuclear family. For example, a widow with her unmarried children plus her dead husband's brother's widow;

fourth, nuclear family (couple and their unmarried children);

fifth, supplemented nuclear family (a nuclear family plus some other widowed, divorced or unmarried relative(s); such as the husband's widowed mother or his unmarried relative(s); such as the husband's widowed mother or his unmarried brother or sister);

sixth, lineal joint family (parents with unmarried children plus one married son and his wife and unmarried children);

seventh, supplemented lineal joint family (a joint family plus some other unmarried, divorced or widowed relative(s); such as the widowed sister of the older man or his unmarried brother);

eighth, collateral joint family (two or more married brothers with their wives and unmarried children);

nineth, supplemented collateral joint family (a collateral joint family plus some other unmarried widowed or divorced relative(s), such as the widowed mother or widower father or unmarried brother or sister of the married brothers);

tenth, lineal collateral joint family (parents, their unmarried children plus two or more married sons with their wives and married and unmarried children);

eleventh, supplemented lineal collateral joint family (a lineal collateral joint family plus some other relative(s) who is (are) not a member(s) of any of the nuclear families involved. For example, a wife's widowed brother or the eldest male's unmarried brother);

twelveth, other (those families categorised as 'other' by the researchers and not further defined or described, as well as some families that did not fit in the types above. Such as a grand mother living with a grand children and a widower living with his widowed daughter- in law.[13]

On the other hand, the family on the basis of the number of spouses or the life mates have further been distinguished as the monogamous and / or the polygamous families. Most of the Indian tribes have monogamous type of family consisting of a husband, a wife and their offsprings. While the latter type, i.e. the polygamous has again sub-divided as the polygynous and the polyandrous type of families. Polygynous family consists of a husband, two or more wives and their children as is observed among the Todas of Nilgiri in Tamil Nadu while the polyandrous families consists of a wife and two or more husbands and their children, for instance the Jaunsari-Khasas of Dehradun in U.P. have polyandrous type of families.

Apart from the various types, the family as a primary group is supposed to perform the social, economic, educational, recreational, religious and cultural functions and also liable to provide every sort of protection to its members and every possible facilities for their development. It is more over an important agency as to provide an established and socially approved base which bears in common the universalistic value for sex-satisfaction to the mates and also the procreation of children and their upbringing. Besides this, the family is one of the most powerful means of socialization and an agency of informal social control. It also makes the cultural transmission possible from one generation to another. But with the course of time the forms and the functions of the families have undergone numerous changes.

In the present study the generalization of the empirical data obtained through direct sources particularly in regard to the family structure shows the existence of ten different types of the families based on the generation depth and the total number of the family members. These are as follows:

1. Nuclear family of traditional type (husband and wife with or without children, nuclearity due to poverty such as absence of land ownership, lack of sufficient and stable means of livelihood and shifting mode of occupation etc.).

2. Supplemented nuclear family of traditional type (nuclear family or traditional type plus unmarried brother(s), sister(s), widowed mother or widower father of the husband and one or more relatives who do not add the generation depth).

3. Nuclear family of modern type (husband and wife with or without children, nuclearity due to positive causes such as education, urbanization, modernization, occupational mobility etc.).

4. Supplemented nuclear family of modern type (nuclear family of modern type plus the husband's unmarried brother(s), sister(s) and widowed mother or widower father and the relatives who do not add generation depth).
5. Collateral joint family (two or more brothers with wives and unmarried children).
6. Supplemented collateral joint family (collateral joint family plus unmarried brother(s), or sister(s) of the married brothers and widowed mother, or widower father and the divorced mother).
7. Lineal joint family (parents with unmarried children plus one married son, his wife and unmarried children).
8. Supplemented lineal joint family (lineal joint family plus some unmarried, divorced or widowed relatives) i.e. widowed sister of the father and the unmarried brother.
9. Collateral lineal joint family (parents two or more married sons with their wives and married and unmarried children).
10. Supplemented lineal collateral joint family (lineal collateral joint family plus other relative(s).

To make the scientific delineation more comprehensive almost all the family types found among the scheduled tribal communities under-reference have been merged into two broad categories. First, the nuclear families, consisting the first four types i.e. from Ist to IVth types and second, the joint families consisting the remaining six types i.e. from Vth to Xth types. The tribe-wise distribution of the families belonging respectively to first and second categories have been presented in the following Table.

Table 16

Scheduled Tribe-wise Distribution of Family Types

Families	*Bhotiyas*	*Buxas*	*Tharus*	*Rajis*	*Jaunsaris*	*Total*
Nuclear families	223 (67.17%)	40 (29.62%)	40 (32.00%)	18 (78.27%)	09 (10.59%)	330 (47.14%)
Joint families	109 (32.83%)	95 (70.38%)	85 (68.00%)	05 (21.73%)	76 (89.41%)	370 (52.86%)
Total	332 (100%)	135 (100%)	125 (100%)	23 (100%)	85 (100%)	700 (100%)

It is evident from Table 16 that 223 (67.17%) Bhotiya families out of the total 332 (100.00%) are nuclear in form and 109 (32.83%) are joint. Among Buxas 40(29.62%) families are nuclear and the rest 95 (70.38%) families are joint in type. There are 40 (32.00%) nuclear and 85 (68.00%) joint families among Tharus. Among Rajis, 18 (78.27%) families are nuclear and the rest 05 (21.73%) are joint. While most of the families i.e. 76 (89.41%) among Jaunsari Khasas are joint in nature and only 09 (10.59%) families are nuclear. Besides the quantitative enumeration of the family types,it is however, more consistent to describe the nature and the notion implied with the nuclear and joint family structure in the frame of reference as they exist among the tribal communities under reference. Since, the social structure of the nuclear and joint family widespread in Indian society exhibits many regional differences and the same is true in reference of the scheduled tribal communities of Uttarakhand.

Although, traditional peasant societies everywhere in the world had a predominance of extended families. Usually such families were patrilocal and patriarchal, in such families women had relatively subordinate position; all members were guided in their activities by an elder family head and interpersonal relations of all the members were authoritarian. Marriage in such families was governed by rules of kinship rather than courtship and was considered a matter of inter-familial and not inter-personal concern. Family in such society was also the unit of economic, cultural, religious and political activities.[14]

Table 17

Ecological Settings and the Distribution of Family Types

Types of Families	Bhotiya			Buxa			Tharu			Raji			Jaunsari Khasa				
	Ru.	*Ur.*	*Both*	*Ru.*	*Ur.*	*Both*	*Ru.*	*Ur.*	*Both*	*Ru.*	*Ur.*	*Both*	*Ru.*	*Ur.*	*Both*	*Total*	*%*
Joint	100	--	09	95	--	--	80	--	05	05	--	--	60	--	16	370	52.86
	(27.02)	--	(2.43)	(25.68)	--	--	(21.62)	--	(1.36)	(1.36)	--	(16.21)	--	(4.32)		(100.00)	
Nuclear	23	165	35	30	02	08	27	08	05	18	--	--	--	09	--	330	47.14
	(6.97)	(50%)	(1.66)	(9.1)	(0.60)	(2.42)	(8.19)	(2.42)	(1.57)	(5.46)	--	--	--	(2.72)	--	(100.00)	
Total	123	165	44	125	02	08	107	08	10	23	--	--	60	09	16	700	100.00
	(17.58)	23.58)	(6.28)	(7.86)	(0.29)	(1.14)	(15.28)	(1.14)	(1.42)	(3.29)	--	--	(8.56)	(1.29)	(2 29)	(100.00)	

There is, however, another form of family called, nuclear family which lacks every characteristic as found in the social structures of the joint families. But the nature of the jointness and nuclearity of the social structure of the families as existed very often in different societies were quite different from one community to another and from one place to another. The following description of the social structure of the scheduled tribe families prove the regional variations of the family structures. For this purpose the family types have been distributed on the basis of the domicile which represent the ecological or the regional variation as follows:

Table 17 depicts that out of the total 700 respondents the maximum 370 (52.86) reside in joint families and the rest 330 (47.14%) live in nuclear families. Out of the total 370 respondents the maximum 100 (27.02%) Bhotiyas belong to the rural communities which is followed by Buxas, Tharus, Jaunsaris and Rajis with as much as 95 (25.68%), 80 (21.62%), 60 (16.28%) and 5 (1.36%) respectively belong to the rural communities. But none of the joint family exist in urban areas, while 9 (2.43%), 5 (1.36%) and 16 (4.32%) joint families respectively from Bhotiya, Tharu and Jaunsari communities exist in rural-urban continuum. On the contrary the majority of the nuclear families exist in urban areas. As out of the total 330 nuclear families, 165 (50%) of Bhotiyas exists in urban areas which is followed by Buxas, Tharus and Rajis with as much as 30 (9.10%), 27 (8.19%) and 18 (5.49%) nuclear families which exist in rural areas. There are, however, some more nuclear families which belong to the Tharus, Buxas and Jaunsaris and exist in urban and rural-urban continuum. But none of the Raji families is found in any urban area.

In fact, the scientific analysis of the information gathered through investigation consistently prove that the joint families side by side with the nuclear families of the traditional type exist in rural areas. But the social structure, inter-personal relations among the family members however, what is more important to prolong this system, that is the basic ground on which based the existence of the jointness of the families, are some what different than the rest of the tribal communities and the non-tribal communities as well. Among Bhotiyas the particularistic socio-economic and ecological factors have imparted a significant role in determining the type of the family. The different means of transportation and communication, the necessity of more and more man power for cultivation, animal husbandry and other traditional type of economic pursuits like trade and the prevalent illiteracy too have been the most conductive factors to strengthen the joint family system among Bhotiyas. Those are the factors amenable for the sojourn of the socio-occupational mobility among Bhotiyas. Thus, they have subsequently been forced by the circumstances to live together in joint families. In fact, the joint family used to prolong unless and until the brothers, whether married or unmarried do not consolidate their position by achieving self reliance. Afterwards, to avoid the family disputes in between the brothers, brother's wives and mother-in-law and the daughter-in-laws, the joint families have broken up into nuclear families. It is the only cause of the small size of the joint family among Bhotiyas which chiefly consists of the members of two generations, i.e. the parents and their married sons and the unmarried grand children.

Having followed the rules of patriarchal, patrilocal and patrilineal the aged male member of the family holds up the status of the head of the family while the women have relatively subordinate position, nevertheless in every field of the socio-economic life both the male and the female equally participate. Theoreticaly, the inter-personal relation between the members are authoritarian and the members are guided in their activities by the head of the family. The head of the family is entitled to avail the various privileges regarding to the different spheres of socio-cultural life and also liable to shoulder almost all the familial responsibilities viz; religious, economic, cultural as well as the political. In Bhotiya dialect the head of the family is addressed as the 'Thokolchyo. It is of course a respectable rank. Hence, almost all the familial tasks are performed with his prior consent. He is the only person in the family who commences every auspicious and inauspicious acts by himself and enjoys the privileges in every spheres of social life. Yet, he works hard, every tedious task goes to his part. He is liable to afford every sort of familial expenses whether petty or the big.

Simultaneously, the aged woman of the family is considered to be as the female head and, this symbolic status is honoured with the title, "Mulin-Rani", that is the queen of the hearth. She is privileged to attend to hearth for cooking food. In case, if any other member of the family cooks food, it is, however, the privilege of the 'Mulin-Rani' to dish-it up to the family members. Besides this she takes care of the household goods, agricultural instruments and also looks after the infants and the milch cattle left at home during the day time. Thus, it may be concluded that the remote most villages have still the predominance of the joint families; because of the professional necessities of the people who for the pursuits of trade, agricultural and pastoral farming used to live under a common roof, cooked food in a common hearth and share the common property. Moreover, the transhumance nature of the Bhotiyas has also conduced to live together the akins belonging to more than two generations.

Since, the Bhotiyas of the sub-Himalayan region of Uttar Pradesh breed yaks and jibus (cross breed of Yak and Cow) and are the itinerant traders, they come down to the plains in winter and go over the hills right upto Tibet in summer.[15] Although the trade between India and Tibet is constitutionally banned, however, the rest conditions as to substantiate the existence and continuity of the joint family system are as usual and it appears that there has been developed a symbolic relationship between the socio-occupational ecology and the joint family type. For this very purpose, the ecological changes have also brought about some remarkable fundamental changes in the traditional joint family structure of Bhotiyas. The ecological variation and the variation in family type are positively correlated. It is evident from the analysis of the data presented in Table 17. Infact, on the one hand the breach of international trade contract with Tibet and China, has caused the shortage of the raw-wool material, subsequently, the existing trade profession prevalent over ages had adversely affected and on the other hand, the welfare schemes of government for the socio-economic development of the tribals and the attraction of the white collar jobs, availability of educational facilities as well as the means of transport and communication have generated a new ecological environment, consequently, a new way for professing newly emerged alien professions developed, which ultimately crackled the traditional periphery of joint family and changed it into the nuclear family type. Today, the joint families of Bhotiyas are observed only in the farthest remote and interior villages, but these rare families have also begun to lose their traditional traits of jointness.

The essential features of joint family viz; the large size, common property, common roof, common hearth etc. have constantly been disappearing among the Bhotiyas. At present most of the Bhotiya families are nuclear in form. There are however some families which are neither joint (in traditional sense) nor absolutely nuclear, such families possess the mixed characteristics of traditionally joint and the modern nuclear families; such a family may be termed as the functional joint family, which are the inevitable outcome of the inter-functional jointness of the collateral nuclear families. Thus, if we look on deeply the nature of the existing Bhotiya families, there we find mainly the four types of families which have been termed in the present description as follows:

(i) The traditional joint family.

(ii) The traditional nuclear family.

(iii) Modern nuclear family and

(iv) The functional joint family.

In brief, the joint family is one of the different types of Bhotiya families which bears all the same basic characteristics as described by I.P. Desai[16] in perspective of the Indian society in general. The traditional nuclear family is that type which grows into the traditional joint family and exist in traditional Bhotiya community in the farthest and remote most habitations. But the nuclearity of this sort is an outcome of adverse agro-climatic conditions, insufficient and instable means of economic subsistence and the pervasive poverty on account of which the family members more than two or more generations can not live jointly and in general the brothers just after their marital alliance get separation and live independently in a small nuclear family, consisting a husband, a wife and their unmarried offsprings. Moreover, such families also bear some characteristics as found in the traditional type of joint families viz; the authoritarian inter-personal relations among the family members, subordinate position of women, observance of child marriages and the excessive dependence on the kinsmen and the elders particularly for decision making in some major familial issues. Such type of families have predominantly been confined within the original habitates of Bhotiyas and, subsist on the agriculture and other subsidiary pursuits.

The modern nuclear family is the type of Bhotiya families which grow into the milieu of modern society. This nuclearity is the out come of the positive causes viz., the education, technological innovation, occupational mobility and the individualistic and particularistic achieved values. In such type of nuclear families the woman holds up a dependent position side by side with man, she also engages herself in some business pursuits and the services. The family members avail greater personal freedom. The family is independent for taking any sort of decision in respect of all the familial matters. Such family type is predominant among those people (Bhotiyas) who have been engaged either in some earning jobs or business pursuits and also have got their settlement either permanently or partly in the town areas. The present study has also proved it (see Table 17). Moreover, it is also observed that the youth generation of Bhotiyas has frequently been moving outside of their ancestral places of residence to acquire education, employment and some other subsidiary jobs and gradually getting their settlement in towns or the places of their present jobs along with their nuclear families. But, however they occassionally visit to their ancestral villages to perform some traditional festivals and ritualistic ceremonies jointly with great enthusiasm, cohesiveness and in a cooperative manner. For instance, all the brothers alongwith their family get-together to perform jointly the marriage ceremony of their sister or brother and also share the expenses incurred on the marriage. Such type of family has been termed as the functional joint family. It is a latent form of the family, which occasionally comes into existence and manifested in the form, to which we have termed as the functional joint family. The Bhotiyas who are passing through the transition of rural-urban continuum present such a peculiar type of family.

Among Buxas the male, theoretically wield greater influence over women folk, because the family has traditionally a patriarchal form, the residence is patrilocal and the descent is traced through the male line. But so far as the type of the family prevalent in common among Buxas is concerned it is observed that the nuclear families are in ascending trend. As it is obvious from Table 17, almost all the joint and nuclear families exist in rural areas. None of the family exist in any town area, which shows the sojourn spatial mobility of the Buxas. Though some Buxas have been engaged in Government services and in some non-traditional occupations, however, they do not keep their families with them due to the insufficient income and the lodging problems in towns. Consequently, the Buxas, working outside in Government services or elsewhere live all alone while their wives and the children live in villages.

Both the joint and the nuclear families bear in common, the traditional characters. The father or the aged male person of the family holds the status of the head of the family and his advice continues to be sought in family matters. Some times the aging father hands over his authority as well as the familial liabilities to his eldest son or the eldest male member of the family and continues to be the nominal head of the family. It is however, observed some times that the nominal head avoids any such situation which can put him in jeopardy and therefore left for the account of the eldest male person in the family. For instance, in taking the decision for the marital alliance of the youngsters in the family, the nominal head impose it on the choice of the acting head. In regard of the right for property ownership the Buxa people follow the rules of 'Dayahhag', because the father is all alone the owner of his property during his life time, unless he himself is not agreed to share the property to his sons. Hence, the father and the son make every possible efforts to live together under a common roof. In fact, the father, to avoid any complications and the libellous situation in community tolerate every hardship of the family, but do not share the land and the property into pieces, because it is considered to be humiliating and disgraceful in community particularly when the father is alive. This act indeed, makes the position of a father ludicrous in community and also invites the misfortune, sufferings and the perplexities in his life. However, the quarrels between the mother-in-law and daughter-in law, estrangement among brothers over property, and the strained relations among the wives regarding the division of labour and sharing the responsibilities of the family have ultimately been bringing about the disorganization of the joint family and the emergence of nuclear family system among Buxas.

Today most of the nuclear families among Buxas are the outcome of the familial disputes. Today most of the peace loving Buxas separate their sons as soon as they are married so that the possibilities of the familial disputes may be stopped and the cordiality among the separating nuclear families can be maintained. But it is noteworthy that the nuclear families possess the traditional nature as is observed among traditional joint families. An average Buxa-nuclear family consists of a husband, a wife, their unmarried children in general and some times the widow mother or widower father or unmarried brother or sister of the husband in particular. Thus, extended nuclear families are predominantly observed among Buxas, who possess the traits of traditional nuclear family as has been observed among Bhotiyas. The interpersonal relations among the family members are authoritarian. An elder person holds respectively a higher position and power to order the youngers. In response, the youngers obey their elders and also pay due respect and veneration to them in the family.

The status of woman in Buxa family is highly venerable. The aged woman in family possesses in practical the equal status to that of the head. Mostly the familial matters are decided with the mutual consent of the head and the aged woman. In fact, the Buxan (the Buxa woman) in practical holds an important position in the family as she is supposed to be superior, because of the royal decent from the queen (Ranis) of Rajasthan while the male were merely the camp followers.

Thus, it may be concluded that the family type among Buxas is predominantly nuclear, and comparatively smaller in size. But the nuclearity, which contains in particular the traditional character of role-structure, is the outcome of some indigenous familial causes. The processes viz., urbanization, modernization, sanskritization, education as well as the professional mobility have no contribution in the transformation of the joint family to the nuclear ones.

For Tharus, the family is a 'Sang' in local dialect, which refers to the collection of nuclear families of the same lineage. The residence of the family is patrilocal and the lineage runs with the male's line and the father holds the supreme authority in the family because the Tharus too follow the rules of patriarchy. Both the joint and nuclear families are simultaneously prevalent over the Tharu community.

Almost all the joint families consist of the parents and their married sons and their children in general. Thus, the collateral joint families are very common among Tharus. Moreover, some extended joint families do exist in the community. In extended joint families, the son-in-law, the relatives from female side also live together. On the contrary the nuclear family consist of the husband and wife and their unmarried children in common. But in some extended nuclear families the husband and wife live along with some dependent members of the family viz; the widow or widower parents of the husband, unmarried brother or sister of the husband and the children of the wife from the former husband. Thus, the joint families side by side with nuclear families of traditional type exist among Tharus. Alike Buxas, the jointness and the nuclearity of the families exist among Tharus implied absolutely the traditional character which is evident from the nature of the interpersonal relations among the family members as well as the factors responsible for the existence of the jointness or the nuclearity of the family.

In the family, the eldest male member is considered as the head (Sayana) of the family. He looks after all the familial properties and the trustee in real sense and also carries out the liabilities pertaining to the interest of one and all members of the family. Every family member is supposed to obey the head in all matters concerning to the family as a whole. The head enjoys in general a number of privileges in almost all the spheres of social life. He works hard to meet out the necessities of the family. But whenever the 'Head' proved to be incompetent and become helpless the powers and the duties are informally transmitted to the next eldest male person of the family, while the former one continues to be a nominal head. The acting head thus took over the charge of all the familial matters and performs them with the consultation of the former head and other family members.

In the same way, the eldest woman in the family equally shares the responsibilities of the household. She invariably happens to be the female head of the family and therefore lends her hand in managing all the economic and social and the religious affairs of family. The Tharu woman is highly venerable in the family. She also claims to be descent from royal origin and therefore the husband uses the honorific plural towards the wife, whereas she uses the singular towards him. In this way the honorific demonstration of the husband towards wife proves the honourable position of woman in family. In fact, a Tharu woman possesses a dominant as well as the respectful status in the family. Besides this, the respect among Tharus is duely shown to the elders.

Today the youngsters utter 'Ram-Ram' as a mark of salutation for the elders, in return the elders utter a blessing term, means "may you live long". The children are expected to show respect to their parents and all the other elder members of the family. The school going children are heard to utter 'Namaskar' as a mark of salutation to the elders. Today, Tharus prefer to have sons in comparison to the daughters. In fact, there was a time when the birth of a daughter was considered more useful to family because she was more hard-working than the male. But irrespective of the sex difference, the youngers are supposed to obey their elders but if there is not much age difference they behave with each other almost as equals. Alike Buxas, the Tharus are also peace loving, hence a least case of family disputes or the bickerings among the family members are observed. However, some exceptional cases of strained relations between the brothers and the brother's wives over property are recorded, particularly in joint families.

The most discarded persons in the family are the step children who command no respect and affection in family. Some times the step children are deprived from all rights of property ownership by their step mother and in such cases the helpless father can do nothing for the protection of their interests for he appears morally, socially, and psychologically to be a depressed creature and can not dare to envisage any adverse situation which can be in the form of separation of the newly wedded better half, by taking the favour of the step children.

Among Rajis the family is 'Kunba' which chiefly consists of a father, a mother and the unmarried children. The 'Kunba' in Raji dialect means a small family, generally termed as a 'nuclear family in reference of Indian society. It is thus proved that the nuclear families are predominantly exist among Rajis. In fact Raji, a primitive tribal community of Uttarakhand has been the most backward nomadic tribe till recently. They used to move in clusters, from jungle to jungle in search of the jungle products. Every cluster was invariably a group of small families consisting of the mates and their offsprings. Thus, even after having a permanent settlement the Rajis have continued to maintain their traditional types of nuclear families. Even today a newly married son is separated to bring up his wife and children independently. Because it is practical difficulty to accommodate the joint family in a small hutment built up of the wooden upright logs and plastered over the mud and roofs thatched with grass. Moreover, the pervading acute poverty too, has deprived the two or more generations to live jointly. Thus, ultimately only a nuclear family, some times with the widow or widower parents and unmarried brothers or sisters of the husband, remains as the alternative shelter for the Raji people.

By residence, Rajis are patrilocal whose lineage runs with father's line. The authority of father in family is superior in principle, however, the wife predominantly dominate the family in its various spheres. She can command a venerable status in family to such an extent that some time an observer mispercept the community as the matriarchy. For instance, she always behave with her husband as a mistress and addresses him without any honorific plural term but by the singular, rather disgraceful term. It appears, that Rajis would have been a matriarchal community in remote past.

Besides this, some Rajis particularly those who are frequently in contact with the neighbouring Kumaun Hindus, have begun to observe the tradition of defilement, mainly when a married female in the family goes under menstruation or gives birth to a child. In the former case the sense of defilement lasts in three or four days, while in the latter for nine days. During this period inter-dining relations with the defiled woman are prohibited. All the family members, particularly the mates and their offsprings have vital, cordial and affectionate attachment with each other, however, they don't have any particular pattern of showing reverence to the seniors. The old age is a curse for Rajis, since, they avail neither any respect nor any support from the rest of the family members. The same is the position of the step children. In the family none of the members is liable for any task, however only the infants are looked after by the parents and the grown up child when attains the age of six years and more is supposed to lend his hands in economic pursuits. Parents are not worried at all about the education and proper personality development of children. All the family members viewed as mechanically governed by themselves.

A most striking trait among Rajis is the absence of the sense of liabilities of the elders to their youngers, since every family member is expected to work according to his capacity thus whatever they acquire through collective efforts is consumed till it comes to an end, afterwards they further made another efforts for food collection. By nature they are idle and undutiful and always remain desirous to manage the food stuffs as much as is essential to keep body and soul together. They don't have aspiration for better living yet except for the fulfilment of the minimum needs of food and clothing. This is exactly a cause of the poverty and the existence of the nuclear families among Rajis.

Unlike Bhotiyas, Buxas, Tharus and Rajis, the Jaunsari-Khasa community, in its broadest sense, is an association of the families. Indeed, the family inspite of being an independent, self sufficient and well organized unit, is indifferent to the community as a whole. If the number of the members of the generation depth is taken into consideration as the basis of family type, we observe in common the prevalence of the joint and the extended joint families among Khasas which consist of a number of nuclear families. Even today almost all the Khasa families are joint in form out of which the majority of the families are collateral-lineal joint, consisting of the nuclear families of three or more lineally and collaterally related akins with or without relatives. The Khasa-family lives under a common roof, cooks food in a common hearth, acts as an economic unit and performs all the ritualistic activities in common. It is observed that the members belonging to more than three generations are equally the share-holders of the common property.

A Khasa family is patriarchal, patrilineal and patrilocal where the eldest male member of the family holds the status of the head (Mukhiya) of the family, the lineage goes with the father's name and a female after marriage is supposed to come to live with her husband's place of residence and also entitle to conjoin herself with the husband's caste-name. In the family, the head is privileged to take arbitrary decisions in every familial matter. It is the head all alone, to deal with the property, income and expenditure of the family and marital alliances of the children. He decides which one of the children has to be educated and which one will not. Even the division of labour in the family is managed by himself. Thus, the authority of the head in family is paramount and supreme, none of the members intentionally can ever wishes to intervene the decisions and the privileges of the family head. Every family member not caring of one's own grievances and the sufferings, mechanically performs one's respective assignments as allotted by the head; unless the head himself do not initiate and wish to know the same.

Moreover, a status of female head, simultaneously exists in the Khasa-family. Mostly the senior most female i.e. the female having the maximum standing in the family, traditionally considered as the female head with corresponding authority. In real sense she is the counsellor of the male head and also looks after all the internal household management and other familial matters, particularly in the absence of the family head, she is the overall incharge of the family management. Both the heads endeavour to operate all the familial matters by the mutual understanding and consent and in every respect the family head is obviously observed to be governed by the latter. Thus, it appears that the Khasa community observes matriarchy in practical side by side with the patriarchy in principle. Polyandry is the main cause of the practice of matriarchy among Khasas.

In fact, the Khasas of Jaunsar Bawar have the polyandrous type of family. Having been the descend of 'Pandavas' the tradition of fraternal polyandrous family has been prevalence among Khasas over ages. Majumdar has also stated that "The Khasa of Jaunsar Bawar live in a joint family. A group of brothers live together with one, two or more wives under the same roof, the brothers sharing the wives without any exclusive right of any brother to cohabit with any one wife".[16] Even today two and more brothers share jointly the same wife. While in some families, particularly when the difference of age is comparatively larger among the brothers, the wives may be two or more but however none of the brothers has exclusive right on any wife. All the brothers have equal right to share any of the wives; but in case of single wife the eldest brother is monopolised to cohabit with her particularly at night. Only the absence of the eldest brother virtually provide the opportunity to the second one to cohabit with the wife at night and in the absence of the former two, the brother coming next to them avails this opportunity.

Besides this an alternative arrangement also exists among Khasas, that is, the common wife used to invite any of the younger husbands during the day time, so that both the husband and wife may give a practical shape to conjugal relations. In such conditions when younger husband indulge himself in sexual intercourse, oftenly put his cap hanged on the door out-side of the room, so that a member entering into the room may be mindful to understand the symbol and could be returned instantly without disturbing the couple infatuated with sexual love. Moreover a more alternative place for the meeting of the wife and the junior husbands is the hutment builtup for animal husbandry in the out skirt of every village. Every day, the wife with her alternate husband visits to the hutment for looking after the cattle and in the meanwhile they also quest the lust along with the work assigned for the day. Thus, the wife carries out her fidelity with the husbands without any difference and partiality and feels proud of being a wife amongst the two and more husbands, who separately make efforts to provide every possible pleasure, comfort and the presents as well to her.

Inspite of being predominantly the fraternal polyandrous family type some instances of the polygynous and the monogamous family types are also observed in Khasa community. But such type of families are absolutely conditional however socially sanctioned to be observed as such by the community. Mostly, in the state of being two and more wives respectively of a group of brothers, the death of one and more brothers virtually provide the privilege to the remaining brothers to have an exclusive right on the wives and thus a polygamous family comes into existence. Besides this, if only one son in the family has no male issue from the first wife, the head of the family and the head (Siyana) of the village persuade him to wed one more wife and this process resultantly brings the polygynous type of family into practice. Subsequently, this process goes on until the man does not reproduce a male issue as a heir for his parental property and also to run the lineage in natural course. Besides this, the prevalent economy is also an amenable factor to establish a family having not more than one male member to wed two and more wives as to seek assistance in agriculture persuits and similar other subsidiary jobs. Comparatively, a well off family, having more ancestral agricultural land, rich live stock population and more immovable property too, set up the family called polygamous.

Besides the traditionally prevalent forms of Khasa families

the monogamous families are gradually coming into existence. During the scientific investigation, it is observed that the new generation, particularly the male youth frequently coming out of their traditional occupation to profess any of the non-traditional professions i.e. the business, government and private services and preferably like to dwell merely with their small family at the places of their jobs. In particular, the service class and business class Khasas, have at least begun to keep their separate wife, yet with the prior consent of the head of the family. Such youths plead for their economic independence and insist to carry out the economic liability of the separate wife and their offsprings. In such exceptional cases, the head along with the male members of the family give permission to a desirous youth male to keep the separate wife to share and cohabit with exclusively while the rest of the familial liabilities as well as the property, hearth and the roof always remain the same as usual i.e. the joint, because the distribution of property may cause the economic deprivation resultantly come out of the reduplication of household equipments and excessive sub-division and fragmentation of land and the house. Thus, what ever been the causes of jointness, but it is uncontestably be asserted that the joint family in this region has such a strong hold on its members that none of the members wishs or thinks of getting separated from its root i.e. the joint family.

It appears that the various forms of families i.e. fraternal polyandrous joint, the non-sororate polygynous joint and the monogamous joint are predominantly prevalent over the Khasa community. It is however a truth to be kept in mind that whatever been the legend or the speculation laid down to prove the prevalent most fraternal polyandrous type of family among Khasas, the economic factor is absolutely a determinant factor to ascertain a particular type of family in the present day context. For instance, the people were asked to narrate the responsible factors of the prevalence of two or more than two types of families in the same community at the same time. The responses generalized objectively goes in favour of the economic factor which constitute the sub-structure of the Khasa community, on which based the family structure of the same community. In fact, in those Khasa families particularly when two or more brothers are engaged in agricultural and its subsidiary pursuits a common wife is sufficiently enough to share by them so that the continuity of the lineage can be maintained and the internal household liabilities and the works in common can be shared by the wife. Even then if the two and more brothers respectively wed the two or more wives, the problem of their up-bringing and maintenance will remain for ever, consequently, the state of scarcity of food and clothes would cause the family dispute, strained relations among the husbands and wives, which once in a while resulted in the separation and the divorce of the spouses. For this very purpose, the brothers to avoid every such adverse situations and to develop cohesive, sympathetic, cordial, vital and cooperative relations among themselves, and to stop the division of the property and the fragmentation of land, and beyond all these factors, to get rid from the intricate problem of nurturing the two and more wives, get married with a common wife and establish a house hold.

Contrary to this, the family, having only one male member without any hand in assistance to perform agricultural pursuits, manage two or more wives as to make cultivation and cattle breeding possible. In the same way the welloff families, having agricultural farming in large scale, and plenty of domestic animals viz., the cows, ox, sheep and buffaloes need eventually the more man power and thus only a way out left to brothers to marry more than two wives. This situation ultimately gives rise to the polygamous type of family. While the monogamous type of family is the inevitable outcome of the economic independence of the persons concerned. Thus, it may be concluded that not the tradition but the economic factor is exclusively responsible for the determination of the family type among Khasas.

The inter-personal relationships in the family are of cohesive nature. The eldest brother or the male member of the family is the supreme authority as to handle the whole of the family and its members according to his own choice. The senior most female member of the family is the female head with corresponding authority particularly in the internal household matters. The strained relations among the brothers are hardly observed, because of the strong hold of the fraternal polyandry system the eldest brother is assigned the highest status with corresponding privileges eventually all the possible causes of dispute which may resulted in the split of a family are eliminated. But the male and female heads of the family are supposed to command due respect from the family members. The status of male child is comparatively higher than the female consequently the male child deserves to get some preferential treatment in the family. However, the younger brothers and sisters are expected to pay respect to their elders and also to obey them. Traditional set up of the family never creates the bickerings between the mother-in-law and daughter-in-law(s) or the sister-in-law(s) and daughter-in-law(s) and between the wife and the co-wives. Thus, the Khasa family is well organized association consisting of various statuses and their respective roles which ultimately bind the family members together by inter-functional relations.

Division of Labour in Family

The patterns of the division of labour among Bhotiyas vary from one family type to the other. Particularly in joint and traditional nuclear families the system of the division of labour is approximately the same. In general, the aged persons of the family are left at home for looking after the infants while the young females are liable to bring water from the nearest water source, wash the clothes, clean the used utensils and, the young males alone are liable to plough the field. This is a general division of labour among the family members which is based absolutely on the age and sex differences. There is, however, any hard and fast rule of following this division of works because all the tasks, except ploughing the field which is all alone the privilege of the males can be performed by any body in the family irrespective of the difference of one's age and sex. Generally, both the male and female work in fields, harvest the crops, bring fire woods and fodder from jungle, the male members of the family go for itinerant trade of the woolen stuffs viz., blankets, 'Thulmas', boltcarpets, 'Chutakas' etc. to the neighbouring non-tribal villages and some time come down to the plains of Tarai and Bhabar and thus earn money. While some Bhotiya males engaged themselves in transportation of various commodities from remote areas to bus terminals and vice-versa through transport animals like hackney or the sheep they rear themselves. Besides this, every family member without the difference of sex and age, remains busy in spinning the woollen yarn and knitting the woollen stuffs all too often. Thus, all the family members actively contribute their role-share for the integration and economically smooth running of the family. The male and female earn money by their joint efforts and keep it under the trusteeship of the 'Mulin Rani' that is, the female head and expend with mutual consent for the interest of one and all of the family members.

But in modern nuclear Bhotiya families, the nature of the tasks of the male and female varied according to the variation of the means or the sources of the economic subsistence, such as in business class and service class families, the woman performs almost all the domestic tasks such as rearing and caring the children, cooking food, washing clothes, knitting and weaving works during the leisure, marketing and some women do peddler jobs at market places, while the tasks related outside of the family are performed by man. However, no differences between the status of the male and female are observed, they hold equal status and enjoy the similar privileges. Every child whether male or female avails equal opportunity and privileges. No one in the family is deprived on the basis of sex dichotomy. Thus, there is some sort of socialistic pattern in the family system. Every member works according to one's capacity and avail the facilities without the difference of sex and age.

Thus, it may be concluded that the sex is only a basis to ascertain the task but only in some particular spheres of life of the family members. Otherwise almost all the tasks are performed equally by the members of the family without the difference of sex and age. There is however, a certain difference between the daily routine works of the males and females belonging respectively to the joint family, traditionally nuclear family and the modern nuclear family, but this difference is merely an inevitable outcome of the physical ecology which ultimately determines the man's material environment, especially the profession determines the pattern of life and the nature of the work of the male and the female as well and this way the Bhotiya people have got the capacity of adaptation with the new environmental ecology, which has been developed from the processes of urbanization, modernization and its supplementary processes.

Khasa is predominantly a agriculturist cum-pastoral community with the backward economy based on the crude type of cultivation and animal husbandry in common. Each and every member of the family supposed to lends one's hand in any sort of the economic pursuits as assigned by the head of the family. The division of labour among the family members has obviously been based on the age and sex, which may be treated as the earliest form of division of labour prevalent particularly in primitive societies. The sex and age based division of labour has not only developed particular type of social solidarity and the cohesiveness among the family members but it has also imparted its determinant impact in the psychological make up of the people and in ascertaining their style of life and the statuses as a whole. The senior most (age) male (sex) of the family is head (status) and expected to manage (function) the family and the distribution of familial works among the family members and also to look after the work done by the respective members. It is the privilege and the liability too, of the head to settle the marriage of youngers in family and also to procure all possible means to perform it. Rest of the aged male persons i.e. the old generation in the family are liable to plough the fields, to strip the buffaloes and the cows, to go for the sale of Ghee, vegetables, including some root vegetables like potato, ginger, turmeric and 'Gaderi' to the nearest market places and purchasing the provisions for daily needs.

Moreover, it is also a duty of the male members to procure the essential material for instance, the stone and the wooden stuff for house constructions. Some times the male members are observed busy on the work of the building construction of their own. The rest of the male members are assigned to graze the sheep and goats and also to bring fodder from jungle. Moreover, the major agricultural works viz., ploughing, irrigation, manuring, sowing, reaping and threshing are also assigned to the male members of the family while the younger generation, ranging from six to fourteen years of age, frequently helps the elders as their assistant helpers in all sorts of the works. Mostly, the children and the adolescents are deputed for grazing the cattle, managing the fodder and collecting the fuel wood and also in agricultural fields to perform small jobs. However, some children have begun to go for schooling, provided the schooling facilities is available in the village or the place under approach.

On the contrary, the senior most female is considered to be a female head of the family. She is indeed, an incharge of kitchen and the managing authority of the internal household matters. She is liable to advise the male head in respect of family matters and make him aware about the shortage of the essential commodities in family. She has exclusive right to make social dealings with the neighbourers, villagers and the guests. Mostly she remains throughout at home to look after the infants, to feed the milch cattle and to entertain the guests. The rest of the females remain busy throughout the day in agricultural pursuits except ploughing. They arrange the fodder for domestic animals, while the younger female members of family go for grazing the cattle, collecting cow dung, fetching water, pressing oil and cutting grass in the baskets made of 'Baint'. Moreover, many other domestic works; sweeping the house, washing the used utensils and the dirty clothes and also to make wash the hands of the male members of the family and of the guests before and after of the meal are also performed by the females in the family. It is also her duty to clean the hearth and to lift the leavings of food and to wipe the dining room.

However, the head, inspite of the general division of works among family members, occasionally make an alternative arrangement for carrying out the seasional works properly. For this very purpose the head at every night generally during meal assigned the duties to the members for the following day. Consequently, as soon as the day breaks the members, mechanically, engrossed themselves in the works as assigned to them previously. Thus, the pattern of division of labour resultantly gives birth to a system among Khasas, which Emile Durkheim has termed as 'mechanical solidarity' in his writings. Thus, the process of division of labour among Khasas bears in common, some functional significance as to develop the coherence among the family members and also to determine the status and roles of a person in the frame reference of the rest of the members in family. The status and the works invariably ascertain the psychological set up of a person and induce to interact in a particular manner with other statuses of the family and the community as a whole.

Apart from the agriculturist families the nature of work of the male and female particularly in monogamous nuclear families belonging to the business or service based economy, is different. Firstly, such families exist in the adjoing town areas of Dehradun district, secondly, the whole of the family subsists on the income earned by the concerning male members of the family through the service or any sort of the business pursuits. In those families the male members perform almost all the work outside of the family, while the female carries out all the familial tasks inside of the household. The children, mostly go for schooling and help in domestic jobs as is desired by the parents.

The nature of division of labour, among Tharus is very simple, even today it is based on the age and sex dichotomy particularly in respect of the agricultural and other subsidiary jobs. Yet, in every collateral joint families, the status of the head of the family is assigned on the basis of the ability of dealing with all the familial and social matters. Mostly, the male member having comparatively more ability in regard of the public dealings, who is shrewd, clever and have the ability to argue with the outsiders and also to get work done, holds the status of the head in family. Virtually, the head is supposed to put the family members to work and to get work out of them. While the rest of the male members of the family are liable to perform all the major agricultural tasks viz; ploughing, irrigating, manuring, sowing, reaping, threshing and also carrying the food grains for sale to market places. Moreover, he also looks after the domestic animals and feeds them time to time. He brings the fuel wood and the fodder from jungle. He builds huts and performs all the tasks outside of the house hold. It is also the liability of the males to manufacture the cot, mates, rope and wooden agricultural equipments only for their personal use.

On the contrary, the females are liable mainly for the internal house-hold jobs. She attends the kitchen, brings viscous soil from the pond for smearing the courtyard and also for plastering and white washing the hut walls and the floor. She traps fishes, collects a special type of the vegetable called, 'Narai', 'Lakura' and 'Bhadhuwa' in local dialect from jungles. Tharu women prepare basket called 'Daliya' by the sticks of the grasses during the end of the rainy season, and oven called 'Chulha' by the clay mixed of husk and, the 'Kuthiya' for the preservation of the foodgrains. Today a Tharu woman can be seen busy with her stitching machine. In fact, the sewing and knitting are also the personal tasks of the Tharu woman.

Besides this, the children both male and the female ranging approximately from six to fifteen years of age perform the small jobs viz., grazing cattle, bringing fodder and transplanting the paddy plants side by side with schooling.

Like Tharus the Buxas also pretend to be the discent from the royal origin in female line and also depend on the agricultural and similar other subsidiary jobs. Besides this the agro-climatic conditions and the ecological settings of the locality they dwell in are almost the same as Tharus have. They observe approximately the same style of living as the Tharus of Kumaun do. Yet the agricultural pattern and the socio-economic standard of Buxas is comparatively lower than the Tharus, for they are introverted by nature and have no meaning of modernization, education and better living in general. They wish to procure only as much as is necessary to keep body and soul together. Consequently, the Buxas, a primitive tribe have frequently been observing the simplest or the oldest form of the division of labour based on sex all along. Unlike Tharus, the Buxa woman in the family retains comparatively a privileged status and therefore confined herself with the easier household jobs such as rearing and caring the children, cooking food, and managing all the household matters. She commands over the men folk, assigns their duties to carry on, the males in response are expected to obey the female by performing all the tedious tasks outside of the household. He is also liable to manage the essential provision for the subsistence of the family by any means. Moreover, the major agricultural jobs are performed simultaneously by the males and the females, yet the ploughing goes to male's part. The children also lend their hands in every sort of economic pursuits side by side with the elder members of the family. They go to the school, yet the main concentration always remains on the economic gains, since every child, as soon as he / she attains the age of six is supposed to be an integral part of Buxa's economic structure, hence a child is preferably attached to any of the jobs having direct or indirect use for economic assistance rather than schooling. However, the various incentives given by the government have attracted the Buxa children for free schooling.

Rajis, another primitive tribe of Uttarakhand correspond the same pattern as well as the bases for the division of labour in family as is observed by Buxas. Like Buxas, it is also a female dominated tribal group. But comparatively the more economic deprivation has shortened the division of works between the male and female in general, however, the ploughing, manufacturing wooden equipments, dealing with outside world, eventually go to the male's part. While the rest of the agricultural as well as the domestic tasks what ever of kind are performed by the males and females without any difference. The male also attends the kitchen, strips the milch cattle, grinds the flour and pestles the paddy. Correspondingly, the children also help the family members in various fields. Mostly the children are deputed for cattle grazing. They bring fodder and fuel wood, fetch water from the water source and some times look after the infants and the house, particularly when the elder members of the family go for collecting jungle products, like herbs, edible roots, and also for trapping the fishes. The aged persons, if any, in the family are mostly left at home to look after the infants and the guarding of the house.

Thus, it may be concluded that the nature of division of labour among the agriculturist families of the tribals under reference is absolutely of the traditional type generally based on the sex and the age difference. It is indeed a simplest and the oldest form of the division of labour as has been observed by the earliest anthropologist and social scientists in various primitive tribes. However, some variations in the nature of the work done by the males and females particularly in those non-traditional i.e. the modern nuclear families, settled down particularly in towns, have come into notice which is inevitably the outcome of the impact of the modernization, which induced the tribals to get education, the urbanization which provides the various occupational opportunities, and the sanskritization which provoked the tribals to imitate the cultural traits and the style of life of the non-tribal Hindus as to make the intra-tribal social intercourse more adaptive and also the desire for social upgradation possible.

Changes in the Structure and Function of Family

The foregoing causative analysis of the various forms and functions of the tribal families demonstrate their adaptive pattern with the varied ecological conditions arisen out of the various processes of cultural transformation. Today we can associate the simple and nuclear families of modern types with relatively urbanized society and the joint types of families, simultaneously the nuclear families of traditional type with traditional agrarian and unurbanised societies.

The transformation from joint families to nuclear families is an example of the structural change in the family which is mainly caused by two major factors; first, the indigenous factors, such as the increasing indigence and the decreasing sources of subsistence of traditional types and the strained relations among the family members over property dealings and sharing the house-hold liabilities; second, the impact of the macro-structures viz; the urbanization, modernization and the sanskritization with the effect of the former factor and the nuclear families of traditional types i.e. the families consisting of the mates and their unmarried children with or without relatives and which bears in common the organizational set up alike of the joint families and confined within the rural areas only have come into existence, while the latter factor has developed the nuclear families of modern type. Consequently, the whole structure which was mechanical in traditional families has been changed into the organismic system which can be observed among the modern nuclear families existing in town areas. Besides this, the age and sex which were the most dominant factors in determining the social status, roles and the privileges of the family members have been replaced by ability, skill and capacity for earning money from different sources as well as the education of the member concerned. The heads of the families, particularly in nuclear families of modern types, are no more all in all in taking decisions about the major issues of the family. For example, in mate selection the personal choice of the boy or girl counts more than the head of the family, hence neither the marriage is settled without the prior consent of the boy/girl nor the family head can take unilateral decision about this matter.

Moreover, the status and role of woman in family has also undergone numerous changes. She is not the subordinate but a co-partner of the male, today she is supposed not only to devote her time in rearing and caring of the children and other internal household tasks but also free to work outside in offices, schools, even in administrative and medical services.

It has also been observed that the traditional forms of framing role expectations have also been changing day by day. For instance, neither the head of the modern nuclear families is liable to perform the socio-economic, religious and political as well as the rest of the familial responsibilities, as is observed in joint and nuclear families of traditional types, nor the wife is supposed to perform all her traditional tasks. In the modern nuclear family the traditional type of division of labour between man and woman has frequently been breaking down. Some times the husband has to share some works which were traditionally assigned to wife and vice versa. Any of the decisions about any major familial issues is taken with mutual consent of the wife and husband. In comparison of the joint and traditional nuclear families, the nature of affection and sentiments in inter-personal relationship of the family members of a modern nuclear families has become more particular and intense and the traditional joint family sentiments and effective bonds uniting the akins are slackening day by day. Thus, it may be concluded that the joint and the traditional nuclear families though still bear some of the traditional features in common while the same are disappearing among the modern nuclear families which are predominantly existant in towns and gradually changeing their style of living as well as the family pattern in the direction of the more civilized non-tribal twice born castes of the neighbouring areas. Thus, it may be concluded that the education, means of transportation and communication as well as the reservation policies of the government for tribals have compelled them to come under the influence of the civilized society. Resultantly, the process of cultural transformation occurred in tribal areas.

Marriage

Marriage is a bio-psychic cum socio-religious institution which makes possible the existence of family institution and its primary functions of reproduction and preservation of the cultural complexes of the varieties of the human groups.

Historical facts and the scholarly conclusions drawn through the comparative and meticulous researchers are sufficient enough to prove the existence of the various forms and the ways of acquiring mates among the tribal communities of the globe. As Majumdar and Madan have remarked, "Marriage can be of several types. All over tribal India and in other parts of the world as well, we come across rules, laying down prohibitions, preferences and prescriptions in deciding the form of marriage."[17] In fact, almost all tribal communities follow some particular sort of rules pertaining to family incest taboo which consequently generate the exogamy or endogamy forms of marriages. The former type leads to the prohibition, on sex relations between closely related kins and in between the members of the clan as well as the locality. "This practice of marrying outside one's clan is called exogamy."[18] The Gond, the Baiga, the Ho, the Korwa, the Oraon, the Khasi and the Naga follow the rules of clan exogamy. For Khasis, as remarked by Majumdar, "A breach of exogamy brings disaster to the Khasi. It entails excommunication, refusal of funeral ceremonies and no resting place in the sepulchre of the clan."[19] While the later form of marriage *i.e.* endogamy is "the practice of marrying within one's tribe, or very rarely clan, is called endogamy."[20] The marital relations are set up within the caste, tribe, class, totem as well as locality in endogamous type of marriages. The Bhil of Rajasthan have two endogamous groups the Ujala Bhil and the Mele Bhil. Majumdar has stated that, "Due to the universal fear to the strange, the novel and the unknown, almost all the Indian tribes are endogamous."[21] In fact endogamy is observed by the majority of the tribal groups in India.

Besides this, some preferential marriages have largely been practised by the tribal communities in India. Such as the cross cousin marriages are performed preferentially by the Gond, the Kharia, the Oraon and the Kadar tribal communities of India. The Gond of Madhya Pradesh call this form of marriage 'dudhlautava' *i.e.* "return of milk."[22] Moreover, some tribal communities *viz.*, Toda follow levirate and sororate preferential marriages which emphasize the acceptance of inter-familial obligations and the recognition of marriage as a tie between two families and not only between two individuals.[23] There are some special types of marriages which are performed in particular situations and reasons. Among Santhals, the widow and the widower generally get married. Among Garos the widow mother-in-law gets remarriage with her son-in-law (daughter's husband) so that the latter can have the possession on the property of the former. In 'Gond' tribe the father-in-law and the daughter-in-law generally get married. Even the widow step-mother is married with her step son among Lakher. So is the case of Sema Nagas.

Apart from the above mentioned forms of marriages, some other forms like, monogamy, polyandry, polygyny and group marriages are also practised in the tribal world. These forms are basically structured on the basis of the number of the spouses. "Polyandry, as Majumdar remarks, is comparatively, much restricted in distribution. It is found among the Tiyan, the Toda, the Kota, the Khasa and the Ladhakhi Bota .... among the Indo-Aryan, as also the Monogoloid peoples, polyandry is reported."[24] Polygyny is found among the Naga tribes, the Gonda, the Baiga, the Lusai clan and most of the other proto-Australoid tribes of Middle India.[25] Monogamy is practised among the Khasis, the Santhals and the Kadars.

In spite of the various forms of marriages, the manner of acquiring mates are also numerous in tribal India. Anthropologists have suggested eight important ways *i.e.* the probationary marriage, marriage by capture, marriage by trial, marriage by purchase, marriage by service, marriage by exchange, marriage by mutual consent and elopement and marriage by intrusion, for acquiring mates.[26] Every tribal community living within the given normative order of one's community follow the different rules of acquiring the life mates.

The tribal communities under reference have thoroughly been studied. It is observed that the traditional Bhotiyas of Indo-Tibetan border used to observe the rules of endogamy. Traditionally, a Bhotiya youth cannot marry outside of his / her community. Any such type of event of marrying with non-Bhotiya or the violation of customary law may level of the social stigma on the whole of the Bhotiya community and some times resulted in the excommunication of the accused. But the sub-divisions of the Bhotiya community i.e. the sibs (sub-caste) are exogamous. Mating relations are strictly prohibited within sibs, such as a Kutiyal male would never marry the Kutiyal female *vice-versa.* It is so because of the same place of residence, after which the nick names of their sib (or the sub-caste) is ascertained. Because the persons from the same caste are considered to be the blood related and therefore possess the ties of brother and sister and prohibit any such type of mating relations within the sub-caste. Monogamy is the general rule which permits mating relationship with any one person, at a time. But the death of any of the spouses may cause the widow/widower remarriage. The divorced (which are rarely observed) remarriages are also take place. Thus, it may be concluded that some prohibitions regarding the settlement of the marital relations are observed among Bhotiyas.

Marriage among Bhotiya has never been a religious sacrament like Hindus. It is rather a contract between the two families which ensure the marital relations between the two opposite sexes for the bio-genetic cum socio-economic gains in life. Although,it extends socially the consanguine ties between the two kin groups but more accurately, it restraints bio-economic function to the mating parties. Thus, the marriage among Bhotiyas is bio-economic institution rather than a religious one. It regulates and socially sanctions the sex relations of the two and also provides better opportunity for economic pursuits.

Apart from the incest taboos or the prohibitions regarding the settlement of the marital relations, some prescription or preferences are also observed for marriage in some particular kin groups. In this regard, the cross-cousin marriages are often preferential and is of the immense importance and consists of considerable degree of reverence in the community. Same is the case with the Gond, the Khasi, the Kharia, the Oraon, the Mikiri and the Bhils. Grigson has found 54% cross-cousin marriages among Gonds. Alike of the tribal communities, a Bhotiya always prefers to marry his/her cross cousin and in the absence of the later a mate is looked among the similar other consanguine kin groups.

Besides this, some other forms of marriage viz; sororate, levirate and widow remarriages are also practised among Bhotiyas. Some exceptional cases of polygyny are also recorded which is generally performed for the sake of the male child to run the descent, provided that there is no any male issue survive from the former wife, the husband with the mutual consent of the wife and other family members married a second wife.

Thus, it may be asserted that 'Bhotiya' is a monogamous tribal group and observes the rules of endogamy (at community level) while the rules of exogamy are followed at sib or sub-caste level. Moreover, some incest taboos and the forms of preferential marriages viz. cross cousin marriages are also observed among them.

Following the different rules for the different forms of marriages, Bhotiyas acquire their life mate by different ways. Historically, there are number of evidence to prove the prevalence of one and more ways i.e. marriage by capture, marriage by elopement and the marriage by mutual consent among the Bhotiyas, as is observed among Nagas, Hos, and Gonds. Among Gond[27] as Majumdar has said, capture takes place at the request of the parents of the girls. This procedure of acquiring mates is called the 'Oportipi' among the Hos and 'Posi-Othur' among the Gonds. Among Bhotiyas, this procedure is known as 'Thachimo-Vekhant' which generally followed at night time beyond the knowledge of the girl's parents. In the capture of the virgin, the villagers, who are previously made known about the case also help the young man desirous to marry the woman. Although, there have been a number of implications in following this savagery and inhumane way of acquiring the mates, but generally the particularistic cause, as observed in several tribal communities in India, is the exorbitant rate of bride price that often leads to marriage by capture, which may often be pre-arranged as is observed among Ho. But the physical capture of Bhotiya virgin is caused due to the economic pauperism of the parents because the ceremonial formal celebration of mating is rather more expensive, hence the indirect acceptance of the parents to the man desirous to marry used to lead the marriage by physical capture. But, the forced capture which has previously been denied and prohibited by the girl's parents may resulted in the dispute and sometimes violence between the two parties, ends up with the desirable implication of the winner and the fine as token of punishment to the looser. At present this method of marriage has disappeared from the Bhotiya community, however there are sufficient evidences even today to prove the popular and customary prevalence of the marriage by capture, as the bride, even today weep and lament and make a pretense of resistance by embracing and clinging with her parents and companions at the occasion of her departure to groom's house.

Besides physical capture, ceremonial captures as has been observed among Kharia and Birhor has also been practised among

Bhotiyas. But the method of performing ceremonial capture is quite different among them which is the cause of the organizational differences of the tribal communities. In Bhotiya community a man failure to acquire the mate by a socially approved manner, captures the virgin to his house and offer her 'Dhalan' (a 'Cake of Sattu') and a cup of 'Chyakti' (wine) at the threshold and the acceptance of a piece of cake and the doze of wine by the girl leads to perform the primary rite of the marriage and thus inspite of being opposed by the loosers, the man thus have a social claim to call her as his wife before the tribal council of elders.

Besides this, the marriage by mutual consent and elopement had also been practised among Bhotiyas. As Mr. Rayapa,[28] has aptly stated that, some times the lover and the beloved get into illicit sex-relation and promise to lead a married life inspite of the disapproval of their parents and therefore get elopement out of the community and lead independent married life, until and unless the parents do not affectionately invite them. But in course of time the parents do call them within the community and once again the formality of the marriage is performed in a usual course. This way of getting mates among Bhotiyas is termed as "Chalvu Deemo" means—the marriage by mutual consent and elopement which is possible only beyond the knowledge and estimation of the parents. But a mediator, termed as 'Taram' outstandingly play an important role in making the abduction possible. The man previously brought about the consent of the girl as well as the parents through the mediator in case of the pre-consent of any of the two (either parents or girls) the capture takes place. But no case of the girl's desirous to marry an unwilling man has so far been found. It is so because of the bashful nature of the female who inspite of the willing to marry a particular man does not expose herself. Thus, it may be concluded that the man, willing to marry a woman takes initiative either by himself or through his parents or the 'Taram' (mediator) and it generally depends on the choice of the girl and her parents to accept the proposal or not. But instead of the disagreement of the latter party, if the man duress over the woman by oppression and the application of repugnant means for her capture, the woman's party resist and oppose the trial which some times resulted in the form of dispute.

But the intensive and thorough observation of the various

ways of getting the mates, exhibits a considerable variations in accordance to the variations of the social, ecological, occupational and education standard of the Bhotiya family in general and the man desirous to marry in particular. It is observed that the part of the population still reside in remote and interior villages do observe the ancient and the traditional ways of acquiring mates as mentioned above, yet with some considerable symbolic and structural changes. Thus, the capture and the 'mutual consent and the elopement' have been transformed into a formal and institutionalized way of marriage. Today, the ancient ways exist no where even in the farthest remote village areas of the Bhotiyas but the traces may viewed symbolically only by a learned and experienced social scientist such as the lament of the departing bride clinging with her kith and kin, to take out marriage procession with beating drums, and shield and sword in hands, the concept of 'Tisya' and 'Sya-Sya' and staying of the marriage party for about three days at bride's place, are the symbolical evidences to denote an ancient type of Bhotiya marriage; i.e. the marriage by capture. Besides this, the concept of 'Dhalan' (the cake of Sattu) and 'Chyakti' (the wine) which is offered by groom's party as a token of proposal for the bride and its acceptance by the parents of girl and the girl herself indicate the ceremonial capture, after which the groom's party may have right to claim on her as inlaw.

Besides, the physical and ceremonial capture, the marriage by mutual consent and elopement has been transformed into socially sanctioned love marriage with some formal proceedings as appeared in formal marriages. Today if a boy falls in love with a girl and both of them like each other and eager to lead a married life, the former then approaches with a suitable medium i.e. through his guardian to the latter's parents and make a proposal for marriage with the formal ceremonies. If, both the parties agree, the marriage of the desirous male and female is settled down and performed according to the suitable dates suggested by the groom's parents. Thus, the amorous and illicit sex relations between the male and female which used to lead a marriage by mutual consent and elopement in ancient time has now got, rather a refined and ceremonial form to regulate the pre-marital sex relations of the parties. It is thus obvious that the way of acquiring mates among Bhotiyas have undergone a tremendous structural as well as the organizational changes which in every possible means is the inevitable resultant of the cultural contacts of the out groups and the nodding acquaintance of the neighbouring Kumaunies.

At present, 'the Bhotiya marriage' which even today implies not a least religious or sacramental sense as is observed among the neighbouring Hindus with some structural and organizational changes is followed with some particular proceedings, which is as follows:

Thomo, *i.e.*, the Betrothal

Marriage ceremony among Bhotiyas is followed by some particular sequential performances, the most important of which is the worship of 'Dhalan' and the acceptance of a brimmer of 'Chyakti' decorated with flower and green grass as a mark of gracious sign. The proposal for marriage with 'Chyakti' and some sweets or 'Dhalan' is offered to the bride's parents. Sometimes the bride's father or guardian makes a false pretension of disagreement as to reserve his discretion about the matter and therefore refuses the proposal by returning the 'Chyakti' and 'Dhalan' to the proposers in that very moment. The proposers then approach the girl's kith and kins and again offer the proposal with the help of the mediators. Often the girl's father or guardian, ultimately gives the consent accepting the brimmer of 'Chyakti' and the sweets or 'Dhalan' and in return arranges a grand-feast to the proposers alongwith the whole of the villagers. At this occasion, the boy and the girl also give their formal consent towards the proposal by having a brim of 'Chyakti' and a piece of 'Dhalan'. This observance is merely a formal ceremony, particularly in most of the cases the girl has already been selected by the boy and his parents either by the pre-marital love between the boy and the girl or being in line with the usual course of marital ties. At the very moment the ceremonial rite of filling the lap of the girl's mother i.e. the 'Godbharai' with some amount of money as much as is decided for the loss of the milk of the mother is also performed. Symbolically, it is nothing but an advance amount for bride price as to make the dealing confirm. Moreover, the date of the marriage is also fixed according to the convenience of the girl's parents. Till the auspicious day of the wedding ceremony, the fiance and fiancee await eagerly the gracious meeting and avoid any direct contact with one another, for the pre-marital meetings of the betrothed mates are socially prohibited because such meetings may cause some amorous relations between them.

Dhami-Syasya , *i.e.,* the Wedding Ceremony

The wedding ceremony among Bhotiyas is followed by some ritualistic performances, the most important of which is the tradition of 'Shakanu' in which a brimmer of 'Chyakti' decorated with flower and green grass (Dub) as a symbol of prosperity and well being and the 'Dhalan' is offered by each and every family of the girl's village as a mark of reception of the marriage processionists (Baraties) on their arrival in the village. Sometimes two or more families jointly observe the 'Shakanu' rite for their own convenience. But lastly, the bride's parents perform the 'Shakanu' rite. At this occasion, the Tisya (an uneven numbers of unmarried girls, may be the sisters or father's sister of the groom) who come alongwith the marriage procession are duly respected by the bride's people and offered 'Chyakti' and 'Dhalan' as the token of offering. In fact, the 'Tisyas, in ancient time were the unmarried girls belonging to the groom's kin group who used to accompany the marriage procession to persuade the girl for marriage. At this occasion they had dual functions; first, to adopt every possible techniques for persuading the girl for marriage and second, to carry the food stuffs and 'Chyakti' (wine) for the people joining the procession and also the essential material for 'Shakanu' rite. But today the traditional functional significance of 'Tisya' has slackened and traditionally the Bhotiyas still observe this pattern only for the sake of the tradition.

Having been the observance of 'Shakanu' rite the 'Lai' or 'God Bharai' ceremony is followed. Since the bride being a reproduct of mother is also brought up by her with great care by feeding the breast milk during her infancy and therefore the marriage of a daughter is considered to be a personal loss of the mother's milk, hence symbolically compensated by paying a certain amount of money as the price of the mother's milk. This tradition proves the symbolic utility of a woman among Bhotiyas.

After the 'Lai-ceremony' the 'Khato' rite is performed. According to the Bhotiya tradition all the bride's kith and kins are presented a white cotton cloth (termed as Khato) approximately one and half meter in length and also to the bride's parents but comparatively better in quality than the general ones by the groom's party. The 'Khato' is wrapped around the head as is the turban instantly as a mark of honour by all the recipients. The 'Khato' ceremony is performed generally at midnight after dinner and with its completion the wedding ceremony is conceived to be completed.

The 'Khato' ceremony leads to the most recreational aspect of the 'Bhotiya' marriage called 'Rang-bang' which is participated by all the people whether married or unmarried, young or adult, male or female. But in general, the young unmarried girls and boys celeberate it by singing and dancing with the full intoxication of 'Chyakti' as well as of the blossoming youth. The ceremonial function of Rang-bang makes the atmosphere so delightfully pleasant that the lonely valleys simultaneously echoed with joy and thus make the expression of pleasure with youths singing, dancing and merry making. The function of Rang-bang is celebrated throughout the night and gradually with the appearance of first light of the day the effect of the intoxication also nullified and the over tired youths then go for relaxation to their houses. At the day time the marriage party is invited by the villagers to have drink and meal, subsequently, during their stay on the following days too. Thus after staying for about two or three days the marriage party come back to the groom's place.

At the departure of the marriage procession the bride is symbolically hidden to follow an ancient tradition. The groom then goes after her and searchs her out. Thus, the marriage procession departs with singing and dancing on the drums as well as the heart touching lament of the bride. This practice of hiding the bride before her departure and her lament is evidently a prove of an ancient way of marriage i.e. the marriage by capture. Thus, the marriage procession after having lunch at bride's place returns with the bride to groom's place. The ceremonial performance of 'Shakanu' rite which consists of a decorated vessel full of 'Chyakti' and the 'Dhalan' is also performed at groom's place. The 'Chyakti' and the 'Dhalan' is offered to all the processionists along with the bride and the groom. This ceremony leads to the reception of the marriage.

A more outstanding characteristic of the Bhotiya marriage is the tradition of 'Sya-Sya' i.e. the unmarried girls who come along with the bride as the female companions to depart her. The 'Sya-Sya' who are three or more in numbers, stay at the groom's place for about two or three days. During this period they enjoy at groom's place with the unmarried boys and girls. They all drink 'Chyakti', sing songs and dance. But the tradition of 'Sya-Sya' has been disappearing day by day due to some incidents of obscene and forceful illicit sex liaison with 'Sya-Sya'.

It is observed that the part of the Bhotiya population, which is still confined in the farthest remote and inaccessible places and generally beyond the impact of the out groups follow the rules of the patriarchal monogamy and some preferences and prohibitions regarding to the sexual liaison or matrimonial alliances in some particular kin groups. While the ancient ways of acquiring mates i.e. the marriage by capture, the marriage by mutual consent and elopement and the marriage by purchase have been transformed into 'Bagiya', the modern unified system of marriage which consists of the symbolic traces of all the types of ancient marriages in refined ceremonial forms which are celebrated at the occasion of the marriage. It is observed that in order in which the contact with non-tribal Hindus extended and as they have begun to come out from their narrow limits of geo-traditional peripheries for trades and business as well as for acquiring education and government jobs, the ancient ways of marital alliance also changed into refined rather more civilized forms.

The researcher has also observed the structural pattern of the marriage performed by those Bhotiyas who have come down and got settled in some urban areas or towns either for business and supplementary economic pursuits or the government services and living in the frequent and constant cultural contacts with out-groups, feeling and observing the cultural variation rapidly occurring due to the emergence of multi-dimensional social and cultural complexes and the material values.

Hence, that part of the Bhotiya population who has got its settlement in the town areas has utterly changed the ancient form of the marriage. They generally call the Kumauni Brahmin priest who performs the marriage ceremony as is observed among Kumauni Hindus. Today, the marriage ceremony among those Bhotiyas who have come out from their traditional ecological settings to the urban areas consists of a number of ritual performances, viz., the 'Kanyadan' (gift of daughter to the bride groom), Sanctifier of the ceremony (vivha-home), holdings of bride's hand by bridgroom (Panigrahan) and walking seven times by the bride and groom around the pious fire and the green branches of pine and cherry affixed on the earth as witness, each round being denoted by a coin placed on the earth. In this process the bride leads to groom by holding the one end of sari follow the bride with the promise to keep himself with her (bride) constantly (saptapadi). Thus, the bride is carried away (vivah) and departed to groom's place of residence. Thus, the Bhotiyas who are educated and serving in urban areas and also have got their settlement with their families in urbans and those who are engaged in some sort of settled business in some town and urban areas follow the Hindu pattern of marriage and also claim to be a Hindu Rajput (Kshatriya). It is merely because of the cultural impact of the big community, i.e. Hindus as well as the education, which indispensably compelled them to come under the ritualistic changes to ensure their social status in Hindu caste hierarchy and to establish a state of coherence and assimilation to flow in the main stream of Hindu social system.

However, the Hindu caste hierarchy did not approve their hierarchical position in its structural frame of reference. Hence, the Bhotiya community has hitherto been an endogamous group on community level and constantly been following the same ritualistic performances to claim their Hindu origin as is observed among their neighbouring non-tribal groups. For instance, a respondent unit named 'X' asserted that "'Yes', we are Hindu Rajput and follow the rules of endogamy because we have got our own circle of affinal kinship relations as is observed in every Hindu sub-caste group, viz., the so called "Chand (Rajpur Kshatriya) of Kumaun have their particular circle of affinal kinship relations and in general they follow the rules of endogamy." Thus, the Bhotiyas particularly, the Joharis of the Johar Valley have emerged as a distinct caste group and therefore avoids any sort of affinal relations with other Bhotiyas, however they have no place in Hindu caste hierarchy so far.

Thus, the picture that emerges from the foregoing analysis reveals that the rural population of Bhotiyas is in the process of following some of the major cultural patterns of the neighbouring non-tribal Hindus. For instance, the Bhotiyas like other twice born 'castes' have begun to take the services of the Brahmin priest at the occasion of marriage who chants the hymn (mantras) and performs the marriage as according to the vedic rite. In fact, some Bhotiyas particularly the 'Joharis', claim to be Hindu Rajputs and follow the various mores, rituals, beliefs, practices and the style of life of the neighbouring Kumaun Hindu Kshstriyas. On the contrary, there are sufficient evidences which show that the twice born Hindus though in minority, dwelling in tribal areas also taking over the different cultural traits pertaining to the tribal's beliefs and practices. For example, the Hindus residing in the adjoining areas of the Bhotiya's villages also observe the 'Sakanu' rite and offer 'Chyakti' and 'Dhalan' in the same manner as is observed by Bhotiyas at the occasion of marriage. Thus, the process of 'Sanskritization' and 'tribalization' simultaneously occurring in the tribal areas of Uttarakhand and resultantly a vertical solidarity has come into existence among the population concentrated in the scheduled tribal areas of Uttarakhand. In fact, the tribal and the non-tribal communities, on account of the contiguous regions of residence not only share the dialect, rituals, beliefs and practices of one another but also observe them in the same manner.

Buxa is a monogamous tribal group. It is an endogamous community, yet observes strictly the 'Gotra' and 'Khera' exogamous rules. Even village exogamy is also followed among 'Pachhmias' in particular and therefore a man and a woman despite the differences of the 'Gotra' and 'Khera' are not permitted to marry with one another unless they dwell in the same village. Moreover, the marriage alliances among the three generations in the mother's line is also prohibited. Almost all the Buxa marriages are duly performed with certain procedures and rituals. For a long time, the Buxa marriages are performed by the Brahamin priest. Atkinson has also stated that, "They (Buxa) are now in every respect in their habits and customs Hindus of the ordinary low caste type and employ 'Gaur' 'Brahmin Purohits' in their marriage and funeral ceremonies."[29] At present the Kumauni Brahaman priest performs the marriage according to the Vedic-custom. The rites of Kanyadan, Saptpadi, Vivha-hom etc. pertaining to the vedic customs as the twice born Hindu castes observe, are also performed side by side with their local or tribal customs viz; the Ratjaga, Chheye Katana, Nyauta, Daudha dhari, Nahawan, Bhat lagana, Dr-Bar and Sag-Bhat.

The transmission of great traditions by the powerful media-agent i.e. the Brahmin priest and the Sanskritizing influences have jointly influenced many aspects of the Buxa culture, however they have been failure to leave their basic cultural patterns. However, the combination of the great and the little traditions has invariably provided the Buxas some new alternative choices to be observed, as to prove their Hinduism and also to make available the clue of their up gradation particularly in the direction of Hindu caste hierarchy. Nevertheless, they have been deprived all along. It is observed that the 'Ghargawain Marriages' are also practised among Buxas. Particularly, when a Buxa has only daughters, he arranges a groom for one of his daughters who would stay at bride's domicile after marriage, so that the bride's parents may seek assistance in agricultural and other subsidiary jobs. In such type of marriages the man rarely visits his parents, for he is socially more liable to the in-laws.

Besides, the above mentioned forms of marriages, widow remarriages are also performed among Buxa community. But in such type of marriages no ceremonial performances are made, only the widow is brought with the prior consent of her former in-laws. A certain amount, as decided between the parties is also paid as a compensatory amount to the loosers.

A formal Buxa marriage is preceded by 'Tika' i.e. the proposal for marriage and the 'Ginauan' or the engagement or the betrothal rite. At first, a proposal from the side of the boy is offered to the girl's party, the acceptance of which is followed by the betrothal ceremony. On this occasion the date of the marriage best suitable to the girl's parents, is decided. Lastly, the marriage is performed with Vedic-custom along with some particular local customs. Generally, the marriage is performed in the month of 'Phalgun'. Besides the formal marriage, some other forms of marriages are also observed among Buxas, out of which the love marriages, marriage by abduction and the Gharjawain marriages are very common.

Love marriages are the outcome of the amorous relations developed between the girl and the boy by mutual consent. In such cases the parents of the both parties, generally give their consent and perform the marriage of the lover and the beloved in a formal way, provided that the families do not come within the prohibited degree of affinal relationships. But if the two families dwell in the same locality or belong to the same 'Gotra', the marriage of the accused can not be materalised and then only a way is left for the boys and the girls to get elopement and to live together as husband and wife. Such cases of the love marriages are put before the tribal council called 'Takhat' who thoroughly looks over the matter and gives its final decision which remains often in favour of the accused and only then they are accepted in the community.

Moreover, if a man, married or unmarried, develops some illicit sex relations with any married woman who is neither divorced nor separated, the only way left for him, is the abduction of the woman. Later on, if the looser husband agrees the separation and demands the compensation, the payment of which make easy the regularization of the relationship. But the objection of the looser husband may lead to the excommunication of the couple, however the children born out of such relationship have no social stigma in Buxa community.

Alike of Buxas, the Tharu is also a monogamous tribal group in general, which follows strictly the rules of community endogamy and the clan exogamy in particular. Unlike Buxas, the whole of the Tharu community has been divided into six major sub-castes, which they name as the 'Jat' a popular distortion of Sanskrit term 'Jati'. These are, the Rana, the Bhukasa, the Garaurha, the Dhanara, the Khunka, the Jugiya and the Saunsa. Each of the sub-castes is an endogamous group in principle. For the members of each sub-caste prefer to settle their marital alliance within the same group as to maintain the purity of the blood and also to enrich and strengthen the affinal relations within the members of the sub-caste. Moreover, almost all the sub-castes have a particular status in the sub-caste hierarchy and therefore the people belonging particularly to the higher status *i.e.* hierarchical order avoid any such alliance respectively with the socalled lower sub-castes. However, the rules of endogamy on sub-caste level are not observed so strictly as is on the community level. In fact, in some exceptional cases the evidences of inter-sub-caste marriages are also observed; particularly when a boy is poor and socio-economically incapable to marry the girl from the same sub caste group, he seeks the bride from the lower sub-caste-group and the people respectively from the lower sub-caste group agree any such kind of the proposal as to acquire the higher status in the hierarchical order through wedding relations. Besides this, the extra marital and pre-marital sex relations or the love affairs between the male and the female of different sub-castes may also lead to the inter sub-caste marriages. But whatever been the cause of sub-caste intermarriage, a grand feast is given to the groom's party by bride's party in which the cooked rice, fish and the wine is served lavishly while the bride serves herself 'Ghee' to the members present on the occasion and this celebration is supposed to accept the bride by the groom's party.

On the contrary, Tharus also observe strictly the rules of exogamy particularly among the nearest consanguineous kinsmen. Cross cousin marriages are strictly prohibited.

The settlement of a formal marriage, in normal course is done by a mediator termed as 'Maspatia'. The mediator who is comparatively a prestigious man generally familiar with both parties and the words of whom carries some weight for them takes initiative on the call of the girl's side and thus makes inquiry for a suitable groom. Often in the settlement of marriage the incest regulation which are traditionally prevalent in the Tharu community are precisely followed. Thus, on getting a suitable boy, the mediator make the both parties agree and induce them to materialize the proposal. On the consent of the both parties the 'Dikhanori' or 'Tika' ceremony takes place at groom's place. The girl's father or the guardian along with some honourable members visits to the boy's place, where they present at least five rupees to the boy and apply a mark of turmeric with rice and sesame on his forehead. This ceremony symbolized as the reservation of the boy for marriage. At this occasion a grand feast is arranged by the groom's people. Later on the same ceremony is performed at girl's place. At this occasion, the father or the guardian of the boy presents some rupees to the girl for putting on the bangles and also put a mark of the red vermillion on the girl's forehead. With this ceremony the proposal of marriage is considered to be confirm.

Mostly the 'Tika' ceremony is solemnized at the childhood of the children. After it, when the boy and the girl grown up and attain the age of puberty the next step towards wedding ceremony is proceeded.

Puchahu or Byah Puchhana

The 'Tika' is followed by 'Puchahu' or 'Byah Puchhana' ceremony. At this stage the boy's father or guardian alongwith his nearest and dearest kith and kins, generally five or more in numbers, approach the girl's father to make enquiry about the date of the marriage as well as to seek the formal consent for the wedding of the betrothed mates. On this auspicious occasion the boy's people carry with them a part of the bride price if decided earlier at the time of Tika and also present the fishes, rice and dal to the girl's parents. The date of the marriage as best suited to the girl's people is fixed and in anticipation of the wedding ceremony (Byah) the people eat rice and fish, drink wine and make merry on this occasion.

Byah or Marriage

The 'Puchahu' ceremony is followed by 'Byah' or marriage which is fixed either on any of the Friday or the Sunday of the 'Paush' and 'Magh' months of the year i.e. from 15th of December to 15th of February preferably considered as the best suitable dates for marriage. It is so because of the leisures of the time from agricultural tasks as well as the moderate climatic conditions during winter seasons. Moreover, they also plea for the best suitability of the winter season to digest every sorts of the heavy diet. The 'Byah' or marriage is preceded by some customary ceremonies both in the groom's and the bride's place which are as follows:

1. ***Chulaha Bethan (to set-up the oven of Sagun)***

At least seven days before the marriage the 'Chulha' (oven) already made of clay brought from the pond are set up in the kitchen by the married women whose husbands are alive. This ceremony too leads to drinking, feasting, dancing, singing and festivity. Almost all the kith and kins take part in the ceremony.

2. ***Bhuyan Poojan (Worship of Bhuyan)***

At least a day before the marriage the people of the both sides go with singing, dancing and beating the drums separately to worship 'Bhuyan' in their own places. The Bharare (traditional priest of the community) performs worship ceremony. He offers the 'Ghee', cloves, sweets etc. to the deity and wishes for the success and well being of the marital alliance.

"Sar Dena" or to Visit Pradhan's House for the Worship of the Gaushala

In this step the groom's as well as the bride's people respectively in their own places visit to the house of the head (Pradhan) of the village and worship the stable of the cows. This tradition shows the dominance of the 'Pradhan' over the villagers as well as the devotion and subordination of the villagers towards the Pradhan as he (the Pradhan) is symbolically an authoritative of the collective force and the outcome of the collective consciousness of the people for which they bow their head in great reverence. In return the Pradhan' extends his blessings and good wishes for the successful mating relations.

"Tel Charhawa" or the Tradition of "Nyota"

The traditional priest i.e. 'Bharare' imparts a magic spell to the turmeric and mustard oil and a part of it is sent to the bride through the advanced party who communicates the bride's people the necessary information about the marriage procession and also hands over them to the turmeric and mustard oil which is applied on bride's body by her mother and Bhabi and other lady akins, while the rest of the spelled turmeric and mustard oil is anointed to the groom's body by his mother, Bhabhis and the sisters. The groom anointed with turmeric and mustard oil is seated near the

'Bhu-sen' in the corridor with a long metallic pointed bar in hand called 'Kararo' and at least seven unleavened bread fried in 'Ghee' i.e. 'Poori' in it and only a underwear on the body and a white turban on head. The invited kith and kins and the villagers observe the 'Nyota' ceremony by applying a turmeric ointment on the turban of the groom offering a short amount of money to the groom as a token of the present. The same ceremony is also observed for the bride at the bride's place.

'Paharava'

The 'Nyota' ceremony is followed by the 'Paharava' rite. The brother-in-law (sister's husband) of the groom cause to dress him the newly stitched costume and a white cloth around the waist. The sister-in-laws (wives of the brothers) apply nail polish on the nails of the feet and hands of the groom and thus the groom is adorned with great care as to make him look more and more attractive. With the end of this ceremony the 'Barat' i.e. the marriage procession depart with dancing, twisting and singing on the bands and the drums.

'Bhaurhi' Tradition

Almost all the ladies of the village also accompany the departing marriage procession (Barat) up to the outskirt of the village. The mother of the groom sits beside the groom in the palanquin up to that mark where the 'Bhaurhi' tradition is observed. The mother in particular and the nearest akin ladies in general wash respectively the mouth of the groom and wipe it with the fringe of their 'Saris' and simultaneously apply the 'Kajal' on his eyelids and thus depart the 'Barat' to its destination.

Thus, the 'Barat' consisting of the male invitees go either in several bullock carts or on the tractors. The most outstanding feature of the 'Barat' implies in the self-sufficiency of the community members who do not appoint neither any Brahmin priest to perform the marriage (Byah) nor they hire the band and the palanquin carriers, because the traditional priest i.e. 'Bharare' performs some of the basic ceremonies while the rest of the ceremonies are performed by the brother-in-law (sister's husband) of the groom. In the same way the community members in themselves beat drum and play on bands and also carry the palanquin to whom they call as 'Kutwar'. On reaching the outskirt of the bride's village the 'Barat' has a short stay there, until the 'Kutwar' i.e. the palanquin-carrier from the bride's side come alongwith the bride's akins to receive warmly the Barat. The groom on palanquin is carried by the 'Kutawars' to the bride's house, where the sister-in-law (Bhauji) *i.e.* the bride's brother's wife putting a brass vessel i.e. 'Lota' full of water on the head called 'kars' sprays water on the groom and the marriage processionists. Until the groom's father or guardian do not pay the price of the 'Karsa' to the bride's sister-in-law, the groom is not brought down from the palanquin. With the payment of the 'Karsa' i.e. the performance of the tradition of 'Karsa Bughana' the groom is seated on the ground in front of the door of the bride's house.

In the first phase of the wedding ceremony the clothes and the ornaments brought by the groom's side are offered to the bride to wear. The bride is attired ornamented and adorned beautifully by the bride's sister-in-law (brother's wife), sisters and the fair-sex associates, after which the Kanyadan ceremony takes place.

Kanyadan, *i.e.,* "Giving away a Daughter in Marriage"

Both the groom and the bride are seated on the chairs kept side by side in a room. The bride takes particularly the right seat to sit on and a wooden board is placed at their feet-ward on which they rest their feet. The hand of the bride is given to groom's hand, which symbolically denotes the transfer of all the liabilities of the daughter from bride's parents to the groom and it is assumed that the fate of the bride will remain in the hands of the groom since the wedding ceremony. The parents of the bride then wash the feet of the bride and the groom and the water thus discharges from washing the feet is applied on the forehead by them and lastly by offering the appropriate presentation to the wedding mates, they give away their daughter to the groom for ever. The same act is repeated by all the kith and kins of the bride's side and the invitees as well. The present offered by the bride's people is kept up by the groom's brother-in-law (sister's husband) who alongwith the bride's sister-in-laws (brother's wives) performs the 'Kanyadan' ceremony. At the end of this ceremony the groom's brother-in-law presents a kind of green grass called 'Doob' to wedding mates as a token of offer which is symbolic as the mark of prosperity and the cheerfulness of the mates.

"Bhawnar"

After the completion of the 'Kanyadan' ceremony, both the bride and groom stand up at their places and get about ten or eleven rounds of the lighting lamp. In the first seven rounds the groom leads the bride while the remaining four rounds are led by the bride. With the end of the 'Bhawnar' ceremony the wedding *i.e.* the 'Byah' is considered to be completed.

All through the wedding ceremony the people gathered at the function cut jokes, pass remarks, make sarcasting remarks to one another. A good deal of use of vulgar and abusive language with the frequent references of genitals and sexual intercourse can precisely be observed between both the parties.

Thus, immediately after the wedding ceremony the groom with his brother-in-law takes the dinner. Almost all the processionists spent the remaining time of the wedding night in singing, dancing and drinking. While some people arrange the V.C.R. for the recreation of the invitees present at function.

On the next morning at about mid day the groom's party after having a short breakfast returns to its village. At the outskirt of the bride's village the tradition of 'Bhaurhi' is observed. Almost all the nearest akin ladies of the bride's family accompanied to the 'Barat' up to that place, where the bride's face is washed and wiped by ladies and thus they depart her with blessings. The traditional priest (Bharare) recites mantras to protect the couple from evil spirits and the evil sights of the people on the way to groom's village. The bride is accompanied by some lady companions particularly sister-in-laws or the sisters in relations. The ladies senior in relations are called 'Dhaya' while the juniors are termed as 'Bhirarhya'. Next day the 'Dhaya' and the 'Bhirarhya' call the bride with them to her natal place from where she is departed only when the 'Gauna' i.e. the second marriage ceremony takes place. Reaching on the groom's place the sisters and the brother-in-laws of the groom detain the way of the couple and put obstacle by standing on the enterance of the house until they are not awarded by suitable reward. This act is to be known as 'Mohar Gherana' i.e. to besiege the door of the house. Immediately after, the couple is seated in the room and offered 'Chhitakora' consisting of cooked rice, curd and sugar to eat. Later on the groom is asked to offer 'Parmal' i.e. the fried rice to all the people present on the function. In the afternoon the couple visits to the house of the village Pradhan, i.e. the head of the village, who gives his blessings to the newly married couple. At evening the village 'Pradhan' comes himself and wishes to have drink served by the bride and also asked her to the dinner. This act is to be known as "Bahuju Ki Daru" i.e. the wine on behalf of the bride. All through the night at groom's house, there is eating, drinking, singing, and dancing. The invitees are served lavishly the wine and the fish with rice. After having dinner the sugar cakes are distributed among the people present on the occasion. On the following day the bride with 'Dhaya' and 'Bhirarhya' return to her natal place.

Gauna: *i.e.*, the Second Marriage

At the occasion of the first 'Charai' festival that occurs during the moonlit half of a lunar month of 'Chaitra' the 'Gauna' (second marriage) ceremony takes place. The groom's father and nearest akins go to bride's village to bring her back. A good feast along with drink is offered to the groom's people and the bride is departed to her in-laws house. The affinal female relatives make warm reception of the bride and ask her to bring a vesselful water, which later on is used for cooking and thus the bride gets partial enterance in her affinal kin group. On the 'Charai' festival the bride helps in cooking and it is her privilege to serve the cooked food to the affinal kins and the invitees, and thus she formally gets admission in the groom's community. The bride is provided every possible opportunity to see and understand her husband and also to cohabit with him.

Besides, the formal marriage, some other forms of acquiring mates are also observed by Tharus. The court marriages which are the inevitable consequences of pre-marital sex relations between the boy and girl who are socially not permitted of doing so by some particular incest taboos, generally get elopement and take shelter of the court which ultimately allowed through the proper proceedings of the court to live with one another as husband and wife. Moreover, the widow remarriages are very common among Tharus. The 'Chutkata' and the "Utharna" are the popular forms of widow remarriages. In the first form the widow keeps her second husband at her house while in later form the widow gets elopement with her second husband and live with him at his house. Besides this some preferential marriages are also followed by Tharus. Levirate and the sororate are the most desirable marriages. A widow is married generally with her levir (husband's younger brother). In the same way a widower after the death of the wife get marriage with his deceased wife's younger sister. Apart from the above mentioned types of marriages, some evidences of polygyny are also recorded. Particularly, the polygyneous marriages are conditional and performed under some unavoidable circumstances. For example; because of the barrenness of the first wife or having no male issue from her, the husband with the prior consent of the wife and other family members weds one more woman.

Rajis the most backward primitive tribe of Uttarakhand have quite different manners of wedding and acquiring mates. In general they practise community endogamy and the village and clan (Dhara) exogamy. At present the total Raji population has been scattered over in nine villages and every village is predominantly inhabited by the families of a single 'Dhara' i.e. the clan. Though with the course of time the infiltration of some families from alien clan groups have got their settlement in the villages due to the observance of the tradition of the "Gharjawain" marriages. However, the village exogamy is strictly observed. In fact, the whole of the Raji community has been sub-divided into five major clan groups (Dharas) i.e. the Askotipal, Dinsipal, Baitara, Kwaintala and the Baluwakoti Aeri.

Almost all the Dharas are exogamous. Quite a few violations of the Dhara-exogamy and the village exogamy are found so far. But such cases took place only in some exceptional circumstances.

For instance, a young man of the 'Gangaun' village has developed some amorous pre-marital relations with a virgin of the same 'Dhara' of the same village. The couple expressed jointly the willingness for the wed lock but instantly refused by the elders of the village. Ultimately, the couple had to abscond the village for ever because the act committed by them was the act conceived as the violation of the rules of Dhara exogamy. Even today the couple resides in an another Raji village. Besides this, Raji is a patriarchal community in principle who follows the rules of patrilocal and patrilineal respectively for ascertaining the residence of the spouses after marriage and the lineage of the offsprings. Rajis who claim to be Hindu Rajput and the descendants of one of the Katur Kings in Kumaun, consider the marriage as a contract between the two families but not a sacrament as is observed among Hindus. As Rajis assert that the marriage is not more than a get together of male and female in a family life which implies various functional significance for the mates, however to provide one another the economic assistance and the sexual pleasure in priority. In fact, the economic factor plays an important role at all stages of the settlement of marriage. Hence, a daughter is wedded at an early age provided, the parents are paid a good amount of bride price.

The marriage among Rajis is preceded by two formal proceedings i.e. the "Mang-Jangi" or the proposal for marriage and the 'Tika' i.e. the engagement. The proposal is offered to the girl's parents or the guardian by the boy's father or guardian. No mediator is appointed to negotiate the proposal, yet the boy' s father with some of his nearest relatives visits to the villages and have information about the marriageable girl and then approach to the concerning family. On the consent of the girl's father the bride price is fixed. In general, the matrimonial relationship is established at an early age and sometimes even to this extent that the infants are engaged by their parents during their gestation period. In all cases the 'Tika' i.e. the engagement is followed after the mutual consent of the both parties. At this occasion, some presents in the form of a dress consisting of sari, blouse and peticot and a nose-stud are offered to the girl by the boy's father who accompanied by some of his relatives visits the girl's house. A mark of red vermillion with rice is also applied on the forehead of the girl. The girl's family manages at least one time meal for the visitors. Thus, the betrothal (Tika) ceremony solemnized.

The betrothal ceremony is followed by the marriage which takes place as soon as the groom's father could manage the bride price. The wedding ceremony is performed at bride's place. Now Rajis have started to appoint the Brahmin priest for performing the marriage, yet in practical the groom's brother-in-law (sister's husband) or the maternal uncle and the bride's sister-in-law (brother's wife) perform the marriage with mutual collaboration at bride's place. The groom's people with their relatives and friends visit to bride 's place. On the arrival of the marriage procession the bride is deliberately sent away towards the jungle. Soon after the groom's people are informed about the bride's absconding. At this the groom himself pursues the bride and searches her out and stoops her to conquer. The groom's brother-in-law and the bride's sister-in-law who are traditionally entitled to perform the wedding rite ask the groom and the bride to sit on mat spread out on the ground floor of the bride's house. A gracious mark of the red vermillion is placed with rice on the forehead of the couple respectively by the groom's brother-in-law and bride's sister-in-law and then the mates are asked to offer some sweets or 'Gurh' to one another. With this rite the wedding ceremony considered to be completed. The invitees and the groom's people (Baratis) then take the dinner. Next morning the groom's people are given a light breakfast. The bride and the groom are attired in the new garments and the bride is departed to the house of the inlaws.

On the return of the marriage procession the groom's mother welcomes the newly married couple and apply a mark of vermillion on their foreheads and gives the sweet (Gurh) as a token of an offering. On this occasion a grand feast is given to the villagers. The cooked rice,dal, meat and the wine are the main items of the community dinner. The bride brings water with her affinal lady akins. The water is used for the cooking and drinking and this act is taken as a symbol of bride's admission to her affinal kin group. Next day the bride is taken back to her natal place by her brothers who come along with the marriage procession to see her off at the groom's residence. Rajis' do not observe any rite like "Gauna" i.e. the second marriage as is observed among Tharus and Buxas. Hence, after some days she comes back to her in laws house. During first one or two years she keeps on visitings her natal place, but these visitings become irregular and long gapped when she gets her first issue.

The method of marriage as discussed above is formal way of acquiring mates which is observed by Rajis in normal course. But there are some other forms too. The love marriages which are the inevitable outcome of the pre-marital illicit liaison of the mates, marriage by mutual consent and elopement, widow remarriages, divorce remarriages,levirate, sororate, polygyny (provided the former wife has no male issue or some times the widow of the deceased brother also becomes the wife of the deceased brother's living brother) and the 'Gharjawain' marriage are the common ways of acquiring mates among Rajis.

Jaunsari (Khasa) had exclusively been polyandrous (fraternal) community where all the brothers were the common husbands of a wife or wives. But with the passage of time the polyandrous form of the community has been transformed to some extent into bi-polyandry, polygyny and monogamy. However, the traditional form of the polyandry is still observed among Khasas.

The whole of the Khasa community has been stratified on the basis of the caste hierarchy like Hindus. The Brahman, Rajput (Ksyatriya), Vaisya and the Sudra are the main castes which have further been sub-divided into a number of sub-castes. In general, every caste is an endogamous group, however, the inter caste marriages, hypergamy and hypogamy are also not restricted strictly. Khasas observe the village exogamy. Infant marriages are very common. Some times an infant before its birth is engaged for marriage and after birth when the child attains the age of five or six (in case of female) is married with the previously betrothed boy who remains generally two or more years senior to that of the girl. It is the eldest brother who is only married with the girl and the rest of the brothers spontaneously become her husbands. The descent, succession, inheritance and residence run with the male line. The wedding ceremony is celebrated with a certain procedure which is as follows:

Proposal for Marriage (Rishta)

It is the boy's father or guardian who with the help of the mediator offer the proposal of marriage to the girl's parents or the guardian. The mediator who may be an affinal or the consanguine akin of the boy's father just gets information about a suitable girl and thus approach to the girl's father. Both the boy's father and the mediator visit at girl's house and stay there for over a night. After having dinner at girl's house the mediator then offers the proposal before the girl's parents. On the consent of the proposal a rupee for engagement (Mangani) is paid to the head of the family (Battha) as to reserve the girl for marriage. At the earliest stage of the proposal it is made clear whether the girl to be engaged would be the combined wife of the brothers or the separate wife of one of the brothers. This contract is carried out in the same form after marriage.

On the occasion of the first festival occurs just after the engagement, the boy's father or the guardian visits to the girl's place and offers a typical kind of bread called "Taurhya Rotee" and a bottle of wine to the girl's family. At this occasion too, the boy's people stay there and next morning return with the girls father or the father's representative to boy's place where the Brahman priest (Bhamana) is invited to calculate the date of marriage *i.e.* the "Doosh Khojai". There is a particular date of 'Doosh Khojai' in a year i.e. the 'Navami' that is the nineth day of the 'Nav Ratri' festival(Dasera) occurred in 'Chaitra' or 'Baishakha' (March or April) of the year. Generally, the marriage is fixed only in some particular months of the year *viz.*, the Baishakh, Agahan, Poos and Magh however these are not the universal months for all the villages of Jaunsar-Bawar because the months as mentioned above may not suit to some particular villages. In such cases the priest is the final authority to decide the month, date and the time of marriage of the respective village.

The 'Doosh Khojai' ceremony is followed by the 'Jojyorho' *i.e.* the wedding ceremony which is celebrated at the groom's place. A day before the wedding ceremony the bride's akins who are at least two in numbers come-along with 'Suhag' which consist of the nose stud (Fulli), pendant of an ear ring called 'Tungal' lucky thread i.e. Mangalsutra', called 'Kanrhurhi' to grooms place. This advanced party make the groom's people aware of the arrival of the marriage procession with bride at the given time already fixed by the Brahmin priest. They are offered warm reception and a grand feast as a token of honour. On the following day the marriage procession blowing trumpets and beating drums reach alongwith duely embellished bride to groom's place. The time of marriage called 'Gharhi' may be fixed during the day, as well as the night time. After arrival of the marriage procession the bride is made to sit on the corridor of the house before the family members of the groom's and the groom himself. The groom's mother brings the burning charcoal in an utensil and throws some dried chillis, Ghee and rice on it to purify the bride by its smoke and to give her blessings. This act is called 'Dhoop-Dena'. The same act is repeated by the bride for the groom's mother. Yet a basic difference in which a sense implies on the same act is carried out by the groom's mother who proceed from head to down ward of the bride as a symbol of the blessings, while the bride give the smoke to groom's mother from feet to upward direction which symbolises for the services which the bride will has to carried out after marriage for her in laws. After it the groom's sister, called "Bayati" washes the feet of the bride and the groom who put their feet on a big shallow pan. After it both the bride (Bhohtee) and the groom (Khawad) are got united by tying with one end of the bride's coloured-over-cloth called 'Chunari'. Then they are asked to climb up in the first floor (Bhitar) of the house through a hole (ugharh) which links the ground floor of the house with a stair.

Here the Brahmin priest recites some mantras, lits up the lamp and asks the couple to take round of the lamp, called "Fere". The groom leads the bride in almost seven rounds. The priest, then offers sugar to the groom and the bride and asks to eat it. Further, he also gives some more sugar to each of the couple and asks to throw it on one another. But in some marriages the bride puts garland round the neck of the groom and the wedding ceremony considered to be completed. The bride then joins to her akins i.e. the marriage processionists and the groom to his own. Thus, the wedding ceremony is performed in a very short span of time while the rest of the time at groom's place is passed in eating, drinking, singing and dancing. In fact. Khasa' marriage is celebrated with great pomp and show, because it is only the occasion when a 'Khasa' family exhibits its status and trys to prove it greater than the other in community. The groom's family expends money lavishly. They offer the wine best of its kind, sacrifice the goats which some time ranges 50 to 60 in numbers and pour the 'Ghee' as per measurement of tumblers or a particular type of water vessel called 'Lota' to the marriage processionists and the invitees in particular. The people from bride's side drink 'Ghee' to one's heart's content as well as the wine, and eat the meat as much as they can digest without suppressing their desire. On the contrary the invitees of the groom's side, particularly the lady relatives drink "Ghee" as much as they think it sufficient and the rest of the "Ghee" is collected in vessels they bring with them and later on they (ladies) sell the 'Ghee'. Thus, with this money they purchase some thing like garments or bangles and some cheaper ornaments because it is treated as the personal money of the ladies and it is their privilege to expend it according to their own choice.

In fact, the 'Khasa' community is the best living example of the ancient systems of cooperative societies existed in the rural as well as the primitive societies. The villagers and the relatives generally contribute the 'Ghee', goats and other essential material needed for the feast on marriage to which the family return in near future on the occasion of marriages in the family of the contributors. Actually to collect the blessings of the kith and kins and of the invitees, the Khasa family make every possible efforts to please them by offering the feast of best kind and drinks as well. The unhappiness of lady relatives in particular deemed to be ominous for the wedding couple hence the lady invitees are served the 'Ghee', wine, meat etc. abundantly. Moreover the ladies are the mistresses of society,the displeasure of whom may be supposed as spoiling a gay occasion. Hence,they are feasted with due respect and honour.

After having a rich feast the guest's and the marriage processionists spend the whole night in singing and dancing. Almost all the people whether married or unmarried irrespective of the differences of age and sex participate in the function. Next morning the invitees are served tea and breakfast which is followed by particular type of out-door folk dance called "jaurha" and then the marriage procession leaves for the bride's village by blowing trumpets and beating drums. But the bride alongwith her two or more akins consist of the father or brothers stay at the groom's house for one more night. Next day the bride, the groom, bride's father, brother and the groom's father leave the groom's place for bride's village, where the "Sarsan" ceremony is performed. The groom is presented with the suitable presents consisting chiefly the money, by the bride's mother and other family members as well. The bride is also presented some money by the groom's people called the money for "kotharhi". Then, the bride is taken back to groom's place by the groom and his accompanied father and others.

Duraunj Ceremony

Sometimes the "Duraunj" ceremony is also performed particularly when the groom's family desired to detain the bride at their place for about five or more days just after marriage. In this ceremony the bride just to the next day of wedding ceremony is departed with her father and brothers till the short distance from the groom's village and instantly taken back to the groom's house. This ceremony symoblizes of the departure of the bride to her natal place as well as her return to in law's house. This tradition is to be known as 'Duraunj'.

Honey Moon or "Sath Sulai" Rite

After marriage the couple is not permitted to cohabit freely and willingly as is observed in every civilized community. The priest is asked to calculate the auspicious day and the time for the cohabitation of the couple only then the mates are permitted for the act called 'Sath-Sulai' or the celebration of honey-moon. Thus, the traditional wedding ceremony which they called "Saulta Byah" in which a bride is supposed to come to wed the groom at groom's place, is considered to be completed.

Unlike the traditional form of polyandrous marriage. Khasa also observe some other forms of marriages out of which the polygyny, the monogamy and "Ulta Byah" i.e. the marriage in which the groom visits with marriage procession to bride's village to wed her, are the main forms which are taking place gradually in Khasa community. Child marriages, particularly among rural and illiterate population are essentially observed as to carry out the traditional formality. In fact, the varieties of the factors are responsible for the different forms of marriages. For instance, the observance of polyandry is caused because of the acute economic poverty of the Khasas. On the contrary, the economic prosperity, the excess cultivable land, barrenness of the wife or the longing for the male issue and the death of the brother or brothers lead to polygyny among Khasas, while the new educated generation is in frequent move towards monogamy as a result of the impact of the civilized and modern societies and also to acquire a place in the main stream of the Hindu society. Thus, the Khasa community has not a particular type of marriage, the economy and the education have simultaneously played a significant role in determining the form of the marriage. There is no hard and fast rule to observe a particular form of marriage, but the family and the individual concern selects the way as one desires.

However, the educated mass, specially engaged in some non-traditional occupations and working in urban and town areas are generally lagging behind the traditional form of marriage and in view of the traditional patterns they are following approximately the same pattern as is observed among the neighbouring non-tribal Hindus. Not only this much, in "sulta marriages" the 'Brahmin priest' performs the marriage as according to the vedic rite, the attire, the ornaments, the feast as well as the wedding pattern as a whole are performed quite similarly to that of the neighbouring Hindus. The polyandrous form of marriage among the literate Khasas, who are in frequent contact with the more civilized outer-world, has been looked down by them consequently they are mobilizing towards the monogamous type of marriage. In fact, the prevalence of the means of transportation and communication and the educational facilities as well, have enabled the "Jaunsari-Khasas" to come in contact of the non-tribal groups and also induced them to make estimation of their own patterns of cultural life in general and the peculiar type of polyandrous system in the present day context in particular with the non-tribal cultural patterns which may be considered to the best suited with modernity, and thus ultimately they think the monogamy as the best socially approved form of marriage particularly for the social adjustment with the Hindu social organization and therefore following this pattern gradually.

Moreover, the urban-ecological setting seems to be unsuitable for the polyandrous type of marriages, hence an individual either lives alone or keeps his personal wife and children with him.

It is observed that the educated 'Khasa' psychologically think polyandry as a social evil amidst of the non-tribal Hindus, so that they request their guardians, particularly to the head of the family for the separate wife and also ensure to bear all the liabilities pertaining to the wife and the children born out of her. Thus,it may be concluded that the educated Jaunsari-Khasas are undergoing gradually with the process of sanskritization, modernization and its subsidiary processes and that the illiterate part of the Khasa population lacks the means as well as the motivation to move towards the modernity. Thus, in bringing about the cultural transformation even in Khasa-community, the economic factor has played an important role because, the economically well off families or marginal family who can afford at least the expenses to educate its children could have educated them and also enabled them to move outside of their traditional peripheries as well as the occupation. Thus, the economic factor alone is determinant in bringing about the cultural transformation among Khasas.

The Status of Woman

In sociological literature it (the status) is often used as a synonym for role.[30] The term 'Status' is used to designate the position which an individual occupies in a given community at a particular time and invariably includes some roles ascribed by the society by virtue of the birth and deeds of the individual. Thus it, (the status) represents the position of the individual in group.[31] The 'Status' therefore, presents a base of social stratification and also make aware the occupants with some of the responsibilities, duties, cultural patterns and values assigned with it by the society. But the determinant factors of the status are defined differently by the different social groups. In its broadest sense the birth which deals with the sex dichotomy, age difference, kinship, caste, race etc. and the deeds which represent to the class, occupation, education and many other achieved qualities, determines the status of an individual in society.

Sex-dichotomy has been an ancient and the biological basis to determine the status of male and female in society. In primitive communities too, the 'sex' had been the main basis of division of labour in family as well as in community life and the natural anatomical and physiological difference among the sexes were the general basis to ascertain the status and role of the both sexes. Besides these biological basis, the cultural norms of the given society in which an individual is born and bred also assigned a particular status of the males and females. In fact, the cultural system of a particular community and its cultural patterns viz., beliefs, attitudes, traditions etc. influence the human behaviour and also mould and shape it in a particular direction as according to the standards set up in the culture as a result of the beliefs and practices. Thus, the males and females occupy respectively a particular status and behave in a certain typical way because the community they live in expects from them to behave in such a manner which is virtually supposed to be performed by the both sexes. Even the character and temperamental traits associated with maleness and femaleness are profoundly influenced and are the resultant of the peculiarities of the culture to which its men and women belong."[32] Thus, it is the cultural system which ultimately determines the status of an individual on the basis of the sex dichotomy. Hence, the differences of cultural norms of different cultural groups lead to the contrary statuses of the individuals belonging to the same sex. A female in one given community holds the higher status than the male and in other community she may have lower status than the male. The evolution of man-kind depicts that the status and role of a woman, irrespective of caste and creed, have undergone a numerous fluctuational changes with the change of time.

There was a time when the male and female had equal position in society, particularly during Vedic period, men and women were regarded as having equally important status in the social life. In the Rig-Veda, the husband and wife are described as taking equal part in the sacrificial rites.[33] The Vedic literature mentions, many a women's name who attained eminence as philosophers along with men. Similarly, the Satapatha Brahmana informs us that woman was regarded as an equal sharer with man of the responsibilities and duties in the home. As has been illustrated in Satapatha Brahamana, "when the husband is about to ascend (the sacrificial altar), he addresses his wife in these words; come wife let us ascend to heaven; and the wife answers, 'Yes let us ascend".[34] On the contrary, a negative aspect of woman which presents her inferior position in society than the man, has also been referred in the Satapatha Brahamana. There are evidences to prove that the woman is more emotional and less rational by nature than man, therefore, she is apt to fall an easy prey to external appearances; she lacks the ability for true appreciation or balance of mind and does not possesses depth of reason.

A.A. Roback has said, it is, therefore, not in the relative strength of the instinct that we shall find the reason, the lack of objectivity in female conduct but in the relative weakness of the fundamental principle of conduct which has its root psychologically in some mechanism making for consistency.[35]

Freud, the eminent psycho-analysist has also said that, "It may be admitted that women have but little sense of justice and this is no doubt connected with the preponderence of envy of their mental life."[36]

Even in Mahabharata, Yudhishthara says, "It is said that woman is the root of all evil and that she is narrow minded."[37] Bhishma, also considered the female as the temptress and a lurer...... hence, woman should not be condemned altogether as a sinner because she naturally lacks the strength of mind to resist temptations. "It is man only who commits offences. By committing an act of adultery, only the man becomes sullied with sin......"[38] On the contrary in the same parva Bhishma says, "woman should always be adored and treated with love."[39] Thus, it is observed in Epics that the attitude towards the woman and her nature varies in place to place resultantly her status and role seems contradictory. Some times she is a temptress, emotional and the root of all sins, who by virtue of her straingthlessness does never commit offence. Even in adultery she does not share the sully of the sin and only the man becomes the sullied with sin. On some places she is a thing to be adored and honoured because the propitiation of Gods lies only on the reverence of the woman in family and the society as well. She is a Goddess of prosperity. The splendour, the growth, the prosperity of the society lies on the respect and love given to the women. Thus, the contradictory opinions have been existed in regard of the position of woman and her nature.

Apart from the Epics we find some similar conceptions about the nature and the status of woman in 'Smritis'. Manu says that, "woman must always be honoured and respected by the fathers, brothers, husbands and brother-in-laws who desire their own welfare."[40] Even the welfare and peace in the family may retain only by being happy of the women -folk of the house. Manu says, "in the family in which the wife is pleased with the husband and the husband feels happy with the wife, prosperity always resides."[41] Hence, it has been ordained that the women play equally an important role in the performance of all the activities related to 'Dharma and Yajna' with her husband. Besides, the women particularly, the maiden is supposed to have the freedom in the matter of choosing her life mate in case of the failure of the guardians in arranging her marriage at her marriageable age. But at other places, Manu and other 'Smiritikaras' are not prepared to allow any kind of independent activity to women..... She is subject to the guardianship of the father during her childhood, of her husband during her youth and of her sons after the death of her husband, she is not allowed to do any thing independently even in her own home.[42] This verse shows the dependence of woman on man which eventually ordained her inferior status in society as well as her deficiency in decision making even in the family matters.

In other context, the woman has been regarded as an untouchable particularly, when she undergoes the menstruation and during this period a man even by merely touching of the woman becomes untouchable and by sharing the bed of woman caused the diminution of his wisdom, energy, strength, sight and life duration. Such woman becomes touchable or pure again by taking bath after the period is over.[43] At other place Manu has said, "it is the nature of women to seduce men in this world."[44] Yet, 'Varahamihira' has treated the woman as the jewel created by the lord of men which alone capable to delight the man by hearing about it, by sight, by touch and by thinking about it. Varahmihira has said, "It is women who adorn jewels, woman are not adorned by the splendour of jewels, ...for women can capture the hearts of men without jewels but jewels without being displayed on the bodies of women can not do this".[45]

Thus, 'Manu' himself has considered the women superior in virtues than the men. He said, "Soma (the moon) gives them purity; Gandharvas (the celestial musicians) gave them cultured speech; Agni (the God of fire) has granted them freedom to eat any thing; hence they are as pure as gold."[46]

It is referred in Brihatsamhita that "women are incomparably pure; they are never defiled; their menses destroy all their blemishes."[47] Hence, the women must be respected.

In 'Sastras' the mutual fidelity between the husband and the wife is strictly expected and its violation by either is censured; but it is observed that the man disregard this while the woman followed and therefore the woman, out of deep fidelity embraces even her dead husband and enters the funeral pyre.[48] Hence, women are superior to men.

In ancient Hindu society the woman could freely avail herself of the 'Asrama Vyavastha' in the same way as man did. But later on, the women alongwith 'Sudras' were not taken into account in 'Asharma Vyavastha' by the 'Dharam Sastras'. It was considered that the marriage ceremony is equivalent to the 'Upanayan' of the boy; serving the husband (pati-seva) is equivalent to serving the teacher (guru) and residing in the husband's house and doing her household duties is equivalent to the daily sacrifices and worship of fire by man.[49]

Thus, the aforesaid delineation about the nature and position of woman in the historical perspective and in the account of Epics, Smiritis, and so present a elusive, complex and in some places the most contradictory evidences. As she is deity (Goddess) as well as the seducer, she must be honoured and respected yet she is a root of all sins. She (woman) commits really no offence yet she leads astray not only the ignorant, but even a learned man and make him a slave of lust and anger, she is pure all over yet a person even by merely touching a woman in her monthly course becomes impure and untouchable, she is untouchable during menstruation to share her bed, for it leads to the diminution of the wisdom, energy, strength, sight and life duration of the male partner, yet her mouth is always pure for the purposes of kissing or other intimacies, man is born of woman and she is mistress of the family, yet she is subject to the guardianship of man throughout her life time.

Thus, in an ancient period the position of woman and the attitudes of the masses towards her existence have been inconsistence as to ascertain her status in the broad matrix of the social system. During Vedic period she had the equal position as the man had subsequently during post-Vedic period her position and the venerable attitudes towards the woman took a contrary turn, resultantly a number of socio-religious disabilities were imposed on her. In the medieval period the woman was deprived from all sorts of socio-religious rights and privileges, consequently, a number of evil practices viz., child marriage, Sati Pratha, Purdha system, polygyny and prohibition on widow remarriages were prevalent in society. Even in British regime the position of woman in India was pitiable. But in the beginning of nineteenth century a number of social reformers worked for the social upliftment of the women folk. Consequently the evil practices like 'Sati Pratha', child marriage, prohibition on widow remarriage, polygyny, Devdasi Pratha' etc. were removed. In this field the efforts made by Raja Ram Mohan Ray, Daya Nand Saraswati, Iswar Chandra Vidhya Sagar, Keshava Chandra, M.K. Gandhi and many other women organizations were valuable. During post-Independence era the voice for women emancipation and women upliftment was raised frequently with the result a number of constitutional provisions were constituted and executed with the view of all round upliftment of the women-folk in the country.

The tribal population which constitute a considerable part of total population of India, has also been affected by the constitutional provisions made for the socio-economic upliftment of the masses in general and the tribal population in particular. In general, the position of tribal women in perspective of the Indian society as a whole was paltry and therefore the attitude of the masses implied with it had been abominable and some times as ludicrous. It was so because of the socio-cultural backwardness, unestablished ethical and moral values and the primitive nature of the tribal communities. Yet the tribal woman has a particular status and role in her respective community she dwells in. But there is divergency in the opinion about the status of woman in tribal communities. There are the anthropologists who take the stand that primitive societies generally assign a high status to woman, whereas other viewpoints support the opposite proposition, namely that in primitive societies women are generally a depressed group.[50] Yet, there are the tribal communities in which men and women are the equal partners in the religio-economic life. Whatsoever, the position of woman even in the tribal communities has also gone under numerous changes with the passage of time.

Among 'Bhotiyas' the woman is called 'Ransya'. She holds comparatively a respectful and venerable position in community. Inspite of the patriarchal pattern of family the woman is socially claimant of her mother's ornaments and clothes after her death. In real she is a trustee and the mistress of all the money, jewels as well as the movable property yet the expenditure is incurred in different spheres by mutual consent and understanding of the wife and husband both. 'Ransya' plays an important role in the economic sphere of 'Bhotiya' community. In rural areas, she may be observed from kitchen to field and its granary. She attains kitchen, almost all the three time, made dine all the family members, rears and cares the children, cleans the cattle sheds and sweeps the cow-dung, brings woods and fodders from the forest and performs all the agricultural tasks except ploughing the field. Her hands are never in leisure. In every moment of her daily life the hands either spin the wool fiber or knit the woolen garment. Lifting the burden on the back, her hands never stop. Thus, subsidiary task of spinning and knitting of woolen stuffs is the particularistic pattern of her role system which ultimately fulfills more or less their clothing needs. But during winter or in any leisure she prepares woolen clothes viz; Pankhi, Chutaka, Dan and the sweaters which are the speciality of the Bhotiya community and sold these woolen goods in Jaulajibee commercial fair celebrated during Diwali festival in every year. Thus, the Bhotiya woman performs a significant role in Bhotiya economy. Thus, she is not only an earning member of the family but also a real trustee of the property who deals the overall expenditure of the family.

Besides the rural areas, the Bhotiya families, which have migrated to the river valleys, market places and the plains of Tarai and Bhabar, the woman may be seen in performing a peddler job in the market streets. While the educated Bhotiya women are engaged in Government Services. They may be seen in medical services, teaching, clerical jobs, even in police services. Thus, it may be concluded that the Bhotiya woman whether illiterate or literate always in every situation earns for her and her family and thus has maintained a venerable position in the community. Thus, 'Ransya' is hard working and assiduous in performing her duty even in any adverse situation.

Besides the economic sphere of social life the 'Ransya' also possesses an equal status in socio-religious spheres of the Bhotiya community as the man. She shares all the socio-religious activities with man. Her married life is happy and cheerful in case of any disappointment or mal-adjustment with her husband, she may seek justice through the honourable council of elders and thus gets divorce from her husband. She has got the social sanction to remarry according to one's own choice yet her social status remains the same. In case of widow-hood she can remarry. There is no dowry system particularly, in the rural area but they merely observe traditional pattern of 'God-Bharai' as a mark of bride-price, while the Bhotiyas who have got their settlement in urban and plain areas and who got education, who are in the constant contact with non-tribal groups have started to present some essential things both in the form of cash and kind. Yet there is not any demand from the groom's side as is observed in non-tribal Hindus.

In every respect her life is not gloomy. She doesn't have to face any sorts of disabilities due to being female. Moreover, she enjoys some privileges in family as well as in community life. She is the best host to attend the guest. She offers open heartedly the cup of wine with her pretty hands and unblemish feelings to the new-comers. She sings and dances before even her family members without any hesitation and social taboos. The most remarkable, rather admirable aspect of her life is observed when she guilelessly, willingly, cheerfully and yet confining herself within the normative order of the community by maintaining the graceful modesty of a woman, sings and dances before her parents, in-laws and every people particularly at the marriage and in any auspicious occasion. She does not observe any 'Purdah' with her in-laws as is observed in many non-tribal savarn Hindus'. No incest taboos are laid down on the Bhotiya-woman. She can interact with any unknown person without any motive but living within the modesty. Thus, the nature, activities and the social norms related with the women-folk, show that the status of women in Bhotiya community is prestigious, venerable and equal to that of man.

Among 'Rajis' the woman, in principle, holds comparatively a low status because of the patrilineal descent, patrilocal residence and the patriarchal community. Since, in a patriarchal society the position of woman is depressed, while she enjoys a high status in matriarchal societies as is observed respectively in Todas and Khasis. In general, the lineage of the offsprings in Raji community runs with the father's line. The property is inherited only to the sons. A son after marriage is responsible for his wife and his parents unless he does not get separation from his parents, while a daughter, after marriage gets the lineage of her husband, she resides at husband's place and shares the property of her husband in common. All these normative conditions bestow a lower position to the Raji-woman in theory. But in practice she possesses a key status in the socio-economic structure of the Raji community. She is the central pivot around which the whole of the system of Raji community revolves. She lends her hand in every sphere of community life and performs every tedious toil with the man. To collect the jungle products, to trap the fishes, to dig up the edible roots or the like and thus brings together the eatable things for sustenance so that the body and soul of the family members may be kept together. Both the male and female work in field, any of them may attend to the kitchen and the cattle, both of them bring woods from the jungle, they observe no particular pattern of division of labour in general. Yet, only a man can plough the field and visit the market place to purchase the provisions for daily needs. Besides this, they both earn livelihood in the form of the daily wages from the neighbouring villages by rendering their services to them as the agricultural labour.

Moreover, she participates in every religious and cultural activities performed particularly on some auspicious occasions viz., worship of deities, performances of life cycle rituals and so on. Yet she does not join the marriage and funeral processions. Thus, it is observed that the Raji woman, in spite of being the patriarchal community, participates in every sphere of the socio- cultural life of the community by going out of the way and beyond her competency and field of work. Besides this an outstanding nature, which is observed particularly in the normal discourse between the husband and wife is that the wife always addresses her husband with some disdainful terms such as, Tu, "Tera' and so, while the husband in response calls his wife with some venerable pronouns viz., 'Tum', 'Aap' and so. This character of the Raji woman has made her position pre-eminent in the community, hence she is respected and honoured by the men-folk. She is never discarded for any offence and the misdeed. Even in some adultery cases the man indulge is considered to be an offender who provokes the woman for seduction.

Moreover, she has the decision making power in any family matter. The man as the husband or the son formally asks his wife or mother respectively to commense any task or to take any decision regarding any family affair whether economical or religious and so on. Thus, only after the mutual consent a matter is considered for its materialization. In this way a Raji woman leads every social-cultural activities of the community and thus holds practically a pre-eminent position in society. She does not follow any taboo like protective or productive as is observed in many patriarchal society in general. No feeling like defilement during her menstruation and child birth makes her unsuited for any social-religious-ceremonial performances. Yet some Raji women, particularly who are in close contact with the neighbouring Savarn Hindus reside in the contiguous regions of Kumauni villages have begun to follow some preventive taboos during menstruation period and therefore do not attend the hearth, do not share the bed of their husbands, do not take active participation in religious ceremonies and in bringing drinking water. But the preventive taboo is not observed strictly because there has not been any hard and fast social norms to execute strictly any such taboos. It is of course, merely a imitation of the neighbouring Kumauni Savarn Hindus which may be reckoned as the step in the direction of cultural transformation.

Thus, it may be concluded that the Raji woman apart from all sort of the impacts of modernity, communication and transportation and education facilities has maintained their traditional high social status inspite of being the patriarchal society, yet only the impact of alien cultural groups has partly affected more or less her behavioural patterns hence a minor variation can be observed among the women who are in close contact with that of the non-tribal groups and the women residing in the aloof and the confined peripheries of their surroundings.

Among the patrilineal and the patrilocal Tharus, women-folk in practice dominate the men folk. The husband is subservient to his wife. As a daughter, whether married or unmarried, she enjoys comparatively more freedom in all respects particularly in merry-making with her companion. No restrictions are laid down on her as long as she is in with her parental place. In every auspicious occasion and ecstasy who sings and dances with her girls as well as the boys companions. But her freedom in in-laws residence abates, yet she is honoured, duly respected and loved by all the family members. A Tharu woman, called 'Bayyar' participates equally with her husband particularly in economic sphere. She performs all the agricultural works. She traps the fishes, cooks food, brings clay from the pond to smear the corridor and the rooms of the house. She keeps house and its surroundings very neat and clean by plastering it with clay mud mixed with wheat rubbish. She prepares basket called "Daliya". She feels proud to talk with any unknown without hesitation and with confidence. She had fine coquetry to captivate any unknown on her beautiful look. It is her privilege to offer a cot covered with 'Carpet' (Dari) to any new-comer as the mark of hospitality. An aged woman looks after the infants and children of the family. Old age is not curse to her as is observed in the neighbouring non-tribal communities, as she is duly respected by the family members and her status is duly maintained irrespective of her age and work. It is the privilege of Tharu-woman to attend the kitchen while at home or in any collective feast. She cooks food and feeds all the family members and the invitees in the case of any collective feast organised for any ritualistic performance and festivals. Thus, the evidences also prove her higher status than male. Every religious function is voluntarily performed by her. She leads the men-folk in religious field too. It has been reported that "....... Tharu women are expert magicians and sorceress."[51] But the present study reveals that the Tharu woman do not make any practice of magic or sorcery rather some aged male persons called "Bharare" are observed to practise the magical spell. Besides this, all the proposals for marriage are always presented on behalf of the male side and it is up to the choice of the female's side to accept or reject the proposal. This evidence also gives weightage to the higher position of Tharu woman. D.N. Majumdar has also remarked that, "Among the patrilocal Tharus of the Nainital Tarai, Uttar Pradesh, woman's status is proverbially high."[52] Majumdar further states that a constant tension and a conflict situation are found among the Tharus........ The property is owned both by men and women and the later spend their income without the advice of their spouses.... The Tharu women are so dominant that their husband have earned the epithet of being incorrigibly henpecked.[53]

But today the situation is some what contrary as the relations between the spouses are neither tense in general, nor the women are so dominant as to call her husband with some inferior nickname or epithet. Both the husband and wife are the true partner of one another, hence both participate in almost all the socio-economic as well as the cultural fields. Yet the wife enjoys some more privileges and leads in socio-cultural field and eventually holds a high status in the community. She holds comparatively more power in property possession mainly the jewels and ornaments are her personal property, the live stock population and the crops are outrightly possessed by her. Although the immovable property which chiefly consists of the land, the house is owned only by the male yet in practice he does not transfer it without the consent of the wife. Even the food grains is sold by the female at market places, the male only accompany her and helps in carrying the food grain to market places for sale. The personal life of the Tharu woman is not so restricted, she does not follow any taboos and 'Pardah' during the social interaction with any member of the community. She freely walks within the village and move in group from one village to another for sheer gossiping and merry making.

On the Holi festival and at the marriage ceremony the female whether married or unmarried sings and dances usually accompanied by the male persons. Thus, the Tharu woman presents her passed royal origin by her beautiful look and free and dominant social status and the decision making capacity in every aspects of the socio-cultural life.

However, there is change in her dress, outlook and functions. Now the unmarried Tharu girls go to school for study. There are 50 percent unmarried girls who have got the education up to fifth standard. The parents, particularly the Tharu mothers are keen to send their children to school. Yet they are not in favour to give the more education to their daughters while possess the contrary opinion in regard of the boys. Mostly the girls are educated upto fifth standard only, a few percentage of the females are educated upto eighth standard. The female whether married or unmarried who belongs to the well-off families use the make-up aids or cosmetics in order to look more beautiful. Their costumes have entirely been changed to 'Sari' and 'Blauja'. No female below 40 years of age can be seen in their traditional attire. Yet the aged women have still adhered their traditional dress and the ornaments. The school going girls generally put on the 'Salwar-Kurta' during school time and take them off when at home.

It is observed that the women, in group, used to visit at the nearest market places for marketing or to sell the food grain in weekly markets and come in contact with the non-tribal women and imitate their fashion and the pattern of their make up. A young Tharu woman views with tempting sight to every outsider woman attired beautifully and also try to imitate the same fashion. But in practice they are unable to follow the modern fashion due to economic poverty. Thus, the women who are in the constant contact with non-tribal groups and frequently visit to market places are unlike to that of their community style particularly in respect of their attire, make up patterns, manners, modes of behaviour and colloquial parlance, yet psychologically they identify themselves with their royal origin and expound in every possible manner the behaviour patterns of their imaginary ancestry. Thus, the imaginary ancestral group is a non-membership group for Tharu women to which they consider a reference group and aspire to relate themselves psychologically and try to behave accordingly. Thus, it may be concluded that the feelings for royal origin have made Tharu woman dominant while the cultural contact of non-tribal cultural groups and desire to become alike, has changed atleast their living patterns in general and the fashion in particular by blind imitation. It is observed that the impact of neighbouring Kumaunis is comparatively more.

The status of woman in Buxa tribe of Nainital Tarai in Kumaun is comparatively higher than any of the rest tribal communities in the region. Basically, Buxa tribe is patriarchal and follow the rules of patrilocal to dwell after marriage and patrilineal for lineage. Yet the women folk is almost dominant. The husband is subservient to her and follows her decisions in socio-economic spheres. She does not observe any 'Purdha', she works and walks freely within the community and outside of the community. She can reprimand her husband, who never maltreat her in response and listen quietly. Woman possesses more rights in the selection of mates and also privileged in divorce matters. Thus, the women wield great influence over their men,........ yet the father is usually the head of the family. The higher position of Buxa woman can not be challenged by theory and practice. Even today she has maintained her dominance over men-folk. All the domestic works falls to the lot of Buxa woman. She cooks food and feeds all the family members. She never takes the meal touched by the man. In practice she pushes the dish of meal by her toe and the husband humbly takes it off and eats. This evidence also exhibits the female dominance over male and the disdainful status of the male than the females in community. In agricultural field, the woman also lends her hand particularly in transplanting, weeding, reaping the crops, threshing paddy and husking the corn with motar and petle. Besides this, she traps fishes, goes to the market to sell the agricultural produce with her husband. But all these works are performed by the woman in themselves but not under the command of the men-folk. Thus, the woman among Buxas holds a higher position and performs all the responsible activities.

Among Khasas a married woman at her in law's place is addressed as "Rain" while at parent's place a female whether married or unmarried is to be known as 'Dhyan'. In other words, a woman like as mother, wife, daughter-in-laws and so is 'Raina' in in laws's place while the same is 'Dhyan' at her natal places the daughter, sister, grand-daughter and so. Thus the 'Rain' of one village will be the 'Dhyan' for another. In both the situations the woman follows the different norms under different measurements and performs different functions, avails different degree of freedom and also follows some certain taboos.

In general, the status of 'Rain' in the community is very respectful, she is honoured and loved by all in the community as well as in family. For instance, at the occasion of the marriage when a bride comes with marriage procession to wed her groom at groom's place, the 'Rains' are invited first to have feast. The 'Rains' come in their best garments and rich make-up (as is best possible) and bring with them their younger children and a big bronze dish and particular type of drinking water vessel called 'lota' in hand. The dish they bring with them is never empty, some grains of rice are kept in it as a mark of auspicious sign. All the 'Rains' are seated respectfully insight of the house and dish up lavishly the cooked rice, meat, wine and specially the 'ghee' which is served as much as the 'Rain' desires. She is entitled to collect the shares of 'Ghee' on behalf of her children and in case of pregnancy the share of the infant situated in the womb is also served to the pregnant mother. The 'Ghee' thus collected is considered to be the personal commodity of the 'Rain' to which she later on sells and the money thus acquired is invested by her in purchasing any thing she desires. This act uncontestably is an example of the venerable status of 'Rain' in 'Khasa' community.

On the contrary the 'Dhyans' on the occasion of marriage are feasted at last with the men and also clean the used utensils, dishes, remainings of the food and also wash the hearth. She (Dhyan) also accompany the men in performing all the arrangements in carrying-out the marriage function. In fact the position of 'Dhyan' seems to be disgraceful and ludicrous too particularly on the occasion of marriage. Moreover, the venerable status of 'Rain' becomes more clear and graceful when her mere visit to the family which is not in good terms with her own family, normalises the tense relations between the both families. In fact, there is nothing more honourable than a visit of a 'Rain' to any of the families in village. One more evidence in favour of the respected status of the 'Rain' is that, no one can dare to misbehave, to tease and to rape her. In such adultery cases the offender is punished badly by the council of the elders while any such act pertaining to sex indulgence against any of the 'Dhyans' is neither culpable nor disgraceful but excusable and therefore any sort of amorous relations with the 'Dhyans' is neither regarded as a social evil nor any social stigma for the family. Thus, there is a clear-cut division of the standard of morality i.e. one for the 'Rain' (wife) and the other for the 'Dhyan' (daughter) is observed in 'Khasa' community.

In brief a 'Khasa' woman at her in law's place is supposed to behave under some certain social as well as the moral values and also expected to follow some particular social taboos and thus leads a very restricted and controlled life, while the same woman at her natal place avails much freedom and does not follow any sort of the moral values and the social taboos as well. Thus, the status of the 'Rain' is comparatively higher than the 'Dhyan' in the community. In general, the senior most 'Rain' in the family holds the position next to the male head of the family. She is incharge of all the internal house-hold matters. She manages all the familial tasks and look after the work done by the female members of the family. The female head is duly respected by all the family members. In brief, the position of the 'Rain' is undoubtedly more respectful, yet she is every where under social resatraints and compelled to follow every social norms and the codes of conduct laid down traditionally by the community in general. It appears some times that the social norms and the code of conduct are merely made for the 'Rains' because the 'Dhyans' are almost free from the social restraints. In this way the status of 'Rain' is very pitiable and seems like a drudge, while the 'Dhyan' is privileged to do every thing she desires in general and to develop the sex relations freely in particular.

Majumdar has also said, "There is a double standard of morality, one for wife and another for daughter. What the wife can not do, the daughter can."[54] The wife is kept in a control and she is supposed to follow the different ethical values while the daughter is free from all sorts of normative conditions. Yet being a polyandrous society the position of woman in her in laws place is not good enough while she enjoys a lot of freedom when comes back to her mother's home.

Besides this, the functions of a woman, so far concern, she, other than the female head of the family, rotates like a wheel in a cart around the agricultural and cattle breeding jobs throughout the day. She works hand in hand with the man, because she is equally responsible to perform the tasks pertaining to the family. Majumdar has aptly stated, "women usually gather fruits and roots and edible leaves and herbs. Women help in agriculture........ all the domestic works falls to the lot of women."[55] However, the functions of those women, who are living separately with their monogamous-nuclear families outside of the rural areas i.e. in the towns, and subsisting on service or business based economy, have almost changed. In those families the women merely look after the children at home and performs only the internal familial tasks. In such families the position of woman is far better than of the rural woman. Even the routine work, the patterns of behaviour, the style of living and talking, the apparel and get-up etc. of the woman living in towns with her nuclear family have almost altered in the direction of modernity. The traditional garments have almost left by her. She wishes to educate her children, she prefers service or business based economy, since it makes the instant-cash return of the labour done by her family members and also provide all the comforts of the life. Thus, not only the material aspects of the woman's social life but also the aspirations, attitudes and the feelings pertaining to her own life and for the future of her family have frequently been changing day by day.

Resultantly, the parents appear to be interested enough to educate their daughters at least upto Junior-High School to High School standard. Today some educated Khasa-women are employed in Government departments and in some private concerns. They are not in favour of polyandry and always prefer to be a wife of a man and to live separately with her husband and children. Thus, it may be concluded that the position of 'Khasa woman' who still has persisted in the remote villages, particularly in polyandrous type of families, is very pitiable while in monogamous type of families, her position is comparatively better than the former.

Youth Club or Dormitory

Ever since the human life has been a complex accumulation of various bio-psychic, socio-economic and cultural needs, basically, the biological drives motivate the human beings to come together and to interact with one another in such a way that they may satisfy their derives to make possible their existence. The yearning to secure the satisfaction even of a single drive, eventually generates an association of two and more individuals and also make them aware to let out the ways of making possible their bio-social existence. Such associations may be based on kinship and residence, and some other factors which 'Lowie' called 'sodality'. Various types of sodalities have been found to exist in different primitive societies, sodalities like; secret societies, exclusive clubs, age classes, economic sodalities and so on........ In various parts of tribal India, age classes in the nature of youth house (dormitories) have been found.[56] Dormitory has been an integral part of the tribal social organization. It consists of the bachelors and the maidens in general.

The married people are debarred from its membership. But in some tribal communities the widows and the widowers are treated as the spinsters and bachelors respectively and therefore permitted to join the dormitory. In the frame reterence of the tribal social organization the youth club (dormitory) performs some indispensable institutional functions. In particular, it imparts the cultural education to the youngsters and also trains them in socio-economic, magico-religious and sexual field. The experienced persons denounce their experiences and folk tales and thus prepare the youngsters for future. Thus, the dormitory have some recreational as well as socio-cultural functions in tribal life.

Almost all the Indian tribal communities have the organization named by anthropologists as youth club or dormitory or age-classes and so on. But in every tribal community this organization has been denoted with a peculiar term. Several tribal communities have mono-sexual dormitory system, while some have the bi-sexual, for instance, the Memi has two names for it, the man's dormitory being called 'ikhuichi' and the women's 'iloichi'. The 'Konyak Naga' designate the boy's dormitory 'Ban' and the girls dormitory as 'Yo' while the tribes of Chhota Nagpur i.e., the Mundas, the Hos, the Oraons, designate it respectively 'Gitiora', 'Jonkerpaor', 'Dhumkuria'. The Bhuiyas and Gonds of Madhya Pradesh denote it as 'Dhangarbassa' and Gotul, while the 'Aos' and the Semas' of Assam call it as 'Morung'. The dormitory may be a hut or a house of an open place situated at the out skirts of the village where the unmarried boys and girls generally get together and make merry of drinking,singing and dancing unless they don't get tired. However, the activities of the members of dormitory are not free and open but regulated with some sorts of customs and observances. Majumdar has aptly remarked, "Life in the dormitory is associated with many customs and observances. Some of these have a traditionally antiguity, others have added in the courses of their experience of the functioning of the institutions".[57] Thus, it may be concluded that the dormitory is an association based on some customary observances and remarked particularly by its predominant recreational functions as well as the agency of socio-cultural learnings in general.

The annotation of different scholars about the social existence and functions of the dormitory organization in tribal communities have presented a clue to comprehend its origin in general and it appears that the functional pre-requisites would have given birth to the organization. Nevertheless, no clear cut theory of the social evolution of dormitory organization has so far been established. Thus, the lacking of the factual analysis of the origin of the presently known youth club or dormitory has led a number of speculative postulations to understand its evolution, existence and functions. The anthropologists have viewed the youth club in the form of sex alliances, romanticism and eroticism among the youths participating in the organization. The earliest scholars are of the views that the unmarried boys and girls either for their unfettered romance or to make available the sufficient opportunity for sexual intercourse to the married members of the family, used to get away from their houses particularly at night time. Thus, the meeting place of all the unmarrieds of the community was designated as the dormitory.

While some scholars have remarked that the prohibited sexual intercourse particularly during busy harvest, menstruation of wife and the child birth have given birth to the dormitory system, so that the married male and female may be segregated to keep themselves alone. While some scholars report the home as improper place for sexual intercourse which led them to have the shelter of dormitory as the proper place for cohibition. Thus, it is observed that almost all the scholars are of the opinion of the sex-based origin of the dormitory system. But it is unscientific and therefore illogical to explain the dormitory system on the basis of queer sex alliances and romance, since any of the social phenomena may not have the unifactor origin. In fact, the urge for sex satisfaction, is a biological instinct found in all kinds of living beings but it is delimited and regulated institutionally among human beings through many physical and social-cultural factors which can not be separated particularly when any social phenomena, like dormitory system, is defined through a single factor, since all the factors are inter-dependent and thus no unifactor delineation of any phenomena in general and the organization like 'dormitory' in particular, is scientific. Moreover, the sex alliances may be a biological prerequisite for the continuity and existence of the society, it may provide a sexual pleasure to the parties involved, but alone, it cannot make possible the survival of the mankind, rather the economic, the social, the religious and the political needs basically motivate the human beings to unite into some sorts of social organizations in general and like the dormitory, as is observed in many tribal communities in particular, which ultimately vitalize the bio-social existence of the human beings and subsequently proved to be helpful in setting up the sexual liaison and some time in marital alliance among the members of the dormitory. Thus, the youth organization like dormitory among the tribal communities has basically been originated for economic pursuits which ultimately developed the new dimensions of psycho-physical and socio-cultural needs and the patterns of their satisfactions.

Thus, the dormitory has been an essential segment of the tribal life which was formed basically for the security of the groups and the cattle from the wild animals at night time. The youths both boys and girls and some times in the supervision of the married men and women jointly get assembled in a proper place and used to look after the crops and cattles throughout the night. To pass the time they used to have some drink and also sing and dance so that the state of their keeping awake may be realized by the wild animals. These organizations were also effective during the day time, some times for hunting, some times for hoeing and weeding the crops, some times for harvesting and also in the celebration of the different ritualistic performances. But at its earliest stage of evolution the involvement of elderly men and women can not be refused for to educate or impart the training to the youngsters regarding to the socio-cultural life, through folk lores, folk dances and folk songs, and also to maintain the discipline among the members, the need of elderly people was always needed. In other words, it may be concluded that the elderly people of the different tribal communities have given birth to a social organization, termed as youth organization or dormitory system for imparting the economic and socio-religious education through verbal utterances of the experiences they acquired and the regulation they laid down for the communal harmony. But gradually some organizational changes occurred because of the amorous affairs between the males and females which eventually segregated the elders and married people from the organization and the dormitory took a new organizational shape as is observed in several tribal communities by the scholars.

In Uttarakhand, Bhotiyas have greatly been appreciated for the uniqueness of the youth club called 'Ranchyim' the corrupted form of which has designated as the 'Rang-bang'. As D.N. Majumdar has said, "among the Bhotiya's 'Rang-bang' connotes a social centre for young boys and girls generally at night in a house or a field for dance, drink and music. There is no particular building meant for the purpose and mostly such gatherings are held either in ordinary houses or open places..... boys and girls of the same clan can not participate in one gathering ..... Liquor has an important place in these gatherings......... Participants in these gatherings compulsorily........... pair off and go to sleep...... Chances of sexual intercourse are considerably minimized....... marriage is not a bar to attend 'Rang-Bang'.......... outsiders are not welcome as the participants in the Rang-Bang......... The function of Bhotiya's Rang-Bang' is purely recreational. It gives fun and joy to the youth boys and girls after day's fatigue and its importance as an agency for pre-marital understanding between boys and girls leading to marriage is obvious".[58]

Chattopadhyay, delineating its nature and functions has stated, "There is a secluded room with in the village called 'Rang-bang' where young men and women congregate after sundown. All adolescents, near adolescents and fully post adolescents, unmarried men and women, put on their best dress and assemble there to spend the night in drinking, singing and dancing and general merry making."[59]

Pant has also remarked that, "..........the young men and boys accompanied by the young unmarried girls and married women...... pass almost the whole night in singing, dancing, eating, drinking and smoking. Sometimes the girls invite the boys of the neighbouring villages....... and supply food and bedding to the guests."[60] Apart from the structural framework of the 'Rang-bang' some particular functions in common have also been referred by the previous scholars. For instance, the marriage is based on the courtship or pre-marital acquaintance and love gained by the bachelors during the time spend together in 'Rang-bang'.[61] Pre-marital sexual experience and compassionate marriages are quite usual.[62] Sometimes, illegitimate children born out of wedlock due to intimacy in 'Rang-bang' between girls and boys are called 'Rang-bang khenta and khenti'.[63] Pant has denoted them as the 'love children'.

Thus, the views of Majumdar and other previous scholars just throw light on some common characteristics of the dormitory organization of Bhotiyas, yet, the aforesaid analysis of the 'Rang-bang' in order to highlight its origin, organizational frame work, and functional adequacy for the tribal community, seems inadequate for the exact and factual interpretation of its socio-cultural and economic existence. For the available scanty references about the dormitory system found among Bhotiyas provide only the recreational rather sexual interpretation while they had been failure to recognize its economic and socio-cultural perspectives. The information, gathered directly during the informal cum exploratory conversation with some experienced old aged persons present some what contrary but logically worth appreciating facts to analyse the so called youth organization in its original definition. Basically, an institution meant for the institutional gathering of the people male-female, married-unmarried, young-old of the Bhotiya community was formerly named as the 'Ran-ban' by the community. The term 'Ran-ban' is derived from the roots of the Sauka (Bhotiya) dialect, 'Ran' and 'Ban', respectively meant for 'Saukas' (Bhotiya) and a particular place and thus connotes the place where only the Bhotiyas may come. In fact, it was a place where the people from Bhotiya community used to gather for some socio-cultural and recreational purposes. With the course of time a house for the convenience of the members of the organization was built by the community. Consequently, the organization was named as the 'Ran-ban-Chyim'. The word 'Chyim' denotes, in Bhotiya dialect, a house. In this way 'Ran-ban-Chyim' was the house for meeting the 'Bhotiya people' alone and institutionally it denotes to the compulsory membership of all the Bhotiyas of the village concern.

Basically 'Ran-Ban-Chyim' was an association, organized separately by different Bhotiya villages on some common values and assumptions. S.D. Pant has also remarked, "Every village has its separate village club, known as 'Ran-ban' but larger villages contain more than one. The club meets either in the house or on a land spot which is known as 'Ran-ban Kuri' or the club house."[64] The villagers of each village were the honourable members of the association without the difference of age, sex and marital status. As Dabral has also pointed out, "Even married women who have not given birth to children may visit 'Rang-bang."[65] The activities of the association were duely associated with many customs and observances. Most of them had a traditional antiquity, since they had been formed in order to run the barbarian, coarse and insecure ancient tribal life. In its earliest form the association was the main agency of socialization by which an individual member of it could have been the functioning member of the community by confirming and observing its usages and traditions and also acquired the cultural contents to adjust himself with the whole of the environment. Thus, to train the youths properly so that they may be liable to fulfill the social liabilities, to develop communal sentiments among the members, to think over the different community problems viz; social, economical and organizational settlement of the quarrels and to suggest the best way out for the smooth and the balanced running of the community life.

Apart from the organizational activities, the association had greatly been popular for its recreational pursuits through folk tales, folk dance, folk songs but compulsorily under the spell of the light intoxication of 'Chyakti' (locally distilled wine). However, no amorous sex alliances were reported due to the incest taboos among the members of the same 'Ranth' dwelling in a same village. It was so because that almost all the Bhotiya villages were 'Uni-Ranth' or uni-sub group. On the contrary in multi-sub-group-villages, the free sexual intercourse among the members of the dormitory were not permitted; however the sexual liaison among the members of bi-sexual dormitories which mainly consists of the bachelors and maidens of different 'Ranth' or sub-groups led to the wedlock. Thus the dormitory has had the function of getting together the opposite sexes into a marital life. The "gandharva vivah" widely prevalent among Bhotiyas in ancient time and even today is the outcome of the 'Ran-ban-Chyim'.

Thus, the information collected through participant observation method from the selected respondents exhibit that 'Ran ban' had been basically an institution where the bachelors and maidens used to learn the various norms and behaviour patterns of socio-cultural life from their elders. It was the controlling agency having arbitrary powers to regulate and control the behaviour of each member. Moreover, it had the recreational significance to its members. The elders in general used to narrate the folk tales, stories, eithical values of the community, fictitious stories, and some times recite the folk songs full of healthy romance, bravery and of sacrifice. Besides this the protection of tribal people from the ferocious denizens of the forest has also strengthened the organizational frame work of the 'Ran-ban'.

At present 'Ran-ban-Chyim' organization of Bhotiya tribe have lost its original identity. There is no house or secluded room or open air spot maintained for the dormitory purpose as has been viewed through the old aged sights by the Bhotiya people as well as the references presented by many pilgrims, scholars and the anthropologists. The aged Bhotiya people referred that the infiltration of the bachelors from the neighbouring tribal villages, the visitors, the cultural contacts with the alien cultural groups and the active participation of the educated Bhotiya bachelors have ultimately polluted the chastity and the piousness of the 'Ran-ban-Chyim' and transformed the organization into a recreational spot where the educated bachelors, raising false hopes to the maidens, began to exploit them. Besides this, the elders and the married people stopped coming and going to 'Ran-ban' and broke off the relationship with the organization.

It was the period when the youths predominantly captured the organization and made it the meeting place for the people goaded by lust. The lustful youths of the tribal community and also from the out-groups began to join the organization, the love talks and love affairs had become the main objectives of the organization. Occasionally, the obscenity and amorous sex indulgence of some libidinous youths begun to come in light. Thus, the transgression of limits of ethical propriety of the 'Ran-ban' cracked its traditional and functional decorum. The frequent visits of new comers, out siders, educated tribal youths under the influence of the 'filmee' style, have caused a commotion in the tranquil atmosphere of 'Ran-ban' and the placidity of the Bhotiya people. The emotional, the vital, the hearty, the sentimental love affairs among the simple, plain and tender hearted lovers and beloveds, which generally caused the 'Gandharva' and the marriage by mutual consent and elopement' the most prevalent way of acquiring mates among Bhotiyas, transformed into vested interests, sexual desire, selfishness, betrayal and the physical exploitation of the virgins. Traditional and socially sanctioned pattern of drinking of wine, mythological postulation of Bhotiyas towards wine (Chyakti) unrestricted, and free from all bondages, however beyond the illicit, unethical and immoral values, the folk dances and the folk songs were replaced by inebriaty, romance, shallow and petty jesting and laughings. Thus, the transformation of the traditional

'Ran-ban' into the abhorrent obscence and sex based organization of youths eventually prepared its coffin for itself and slept the eternal sleep, dreaming for the perpetual peace.

Thus, it may be concluded that the socalled youth organization i.e 'Ran-ban' has socio-cultural significance in Bhotiya's social organization which now have disappeared from all parts of the Bhotiya community. Though there are number of evidences of the existence of 'Ran-ban' in almost all the valleys of Pithoragarh i.e. the Vyans, Darama, Johar as well as of Garhwal i.e. Niti and Mara. But at present this institution has become a historical phenomena and passed away in the graveyard of the conventions. However, the traces of 'Ran-ban' are still observed particularly on the occasion of the functions and festivals. But this may be termed as the most refined and sophisticated form of the traditional 'Ran-ban'. More accurately, it is the queer reminiscence of the most functional and immensely important basic unit i.e. the 'Ran-ban' of the Bhotiya tribal organization which had the multi-dimensional functions viz. social, cultural, economic, political and religious as well as the recreational. But at the end only the recreational motive can be maintained, the corrupted form of which invited its diminution.

Today the basic concept of the dormitory system has completely vanished from the Bhotiyas community. The major causes amenable for its decay are though numerous but the impact of education, commercialization of Chyaki (wine), attraction of Bhotiya educated youths towards urban and urban culture, their elopement towards cities, attraction of white collar jobs, impact of non-tribal culture and the feeling of Bhotiyas that the out groups looked down upon their tradition of 'Ran-ban' are main. Besides this, education is supposed to be a most responsible factor for its disappearance. The Bhotiya youth who had been out side for education and economic pursuits, when come back to their community, looked at 'Ran-ban' as the most sloven, rustic and the backward way of recreation particularly the educated virgins, who used to be the main attraction of the 'Ran-ban' stopped to join the institution. Even the uneducated women in youthful bloom, by nodding acquaintance of the educated ones have also stopped to join 'Ran-ban' so that youthful womenfolk may save themselves from the usual allured and lustful sights of the sex hungers.

However, it has the clue for the needy and the shrewd people who ultimately transformed the traditional pattern of 'Ran-ban' into the commercialization of the girls and Chyakti and the allured and lustful youths from the same community as well as the personnels posted in different government posts, military and semi-military posts in the borderland began to attract towards such spots or places or houses where the young girls used to serve the 'Chyakti' (wine) to every visitors or new-comers and thus the original form of the 'Ran-ban' lost its originality. Thus, it may be concluded that the impact of the education, the modernity,the infiltration of out-group members, the commercialization of 'Chyakti' have been the responsible factors for the disorganization of 'Ran-ban'.

At present, 'Ran-ban' as a ritualistic celebration is performed particularly at the occasion of wedding ceremony. Almost all the bachelors and the maidens as well as the 'Tisya' and the members of the marriage party collectively celebrate the 'Ran-ban', generally after the completion of the marriage ceremony. The unmarried boys and the girls sing, dance and make merry with joint hands. The old aged persons also participate but only as an observer and some times pass sarcastic comments or jokes on the activities of the youths. They all drink 'Chyakti' as the mark of the sacred and socially sanctioned drink. They celebrate 'Ran-ban' throughout the night till the day break. Romantic songs are sung by the youths, some times in filmee tune. The educated youths and the persons working in some urban and city areas outside of their locality, generally sing film songs and also present some cultural programmes generally played in urban areas, in colleges and such activities seem to be more and more exciting and captivating to the tribal people and admired by the local youths. But this changed and most sophisticated form of 'Ran-ban' may be considered as the remains of the traditional youth organization of Bhotiyas which is still observed mainly in Darama, Vyans and Chaudans valleys.

But the Bhotiyas of Johar, Niti and Mana refuse to have ever been existed any youth organization like dormitory in their localities and therefore looked down upon the tradition of 'Ran-ban' which had been considered as the synonymous of the group of youths organized for amorous sex indulgence. Nevertheless the traces of the existence of 'Ran-ban' in those valleys are available. As 'Ram Singh Johari (Johar Ka Itihas and Bansawali 1936) has stated that the ancient Joharies used to observe 'Ran-ban' like as Darmias and Vyansis .... with the arrival of new Joharis, the socio-economic and political conditions of Johar has changed. Subsequently, the traditions of 'Ran-ban' and 'Dhurun' (a festival) have also ended. In the same way the traditional form of 'Ran-ban' has also lost its ancient and the original existence. It seems that the dormitory system among Bhotiyas has constantly been changing its form and functions with the course of time. The impact of education, which ultimately induced the educated tribal youths to follow the civilized patterns of social life and also developed an anti attitude towards the savagery style of tribal life on them, has played an important role in throwing away the tradition of 'Ran-ban'.

Besides this, the cultural contact with non-tribal Hindus has also been proved to be powerful media as to brought out some fundamental changes on the cultural patterns of Bhotiyas. Since the neighbouring non-tribal communities are sheer the first contact out groups regarded as the reference group by the Bhotiyas. And they always appear interested enough to follow every possible manners or the style of cultural life as are observed by the non-tribal Hindus of the contiguous regions of the tribals. For this very reason, the Bhotiyas who are educated and frequently come in contact with the non-tribal Hindus, claim to be the Rajput or Kshatriya Hindus and seem restless to be adopted in hierarchical order of the Hindu caste system. For instance, the Joharis and the majority of the Bhotiyas belonging to the Niti and Mara valleys have started to call themselves as non-tribal Kshatriya Hindus, yet it is rather ridiculous that they still avail the reservation facilities in the name of the Schedule Tribe. This tendency is the manifestation of the mental detachment of Bhotiyas with their own community as it implies the sense of universal backwardness in the mind of the people of non-tribal communities yet they are too shrewd to have a stake in the facilities provided by the government to the Scheduled Tribal communities under some certain provisions in general. Thus, it may be concluded that the impact of education, non-tribal culture and the different processes of modernization are positively correlated with the process of cultural transformation among the Scheduled Tribal communities in Uttarakhand.

Kinship System

"Kinship system may include socially recognized relationship based on supposed as well as actual genealogical ties."[66] In fact, the people in every society have some sorts of relations which unite them into groups and also ascertain their relational statuses and roles. Generally, a number of institutional bases viz., the blood, the parentage, the marriage and the contiguity of residence may be regarded as the determinants of the relations among social beings. Thus, the relations may be lineal or collateral, the matrilineal or patrilineal, by descent or by marriage. The organizational frame work of all these relations constitute the kinship system of a given society. Basically, the inherent drive for reproduction generates the two kinds of bonds among the people, viz., the consanguineous kinship and the affinal kinship. Majumdar aptly remarked that, "The first kind of bond, which arises out of a socially or legally defined marital relationship, is called affinal kin........ The relationship based on blood ties is called consanguineous (same blood) kinship.[67]

However, the social recognition is more important than the biological fact in the determination of consanguineous kinship. For instance, the over riding nature of social recognition is the practice of adoption. As Majumdar has stated that an adopted child is every where treated as if it were one's own biologically produced offspring.[68] But some thinkers included seer affinal kinship relations into kinship organization. As Rivers has remarked, "Marriage is only one of the social institutions which have moulded the terminology of relationship."[69] Kroeber has formulated some categories of relationships which ordered the relationship among a given community. These are as follows:

1. The difference between persons of the same and of different generations is recognized; father and grand father, uncle and cousin are the examples.

2. The difference between lineal and collateral relationship is maintained. Father is distinguished from father's brother.

3. Difference of age within one generation is recognized as, for example, the distinction between the elder and younger brother.

4. The sex of the relative except cousin the english terms of relationships are all discriminative of sex.

5. The sex of the speaker is recognized in the terms of kinship. The father and mother may receive one designation from a man and another from woman...... as among Bhotiyas the man addressed his elder sister as 'Pata' and woman called her elder sister as 'Lata'.

6. The sex of the person through whom relationship exists. In most of the advanced systems this category is not operative and conventional qualifications are added to distinguish relations as for example "Paternal grand father" and "maternal grand father".

7. Blood relatives are distinguished from connections by marriages, father in law from father.

8. Recognizes the conditions of life of the person dead or living, married or unmarried, through whom relationship exists. This is not operative in advanced societies.

Thus, the categories of the relationships as propounded by Kroeber, seem most appropriate particularly in reference to Indian tribes.

Generally, kinship terminology have been divided into two principal types; first, the classificatory kinship terms, second, the descriptive kinship terms. In the former type, "the term is used to denote a large number of individuals while in the latter, a term refers ordinarily to one single individual."[70] Moreover, the kinship relations, in regard of the contact, propinquity, intimacy and vitality may be categorised into different degree which are as follows:

1. Primary kins-which consists of the direct kins; (both consanguine and affinal) e.g. one's mother is one's primary consanguineous and one's wife is one's primary affinal kin.

2. Secondary kins-the primary kin of the primary kin will be one's secondary kin *e.g.* one's sister's husband and the brother of one's father will be one's secondary affinal kin and secondary consanguineous kin respectively.

3. Tertiary kin-the secondary kin of one's primary kin will be the

tertiary kin for one's *e.g.* the father's brother's wife and wife's brother's wife will be the tertiary consanguineous kin and affinal kin respectively. Likewise the degree of kinship, as Majumdar has remarked, can thus be calculated at least theoretically to the ninth degree.[71]

Thus, the kinship system determines the consanguineous and affinal kins of the bilateral groupings and also calculates theoretically the degree of kinship. Besides this, the kinship terms both classificatory and descriptive have also given birth to address the kins by the kinship system. In this regard, kinship system has some functional significances to a given kin group, particularly in the determination of the certain types of behaviour patterns which jointly constitute the kinship usages. Thus, the kinship terms are used to determine the designating kin of various types, while the kinship usages ascertain the nature and the patterns of behaviours, verbal or non-verbal which broadly may be generalized into six major types, i.e. the avoidance, the joking, the teknonymy, the avunculate, the amitate and the cauvade.

The kinship organization which mainly consists of the various types of kinship categories of kinship, degrees of kinship relations, kinship terms and usages vary from tribe to tribe because of the variations of the rules of affinal and consanguineous bonds among the members of the tribal communities. For instance, the tribal communities under study present the variety of the kinship organization which can be proved by the following delineation presented on the basis of the exact and the scientific facts obtained through participant observation.

Bhotiya, an endogamous tribal kin group follows in general the rules of patrilineal and divided into a number of sub-group, named after the original place of their residence and each subgroup is thus an exogamous group for the similarity of the places of residence has bounded the people of one locality in socially recognized consanguineous bonds. However, the tradition of cross cousin marriage (non-parallel) has given birth to a particular and unique type of kinship system among Bhotiyas. But in general, the affinity and consanguineity are the two major types to determine the kinship relations among the Bhotiyas. For instance, the marital alliance of the Bhotiya male and female generates the bilateral i.e. both in the male line and female line kinship relations viz., a male after marriage becomes not only the husband of a female but also he becomes a son-in-law and brother-in-law and a father and so on. In the same way, a female not only acquires the status of a wife, but also she becomes the daughter-in-law, sister-in-law and mother at husband's place. Thus, the affinal bonds, consequently ascertain the consanguineous relations viz., after the affinal ties, the reproduction of offsprings simultaneously produces the blood relations among the parents and their offsprings i.e. either of the spouses and their children, father-son, father daughter, mother-son, mother-daughter, brother-brother, sister-brother, sister-sister and so on.

One remarkable thing that was observed during the study is the consanguineous kinship relations between the two persons, one who have got the ceremonial friendly ties and their offsprings having no biological base observe the socially recognized consanguineous relations. Virtually, when ever two persons (in general the two male each from different sub groups or the two female vice versa) respectively get into the ceremonial friendly relations by offering some presents in the form of a couple of sheeps or goats on the particular occasion of the full moon to one another they observe the consanguineous bonds based on socially recognized kinship. Thus, it may be concluded that the social recognition overrides the biological facts in consanguineous kinship among Bhotiyas as is observed among the polyandrous Todas. The relations thus, determined are strictly calculated upto the nineth generations. But all sorts of the kinship relations consists of the various kinship terms which have been categorised into two divisions; the first, classificatory and the second descriptive. For example, the Bhotiyas use the term 'Chhamei' to denote the elder sister of the wife, elder brother's wife, husband's elder sister, daughter of maternal uncle. Again they use the term 'Puni' to denote the elder sister, maternal aunt, father's sister, wife's mother and husband's mother. Likewise the term 'Chheju' is used to address the wife's elder brother, husband's younger brother, maternal uncle's son, elder sister's husband, and the elder brother of sister's husband. Thus, it is observed that the classificatory kinship terms are used to denote two or more individuals by a common term. In the same way, Raji also use some classificatory kinship terms to indicate the relations with number of individuals for instance, the term, 'Niyan' is used to denote the wife of mother's brother (maternal aunt) and father's sister. In the same way the term, 'Chima' is used to denote the mother's younger sister and father's younger brother's wife. Besides Bhotiyas and Raji's, the Tharus, Buxas and Jaunsaris also have classificatory kinship term to denote the large number of individuals. The detailed delineation of the classificatory terms of all the tribal communities have been presented in following table:

Kinship Terminology

Term Used in English	*Term Used in Bhotiya Dialect*	*Term Used in Tharu Dialect*	*Term Used in Buxa Dialect*	*Term Used in Raji Dialect*	*Term Used in Khasa Dialect*
1	2	3	4	5	6
Mother	Mina	Ayya	Aiya	Ihha	Eejee
Father	Ba	Baba	Abbu	Baba	Baba
Brother (elder)	Po	Dada	Dada	Dadda	Dada
Brother (younger)	Nanu	Bhaiya	Bhaiya	Bhulee	Bayya
Sister (elder)	Punee	Dedee	Jijja	Diddi	Dadi
Sister (younger)	Chinee	Laloo	Bhahaniya	Bhanya	Bhaitee
Sister (Middle)	Gunada	—	—	—	—
Sister (Middle elder)	Punee Gunani	—	—	—	—
Sister (Middle (younger)	-- Chinee Gunani	—	—	—	—
Husband	Warasiri	Loga	Khasam	Pariyar	Khwand

Contd.

1	2	3	4	5	6
Wife	Baja Chimai	Bayyar	Baiyar	Metai	Jooru
Husband's mother	Pune	Maya	Sas	Pani	Sasu
Husband's father	Puwa	Buba	Buba	Sasur	Sirsa
Husband's bother (elder)	Chheju	Barhe	—	—	—
Husband's brother (younger)	Cheju/ Chheyan	Dyura	Dewar	Daur	Devar
Husband's sister (younger)	Chhame/ Salisya	Nand	Nanad	Nanad	Dyani
Husband's sister (elder)	Chhame	Nand	Nanad	Jethsasu	Dyani
Wife's mother	Punne	Maya	—	—	—
Wife's father	Puwa	Buba	—	—	—
Wife's brother (elder)	Chhaju	Jetharo	Jethar	Jethu	Mittar
Wife's brother (younger)	Chhayan	Saro	Sala	Salo	Mittar
Wife's sister (elder)	Chhamai	Barhi	Barilia	Pani	Vabi

Contd.

1	2	3	4	5	6
Wife's sister (younger)	Salsya	Salce	Sali	Sali	Bauji
Mother's father	Babu	Nanna	Nana	Babu	Nana
Mother's mother	Amma	Nanni	Nani	Ama	Nani
Mother's brother	Puwa	Mooma	Mama	Guwa	Mamma
Mother's sister (elder)	Punmya	Barhi	Tai	Ekka	Maui
Mother's sister (younger)	Minmya	Mausi	Mausi	Chima	Mausi
Son	Syaree	Lorha	Beta	Paya	Laraka
Daughter	Chime	Laurhia	Betee	Garuni	Larkee
Mother's brother's wife	Puni	Mayi	Mai	Niyan	Mammi
Mother's sister's husband (elder)	Chuwa	Mausa	—	—	Mausa
Mother's sister's Husband (younger)	Minba	Mausa	—	—	Mausa
Mother's brother's son	Chhaju	Bhayya	—	Bhai	Dadda/ Bhayya

Contd.

1	2	3	4	5	6
Mother's brother's daughter	Chhame	Dedde/ Lalo	—	Bahan	Diddi/ Bayati
Mother's sister's son	Poo	Bhayya	—	—	Dadda/ Bhayya
Mother's Sister's daughter (elder)	Ata	Deddee	—	—	Dadi
Mother's sister's daughter (younger)	Sansya	Laloo	—	—	Bayati
Father's father	Baba	Dada	Dada	Bubu	Nana
Father's mother	Amma	Dadi	Dadi	Ama	Nani
Father's brother (elder)	Pun Ba	Dhaee	Tau	Baa	Babu
Father's brother (younger)	Min Ba	Kakku	Chacho	Kakka	Baba
Father's sister (elder)	Funi	Fuwa	Peuju	Phufi	Phuphi
Father's sister (younger)	Chini	Fuwa	Pauju/ Niyan	Phúfi	Phuphi
Father's brother's wife (elder)	Punmya	Amma	Tai	Ikka	Kaki/Eeje

Contd.

1	2	3	4	5	6
Father's brother's wife(younger)	Minmya	Kakee	Chuchi	Chima	Kaki/Eeje
Father's sister's husband	Pyama	Fuffa	—	Bhima	Poofa
Father's sister's son	Chheju	Dadda/Bhaya	–	–	–
Father's sister's daughter	Chhemai Punpu	Dedee/Laloo	—	—	–
Father's brother's son	Pu/Nunu	Dadda/Bhaya	—	—	—
Father's brother's daughter	Ata, punu Ata Gunda Ata	Deddi/Laloo	—	—	—
Brother's wife (elder)	Menchee	Bhaujee	Bhauji	Bauji	Bauji (in case of seperate wife)
Brother's wife (younger)	Namsya	Bhabo	—	Bahu	—
Brother's son	Chhai	Bhatiya	Bhatija	Bhajya	Bharcha
Brother's daughter	Chhesya	Bhatijee	Bhatijee	Bhajjee	Bharchee
Sister's (elder) husband	Chhaju	Jeeja	Jeeja	Bhina	Mittar
Sister's (younger) husband	—	Jeeja	Jeeja	Jawai	Mittar

Contd.

1	2	3	4	5	6
Sister's son	Chhai	Bhanaj	Bhanjo	Bhanja	Vanja
Sister's daughter	Chhasya	Bhanaji	Bhatiji	Bhanjee	Vanji
Husband's sister's (elder) husband	— —	Nandoi (Jeeja Sasaru)	—	—	—

In fact, as observed and proved with the sufficient evidences, the classificatory terms are used to denote only those kins who possess approximately equal position in the kin group and also supposed to have the equal functional significance, such as the term 'Puni' among Bhotiyas is used to denote the elder sister, wife's mother, mother's brother's wife and father's sister, who possesses approximately the equal position as well as the functional significance in the frame of kinship organization. In fact, as the result of the prevalence of cross cousin marriage among Bhotiyas, the kins, denoted with the classificatory kinship terms possess the equal position and functional significance for the speaker. "Thus, social functions often explain the use of terms but the use of terms can also determine social relations."[72]

Besides, the classificatory kinship terms some particular kins mainly consists of the lineally collateral as well as the marital relations are denoted with some particularizing kinship terms. Such as the terms 'Mina', 'Ba', Bada, Chimai', are used to denote respectively the mother, the father and the wife among Bhotiya community. Moreover, the terms beyond the nearer relatives are descriptive, i.e., the terms, uncle, sister, brother, cousin or niece though specify the particular kins but used as the general term 'Minmya' is used to denote particularly the wife of father's brother, but in general Bhotiyas use this term for the woman specifying as 'Minmya' inspite of being far beyond of the nearer kinship relations. Thus, descriptive kinship terms specify the particular kinship relations whether lineal, collateral or the general, between individual rather than groups.

Moreover, some socially sanctioned factors viz; sex, age as well as the condition of the life of the person concern; *i.e.* the dead or living, married or unmarried, also play an important role as the determinant factors of kinship terms. Among Bhotiyas the terms i.e. 'Punee', 'Gunani'. 'Chinee' are referred to denote respectively the eldest sister, next to eldest sister and the youngest sister. Thus, kinship terms are decided on the basis of the age of the kin. Likewise the term 'Minimya' and 'Punimya' which refer respectively to mother's younger sister and the elder sister are also based on the age. The same pattern is also observed among Rajis. Tharus, Buxas and Jaunsaris. Thus, it is observed that the age of the speaker is recognized in the terms of kinship. The sex of the person through whom relationship exists also recognized among Bhotiyas as the determinant factor of the kinship terms. Such as the term, 'Buba', is denoted to refer the father's father is denoted with the term 'Nana'. In the same way the term 'Puna' is used to address the mother's brother while the father's brother (elder/younger) is denoted with the term 'Punba/Minba'. Thus, both the biological bases *i.e.* the age and the sex are socially recognized for the determination of the kinship terms among Bhotiyas. Besides Bhotiyas, the rest of the scheduled tribal communities under reference also take into account the sex and the age factors as the biological bases in determining the kinship terms.

Moreover, the kinship system also includes the various behaviour patterns which an individual performs or expected to perform to a particular kin within the kinship group. Every behaviour pattern, possesses a specific social definition which generally consists of the customary and the traditional sanction. Thus, the rules or the usages which regulate the behaviour patterns between the two and more individuals within the kinship system, may broadly be termed as the kinship usages. Every society in general and the tribal communities under study in particular also observe some sorts of kinship usages to regulate and control the behaviour patterns of the individual within the respective community. But an exact observation of the tribal communities exhibits the varieties of the kinship usages as according to the variations of the communities. For instance,some specific but universal kinship usages, regarding to the avoidance and joking relations vary from one tribe to another. In Bhotiya community no avoidance relations are observed among the kins. But the joking relations are excessively observed among the different sets of relations. Generally joking relationship consists of the traditionally and customary permitted relations by which both the parties may tease, make fun of the other and sometimes may extend to the obscene and the sex indulgence. Among Bhotiyas the most prevalence joking relations are practised between the Bhabhi (elder brother's wife and the younger brother of the husband) and Devar, which they termed as 'Minchee' and 'Cheju'. Besides the joking relations between 'Minchee' and 'Cheju' some other sets of kinship relations viz; the husband and his wife's younger sister, the man and his maternal uncle's daughter, the man and his father's sister's daughter, the wife's parents and the husband's parents also come within the joking relations. The joking relationships between the different sets indicate an equality and mutual reciprocity among the people and also symbolize the potentiality of the sexual relationship and generally, the two kins in each sets may be potential mates or may come under the parallel marital alliances. In regard of the joking relationship the joking may extend from the general ridicules to the obscene and vulgar references to sex. But in general, only the joking comments are extended from the both sides, but in some particular occasions; viz; the marriage ceremony, the local festivals, the meeting of the two in an aloof place and the Rang-ban, joking relationships may amount to the exchange of the sexual pleasure or the references of the sexual jokes and sex play. But the joking relations particularly in between the unmarried sets, provokes both parties for marital alliances or the either of the party sometimes exhibits one's inclination for mating the other. Thus the joking not only provides a healthy enjoyment to parties involved but some times functionally paved the way for mating alliances. A outstanding trait of the joking relations as has been observed during the research work is the sex indulgence only of those kins who are related with one another by affinal kinship relations and mutually reciprocate of the same behaviour patterns to one another. Besides the unmarried sets of joking relationship, the married sets, as mentioned above, also practise the jokings only for the sake of the jokes. The instance of the sex indulgence in such sets hardly come in light.

However, the joking relationship whether among married sets or unmarried sets are not practised to inherit something like the property ownership from the either party but surely for the extra-marital/pre-marital sex relations. As is observed among the matrimonial Hopi Tribe who by virtue of the joking relationship with the maternal uncle's wife try to inherit all the property of one's maternal uncle including his wife.[73]

However, some joking relations are also exist between those people who really do not come under the definition of joking relations. Such as the elder/the adult/the old people pass remarks/taunts and ridicule to the younger ones who in general do not reciprocate but pays no head to the taunt and avoids it with slight smiling. But such type of joking relations, in particular, assume the role of social control and thus correct the behaviour pattern of the latter one by ridicules. In the state of collectivity when the male and female within the intoxication of the 'Chyakti' sing and dance with joint hands in circle, they irrespective of their joking and non-joking relations, extend the ridicule, remarks and jokes through folk songs and other parodies to one another which some times extend to wink and similar other expressions indicative to the extra-marital sex relations. But the most remarkable fact, worth noting is that the joking relations in its rudest as well as the corrupted forms are still observed in the remote and interior villages of Bhotiyas while the people gnerally dwell in some urban/notified/city areas and literate, though observe these joking relations but absolutely in its refined forms. The joking relations seem to be confined only with smile and some sort of light jokes lacking the sense of the sex as is observed in some non-tribal, comparatively more advanced/civilised/cultured societies. It is observed that the people who are still confined with their traditions and the original habitates, having less mobility, isolated from the outer world and still follow the traditional pattern of life also practise the rudest form of the joking relations. The people, who have come out from their traditional peripheries, begun to move with the non-tribal communities and thus following the alien cultural traits, have gradually been lagging behind the ancient rather traditional patterns of joking relations.

In this connection the education and the impact of the different cultural groups have played a vital role even in the transformation of the patterns of the joking relations. In fact education has not only inspired the tribal people for white collar jobs but also speeded up their social mobility towards urban and the plains, consequently they come under the unavoidable impacts of the socio-cultural contacts which is supposed to have slacken its traditional rigidity by acquiring the sophistication of the modern society, concealment of the originality of the behaviour patterns and of the secrecy from the outer world. This pattern of cultural transformation should be understood as the process of cultural annulation.

Moreover, the usage of teknonymy among some particular sets of kinship relations is prevalent among Bhotiyas. Generally, in such type of kin sets a kin referred to other one with some medium and, neither addresses his / her name nor is he entitled of doing so. Particularly, the husband and wife observe teknonymy to address one another. For instance, the wife referred her husband as the father of x, y, z and so as the husband addresses his wife as the mother of so and so. In teknonymy only the children and sometimes the grand children of the family are teknonymously used. But sometimes the teknonymy is also partly observed by other kins. For instance, the father-in-law (husband's father) addresses his daughter-in-law (son's wife) even through the sons or daughters teknonymously. The same is observed by several other kins but in all respect only the children become the medium of address. The prevalence of the pattern of teknonymy basically bears a sense of respect and is an honorific way of addressing to one another. But there is a little variation in following the usages regarding teknonymy. Mostly that part of the Bhotiya population which still confined to their traditional peripheries observe strictly the teknonymy usages while the educated mass who have got their settlements to urbans or of their working places as well as the business class people who have settled down their business in some market places do partly observe the teknonymy usages. For instance, the husband addresses his wife by her name / nickname while the wife still follow the teknonymy usage and addresses her husband through the medium of their eldest child. This changing form of teknonymy prove patriarchal form of family where the male holds the higher status and duly respected by the female (wife). However, it is equally true that the wife is also honoured in the family even by the husband with due respect. Calling the name of the wife doesn't degrade her position but enhance the emotional attachment, intimacy, informality and uniformity between the two and thus strengthen the conjugal life.

But the Bhotiya tribe do not follow any other kinship usages. For example, the avunculate, amitate, and cauvade type of usages are not in prevalence among Bhotiyas and the rest of the tribal communities under study.

However, the kinship system of the 'Khasas' or the Jaunsaris is quite different from that of the rest of the scheduled tribal communities under study. It is so because of the polyandrous family structure of Khasas in which the horizontal sibling relationship is most important. Among Khasas the lineal relationship between father and sons determines the structural base of the familial relationship. On account of the fraternal polyandry the terminological system of 'Khasas' vary from the rest of the tribal communities. Among the relatives the mother's brother i.e. 'Mamma' has a venerable status in the community. He is treated as one of the most important relatives who is invited in almost all the ritualistic ceremonies; particularly at the occasion of the marriage, it is the mother's brother or the maternal uncle of the groom bride who presents the essential commodities called 'Bhoja' consists of Ghee, rice, goats etc. abundantly for the marriage. Only the maternal uncle is invited to dine with 'Rain Jimai' (with the ladies Rani's) which is considered as the most honorific status in Khasa community. Moreover, the heart of the slaughtered goat sacrificed at the occasion of Magh-festival during 15th January to 14th Feb. is respectfully offered to the maternal uncle as a mark of honour.

The maternal uncle is cordially invited by the sister's son at the occasion of the Magh-festival and respectfully offered the cooked heart of the slaughtered goat sacrified at that occasion. In case of the absence of the maternal uncle the heart of the goat is safely kept in dried form by tiding it with the wooden staff inside the roof of the house as long as he does not come. In near future the maternal uncle is specially invited and feasted the cooked heart in honour of him. So far as the joking relations are concerned, the sets of relations *viz.*, sister's husband and the sisters of the wife, elder brother's wife and the younger brother of the husband are regarded socially the most suitable pairs to make jokes with one another. But some times the grand parents are made the objects for ridicule while the children are told whether their 'grand parents' have died (Kya tera Nana-Nani mar gaya hai). Likewise, to say the grandparents whether they wish to be married with their grand children (Kya tumhara byah pota-poti se kar dain). In consanguineous relations no distinction is made in between the father's father, mother's father and the father's mother, mother's mother, hence the common terms 'Nana' and 'Nani' are used to address the grand fathers and the grand mothers respectively. Since the father and father's brother are grouped together in a class hence the siblings have same particular kinship terms while no specific terminology is used to address to the cousins. The father and the father's brothers are denoted by a common term 'Baba' by the children. However, to make the address more clear, comprehensive and specific the fathers are callled with their functional names viz; father-who manages the family, father who look after the sheep and goats, father-who works in the field and looks after the cattle and so.

Thus, the number of kins and relatives are grouped with in a class and a common term is used to address them. Nevertheless the polyandrous form of the 'Khasa' community is changing day by day. Although the 'Khasa' community has never been exclusively the polyandrous, as the historical references exhibit, yet the changing process has got its speedy momentum particularly since the introduction of the education and many other government welfare policies and their implementation for the overall development of the 'Khasa' community. At present the polyandry has been changing in the form of bi-polyandry, polygyny and monogamy. The inter-caste marriages, hypergamy and hypogamy are greatly taking place. Resultantly, the descriptive system of kinship is simultaneously coming into existence side by side with the classificatory system of kinship. For instance, with the practice of bi-polyandry, polygyny and monogamy, the specific terms to address respectively the father and father's brother, the mother and the step-mother and the aunt have come into existence.

Thus, it may be concluded that some fundamental differences among the Scheduled Tribal communities exist on account of the difference of the social motif resultantly an apparent discordance is viewed on the kinship terms and the kinship usages of the different tribal communities. However, both the consanguineous and the affinal kinship relations constitute the kinship organization of the tribal communities in general. But some certain kinship terms are associated with the certain relations and every relation has socially assigned some certain duties to which one carried out in some particular occasions as is supposed by the respective community. Moreover, some certain sets of relations also exercise some sorts of joking relations but none of the Scheduled Tribal community except Rajis follow the rules of avoidance. Thus, the kinship system has since ever a functional utility in determining the nature of the relations and the modes of behaviour of the members of the given community.

References

1. Elliott and Merrill, Social Disorganization, Harper and Bros. , New York, 1950, p. 14.
2. Majumdar, D.N. and Madan T.N., An Introduction to Social Anthropology, Asia Publishing House, New Delhi.
3. *Ibid.*, pp. 245-246.
4. *Ibid.*, p. 246.
5. Piddington, Ralph, An Introduction to Social Anthropology Oliver and Boyd, London, 1952, pp. 103-107.
6. Herskovits, M.J., Cultural Anthropology, Oxford and IBH Publishing Co. New Delhi, 1950.
7. Singh, Y., Modernization of Indian Tradition., Rawat Publication, Jaipur 1986, p. 174.
8. Mac-Iver, R.M. and C.H. Page, Society, London: Mac Millan, 1959, p. 240.
9. Morgan. L.H., Ancient Society, New York, 1877.
10. Mac-Iver, R.M. and C.H. Page, Society, London: Mac Millan, 1953, p. 245.
11. Majumdar, D.N., Races and Cultures of India, Asia Publishing House, Bombay 1958, p. 163.
12. Desai, I.P., Some Aspects of Family in Mahuva, Asia Publishing House, New York, 1964, p. 34.
13. Kolend, Pauline M., "Regional Difference in Indian Family Structure", ed., Robert I, Crane, Regions and Regionalism in South Asian Studies; An Exploratory Study (Duke University, Programme in Comparative Study in Southern Asia, Symposium Papers, 1967), pp. 149-150.
14. Singh, Y., Modernization of Indian Tradition., Rawat Publications, Jaipur, 1986, p. 174.

15. Majumdar, D.N. and T.N. Madan, An Introduction to Social Anthropology, Asia Publishing House, Delhi, 1963, p. 190.

16. Desai, I.P., The Joint Family in India, Sociological Bulletin, Vol. V. No. 2, Sept, 1956, p. 148.

17. Majumdar, D.N. and T.N. Madan, Social Anthropology, Asia Publishing House, Delhi 1963, p. 80.

18. *Ibid.*, p. 80.

19. *Ibid.*, p. 81.

20. *Ibid.*, p. 80.

21. *Ibid.*, p. 82.

22. *Ibid.*, p. 82.

23. *Ibid.*, p. 83.

24. *Ibid.*, p. 84.

25. *Ibid.*, p. 84.

26. *Ibid.*, p. 84.

27. *Ibid.*, p. 87.

28. Rayapa, R.S., Sauka, Rayapa Bros., Dharchula, Pithoragarh, 1974, p. 77.

29. Atkinshon. E.T., The Himalayan Gazetteers, Vol. II, Part I, Cosmo Publications, 1982, p. 371.

30. Majumdar, D.N. and T.N. Madan, Social Anthropology, Asia Publishing House, Bombay, 1963, p. 141.

31. Ogburn, W.F. and M.F. Nimkoff, A Hand Book of Sociology, Routledge and Kegan Paul Ltd., London, 1960, p. 18.

32. Mead, M., Quoted by P.H. Prabhu, in Hindu Social Organization, Popular Prakashan, Bombay, 1961, p. 261.

33. Rig Veda, viii, 31,5.

34. Sat. Br. XIV, 3, 1, 35; Patni Karma eva etc. Kurvanti Yad Idgatarah.

35. Robback, A.A., The Psychology of Character, 3rd Ed. pp. 609-611; London, Kegan Paul, 1952.

36. Freud, S., New Introductory Lecturers on Psycho-analysis, 1934, pp. 134.

37. Mahabharata, Anusasan-Parva, 38 Quoted by P.H. Prabhu in Hindu Social Organization, Popular Prakashan, Bombay, 1961, p. 265.

38. *Ibid.*, 19-21.

39. Prabhu, P.H., Social Organization, Popular Prakashan, Bombay, p. 269.

40. Prabhu, P.H. Social Organization, Popular Prakashan, Bombay, 1961, p. 265.

41. Manu Smiriti, iii, 60.

42. Manu, V., 147-148, Quoted by P.H. Prabhu in Hindu Social Organization, Popular Prakashan, Bombay, 1961, p. 270.

43. *Ibid.*, p. 272.

44. Manu 11, 213.

45. Brihat Samhita, 74, 2 (Quoted by Prabhu, R.H. in Hindu Social Organization), p. 274.

46. *Ibid.*, p. 7.

47. *Ibid.*, p. 9.

48. *Ibid.*, p. 17.

49. Manu. ii. 67.

50. Majumdar, D.N. and T.N. Madan, Social Anthropology, Asia Publishing House, Bombay 1963, p. 141.

51. Majumdar, D.N., The Fortunes of Primitive Tribes.

52. Majumdar, D.N., Races and Cultures of India, Asia Publishing House Bombay, 1958.

53. *Ibid.*

54. Majumdar, D.N., Races and Cultures of India, Asia Publishing House, Bombay, 1958, p. 168.

55. *Ibid.*, p. 160.

56. Majumdar, D.N., Social Anthropology, Asia Publishing House, Bombay, 1963, p. 129.

57. Majumdar, D.N., Races and Cultures of India, Asia Publishing House, Bombay.

58. Majumdar, D.N., Races and Cultures of India, pp. 272-274.

59. Chattopadhyay, P.K., Himalaya Pare Kailash Mansarovar, Calcutta: Orient Book Co., 1962, p. 138.

60. Pant, S.D., The Social Economy of the Himalayas; London; George Allen and Unwin, 1935., p. 204.

61. Chattopadhyay, P.K., Himalaya Pare Kailash, Mansarovar, Calcutta, Orient Book Co. 1962, p. 138.

62. Pant, S.D., The Social Econony of the Himalayas, London. George Allen and Unwin, 1935, p. 204-205.

63. Dabral, S.P., Uttarakhand Ki Bhotantik, Dogadda Veer Gatha Prakashan, 1965.

64. Pant, S.D., The Social Economy of the Himalayas, London; George Allen and Unwin, 1935, p. 205.

65. Dabral, S.P., Uttarakhand Ki Bhotantik, Dogadda Veer Gatha Prakashan 1965, p. 161.

66. Winick, Charles, Dictionary of Anthropology, p. 302.

67. Majumdar, D.N., Social Anthropology, Asia Publishing House, Bombay 1963, p. 98.

68. *Ibid.*, p. 98.

69. Rivers, W.H.R., Kinship and Social Organization, Constable and Co., London, 1914, p. 17.

70. *Ibid.*, p. 240.

71. *Ibid.*, p. 100.

72. Majumdar, D.N., Races and Cultures of India, Asia Publishing House, Bombay, 1958, p. 244.

73. *Ibid.*, p. 105.

6

STATUTORY PROVISIONS AND CULTURAL TRANSFORMATION

One of the most significant development after Independence is the emergence of democratic pattern of Indian Government that characterises the emergence of the struggle to transform the social, cultural, economic, political and the technological system of the traditional agricultural predominant society into the modern society. At present almost all the sections of the society have equally been treated before the Constitution and some additional special provisions are also framed for the socio-economic development of the socially backward and disabled section of the society so that they may flow in the mainstream of the national life. With this end in view, some tribal groups have been taken into account as the scheduled tribal communities and the responsibility for their welfare has been shouldered by the welfare government of India.

Since the adoption of the Constitution of free India, the entire gamut of the tribal problems has been seen in the broad constitutional frame of reference. The Government of India has adopted a policy of sustained efforts for greater inter-community inter-relations, greater understanding of human being and also to bring the tribal communities into the national context, various constitutional provisions for the safeguard of Scheduled Tribes in India have been formulated. As G.S. Ghurye has termed the "ethno-social groups" as a whole category may be said to have been subsumed under, "the weaker sections of the people". Promotion of whose "educational and economic interests" is declared by Article 46 to be one of the Directive Principles of State Policy. The same article further mentions the Scheduled Castes and the Scheduled Tribes as particular varieties of the category of the weaker sections of the people. Article 46 of the Constitution declares that, "The State shall promote, with special care, the educational and economic interests of the weaker sections of the people, and the particular of Scheduled Castes and the Scheduled Tribes and shall protect them form social injustice and all forms of exploitation."[1]

The 'weaker section' of the Indian society in general and the Scheduled Tribal Communities in particular has highly been privileged under the Constitution. The fifth schedule, which is the charter not only of the scheduled areas but also of scheduled tribes, stands as the clearest testimony to the full appreciation of the nature and extent of the problems of the scheduled tribes by the framers of the Constitution. Article 244[2] of the Constitution empower the President of India to declare any area where there is a substantial population of tribal people, as a scheduled area under the fifth schedule or in Assam as a tribal area under the sixth schedule. Article 339 lays down that, "The executive power of Union Government extends to the giving of directions to a State as to the drawing up and execution of schemes specified in the direction to be essential for the welfare of the Scheduled Tribes in the State."[3] Article 275 of the Constitution provides for assistance to the states for the implementation of the provisions of the Constitution. There shall be paid out of the consolidated fund of India as grants-in-aid of the revenues of a State such capital and recurring sums as may be necessary to enable that State to meet the costs of such schemes of development as may be undertaken by the State with the approval of the Government of India for the purpose of promoting the welfare of the scheduled tribes in the State or raising the level of administration of the rest of the States."[4] Article 330, 332, and 334[5] provide for reservation of seats for Scheduled Tribes in the house of the people and the State legislatures. Article 335[6] provides for reservation in the services. Articles 15, 16 and 19 safeguard the interests and the way of tribal life.[7] Besides this, the fifth schedule of the Constitution gives certain powers and lays certain duties on the Governor of every State that has scheduled areas. Part B, para 5 of the fifth schedule says: "The Governor may make regulations for the peace and good government of any area in a State which is for the time being a scheduled area." Such regulations may;

(a) prohibit or restrict the transfer of land by or among the members of the Scheduled Tribes in such area;

(b) regulate the allotment of land to members of the Scheduled Tribes in such area;

(c) regulate the carrying on the business as money-lender by persons who lend money to members of the Scheduled Tribes in such area..........."

Moreover, the fifth schedule, part 'B', paragraph 4 provides for the compulsory setting up of Tribes Advisory Council in each State, having or not having Scheduled Areas but containing Scheduled Tribes..... The duty of the Tribes Advisory Council is to advise on matters pertaining to the welfare and advancement of the scheduled tribes in the State. There is an important provision under the Article 338[8] which provides the commissioner for Scheduled Castes and Scheduled Tribes for implementing the safeguards for the Scheduled Tribes and the programmes for their development. Besides these constitutional provisions, a special emphasis has constantly been given in every five year plan for the upliftment of the standard of the tribal people. In the fifth five year plan, a serious effort was made for an integrated development approach in planning for tribals and tribal majority areas. In view of the tribal development a tribal sub-plan concept has also been introduced. Presently, about sixty five percent of the scheduled tribal population in the 18 States / Union Territories are covered by the tribal sub-plan approach in 180 Integrated Tribal Development Projects (I.T.D.Ps.).[9]

Thus, it is observed that various measures have been adopted to tackle the problems of tribals in India and some special clauses have been incorporated in the Constitution for the creation of Scheduled Areas and Scheduled Tribes for their intensive developments. A reservation policy has also been adopted to provide some relaxation to the tribal people in the Government services, in educational institutions and in the Parliament and legislative assemblies.

Apart from the statutory provisions, a number of voluntary organizations have also intensified their efforts for the reformation of the socio-cultural conditions of the tribals. In this regard the scientific studies of the social scientists with a view to redress the grievances of the tribal population are of immense importance.

Under the constitutional provisions, the five tribal communities of the Uttar Pradesh have also been declared as the Scheduled Tribes in 1967. Since then a number of efforts have been vigorously launched for the socio-cultural development of the scheduled tribal communities. In this direction, the State Government has also established a department namely Harijan and Social Welfare Directorate so that the welfare policies can effectively be implemented. In the Scheduled Tribal areas, on 6th November, 1984, the State Government of U.P. by its government order number 971/J-26-3-84-8(30)/84 dated 6-11-84 has established a separate Tribal Development Directorate to concentrate, separately the welfare measures for the welfare and advancement of the Scheduled Tribes in the State. At present, numerous programmes have been launched by the Tribal Development Directorate for the educational development, economic development, social welfare, rehabilitation on agriculture, cultural protection and for the improvement of the health and nutrition of the tribal people so that the backward and socially disabled and deprived tribal communities can live within the broad matrix of the civilized social life. The development schemes pertaining to the Scheduled Tribal communities of the State have been implemented, particularly in the field of education, socio-economic, health and nutrition, housing and rehabilitation.

The author attempts descriptively to analyse and verify the correlation between the statutory provisions and the process of cultural transformation among the Scheduled Tribal communities of Uttarakhand in Uttar Pradesh. Further, it also proposes to seek to what extent these constitutional provisions and the reformatory agencies might transform the tribal culture and in what respect these cultural changes have been occurred. In this regard the following hypothetical propositions have been framed:

(a) "The statutory provisions are positively correlated with the process of cultural transformation of the Scheduled Tribal Communities of Uttarakhand."

(b) "The expansion of education, means of transportation and communication have brought about changes in the social organization and the occupational structure of the Scheduled Tribal communities of Uttarakhand."

To verify the above hypotheses the attitudes of the sampled units of the tribal population of Uttarakhand have thoroughly been studied. To understand the influence of various statutory provisions, almost all the scheduled tribal population living in the Kumaun and Garhwal division of U.P. have been studied with the help of the participant observation method and the sampled respondent units have thoroughly been interviewed with the help of an interview schedule. The respondent units have been asked the following questions to test the designed hypothesis No. (1) :

Questions	Reactions
(a) Are you aware with the statutory provisions made for the socio-economic development of the Scheduled Tribal communities?	(a) Completely aware, partly aware, neutral, completely unaware, unknown.
(b) What is the impact of welfare measures on the socio-economic life of the Scheduled Tribal Communities?	(b) More development, partly development, neutral, no impact towards development, adverse impact.
(c) The statutory provisions and the developmental plans are essential for the welfare of the Scheduled Tribal Communities.	(c) Completely agree, agree, uncertain, disagree, completely disagree.

(d) Reservation policies have been helpful in providing more opportunities to the Scheduled Tribal people in services.	(d) Completely agree, agree, uncertain, disagree, completely disagree.

The answers obtained in regard of the above mentioned statements are classified and tabulated as in Table 18.

It is observed that 3 (0.81%), 13 (10.40%) and 117 (57.07%) respondent units respectively from first, second, and third categories are completely aware with the statutory provisions formed for the welfare of the Scheduled Tribal population in general. Yet there are respondents particularly in first and second categories i.e. 161 (43.51%) and 32 (25.60%) who have expressed their complete unawareness about the provisions, hence they show their negligence towards the statutory provisions, and similar other welfare activities. The lack of awareness prevalent among a nominal part of the Bhotiya population, who either confined, particularly to the rural areas or in some "Kasbas" is due to the apathy and self centered nature caused by the illiteracy and the social isolation. Approximately the same results have been achieved in case of Tharus, Khasas, and Buxas. Maximum 117 (57.07%) respondent units from the third category have shown their complete awareness and 41 (20.00%) are partly aware towards the statutory provisions it is so because of the high percentage of the literacy. Yet there are 47 (22.90%) respondents who do not express any kind of reactions and thus remained neutral on this matter. The third category which chiefly consists of the respondents of service class are literate and hence possess the essential knowledge with the provisions made for them and continuously seem to get the maximum benefit of it.

Thus, in the first category out of the total 370 respondents the maximum 43.51 percent (161) have complete unawareness while 28.92 percent (107) have made no reactions, 13.78 percent (51) expressed their unawareness while 12.97 percent (48) are partly aware and only 0.81 percent (3) respondents are completely aware. In the second category out of the total 125 respondent units the maximum 44.80 percent (56) respondents are partly aware,

Table 18

Awareness of Respondents Towards Statutory Provisions Made for the Socio-Economic Development of Scheduled Tribes

Reactions	*Bhotiya*	*Buxa*	*Tharu*	*Raji*	*Jaun.*	*Total*	*%*
First Category							
Completely aware	02	—	01	—	—	03	6.81
Partly aware	22	03	19	02	02	48	12.97
Neutral	30	30	32	06	09	107	28.92
Completely unaware	62	53	22	12	12	161	43.51
Unaware	16	17	08	03	07	51	13.78
Total	132	103	82	23	30	370	100.00
Second Category							
Completely aware	09	—	—	—	04	13	10.42
Partly aware	46	03	05	—	02	56	44.80
Neutral	04	03	03	—	05	15	12.00
Completely unaware	17	04	04	—	07	32	25.60
Unaware	04	02	01	—	02	09	7.20
Total	80	12	13	—	20	125	100.00
Third Category							
Completely aware	100	02	15	—	—	117	57.07
Partly aware	13	13	11	—	04	41	20.00
Neutral	07	05	04	—	31	47	22.93
Completely unaware	—	—	—	—	—	—	—
Unaware	—	—	—	—	—	—	—
Total	120	20	30	—	35	205	100.00

25.60 (32) are completely unaware. 12.00% (15) are neutral, 7.20% (9) are aware and the rest 10.40% (13) have complete awareness towards the statutory provisions made for the socio-economic development of Scheduled Tribes in common. In the third category the maximum 57.07% (117) out of the total 205 respondents, are completely aware with the statutory provisions, while 22.93% (47) respondents did not made any reactions. They were almost neutral in this statement while 20.00% (41) respondents have expressed their partly awareness. Thus it may be concluded that most of the respondents belonging to the third category are aware with the statutory provisions made for their socio-economic upliftment. The percentage of the aware respondents gradually decrease respectively in the second and third categories. In fact, the literacy percentage comparatively higher in the third category respondents. Moreover, they also come in frequent contact with the out groups i.e. non-tribal groups and appear always to acquire the maximum benefits provided under the statutory provisions, so they are more conscious with statutory provisions. While the literacy percentage is comparatively low respectively in second and first category respondents moreover, they have lesser contact respectively with the outer-world, since they remain busy with their business, hence, they have been unaware with the statutory provisions particularly made for the socio-economic development of Scheduled Tribes. It is so because of the isolated socio-cultural life and the prevalent illiteracy among the tribals. This fact may be verified from the following Table 19.

Table 19

Literacy and Awareness Pattern

Scheduled Tribe Literacy	*Nos of Completely Aware and Partly Aware Respondents*											
	Bhotiya		*Buxa*		*Tharu*		*Raji*		*Jaunsari*		*Total*	
	Lit.	*Illi.*	*Lit.*	*Illi.*	*Lit.*	*Illi.*	*Lit.*	*Illi.*	*Lit.*	*Illi.*	*Lit.*	*Illi.*
First Category	24	—	03	—	20	—	02	—	02	--	51	--
Second Category	55	—	03	—	05	—	—	—	06	—	69	—
Third Category	113	—	15	—	26	—	—	—	04	—	158	—
Total	192	—	21	—	51	—	02	—	12	—	278	—

The data shows that almost all the completely aware and partly aware respondents belonging to different Scheduled Tribal Communities are literate. (Here; by literate we mean every that respondent unit who is at least primary standard pass and possesses the qualification of reading and writing). None of the illiterate respondents found aware with the statutory provisions made for the Scheduled Tribal Communities. Thus, it is concluded that education and awareness towards statutory provisions are positively correlated with one another.

Besides this, the impact of various development and welfare measures launched by the government particularly for the over all development of the Scheduled Tribal Communities, has also been observed and the reactions of the respondents have been acquired through direct contact with the help of the interview schedule. The data thus collected are presented in Table 20.

The data depict that out of the total 370 respondent units belonging to the first category, the maximum 132 (35.68%) respondents are in the state of uncertainity. 131 (35.41%) respondents assert that there is no impact towards the development of the socio-economic standard of the tribal communities hence they are still flowing in same stream as they used to flow many years back. There are 44 (11.89%) respondents who admit the adverse impact of the welfare measures in the socio-economic development of the tribal communities. Yet there are 44 (11.89%) and 19 (5.14%) respondents who respectively admit the partly development and more development caused by the welfare measures. But, in general it can be concluded that the majority of the tribal population who still reside in an interior most and inaccessible rural areas completely cut off from the outer civilized world are unknown with the welfare measures, neither they ever try to avail the government facilities, they, in real lack, the efficient volunteers to represent them, resultantly they have neither any knowledge for welfare measures nor any aspiration for better future nor they think for any sort of socio-economic development. In fact, whatever been done in the name of development of the Scheduled Tribal Communities, its real benefit has not been reaching upto the last man of the bulk of the tribal population habitating particularly in the rural areas.

Besides this out of total 125 respondents of the second category, the maximum number i.e 51 (40.80%) are of the opinion

Table 20

Impact of Welfare Measures on the Socio-Economic Life of Scheduled Tribes

Reactions of the respondents	*Bhotiya*	*Buxa*	*Tharu*	*Raji*	*Jaun.*	*Total*	*%*
First Category							
More development	06	—	13	—	—	19	5.14
Partly development	18	03	07	09	07	44	11.89
Neutral	30	45	39	06	12	132	35.68
No Impact towards development	53	49	18	07	04	131	35.41
Adverse Impact	25	06	05	01	07	44	11.88
Total	132	103	82	23	30	370	100.00
Second Category							
More development	45	—	—	—	66	51	40.80
Partly development	24	06	07	—	02	39	31.20
Neutral	01	02	01	—	04	08	6.40
No Impact towards development	06	04	05	—	07	22	17.60
Adverse Impact	04	—	—	—	01	05	4.00
Total	80	12	13	—	20	125	100.00
Third Category							
More development	107	04	09	—	01	121	59.02
Partly development	11	08	07	--	21	47	22.93
Neutral	02	03	04	—	03	12	5.85
No Impact towards development	—	05	10	—	07	22	10.75
Adverse Impact	—	—	—	—	03	03	1.47
Total	120	20	30	—	35	205	100.00

that due to the welfare measures launched by the government for the socio-economic development of tribals, the socio-economic standard of the tribals has developed more. There are 39 (31.20%) respondents who accept the partly development of the socio-economic conditions of the tribals through the introduction of the welfare measures. Yet there are 22 (17.60%) respondents who say that there is no impact of the welfare measures towards development while 5 (4.00%) respondents argue for the adverse impact of the welfare measures and only 8 (6.40%) respondents are neutral and neither admit any sort of the development nor accept about the adverse impact of the welfare measures. But it can be asserted that the most of the respondents belonging to the second category admit for the positive impact of the welfare measures. In fact, the respondents belonging to the second category have either completely or partly come out from the isolated places of their traditional abodes and begun to reside in the same towns or 'Kasbas' where they become familiar with the statutory provisions, welfare measures formulated for them and thus gradually, trying to achieve their benefits and mostly the success goes to their part.

On the contrary, there are total 205 respondents in third category out of which the maximum 121 (59.20%) accept that there is more development with the effect of the welfare measures and 47 (22.93%) respondents admit with the partly development caused by the government welfare schemes. On the contrary 22 (10.73%) respondents disagree with the positive impact of the welfare measures and assert that no development has been done so far. They assert that the Govt. has constantly been befooling the simple, native or the ingenuous tribal people by showing them the false hopes as an inducement. This is exactly the cause of the general deprivation of the majority of the tribal population who are uneducated and still confined with their traditional abodes and subsist on the stereo typed means of subsistance. Moreover, there are 12 (5.85%) respondents who are not in the state of evaluating the impact of the welfare measures while 3 (1.47%) respondents agree for the adverse impacts of the welfare measures of the government and assert that with the introduction of the welfare measures the Government has developed idleness, inactivity as well as shrewdness among the tribals who always look intently and sit like an idler all the time awaiting for the well ripen fruit to gulp down. But they are not aware with the ever lasting waitings that have subsequently made them idle, inactive and apathetic for future.

Thus, it may be concluded that the reactions of the different respondents of all the three categories vary from each other, yet the comparative assessment of all the respondents belonging to the different categories exhibit that the majority of the respondents belonging to the first category have negative opinion about the impact of the welfare measures, while the majority of the respondents belonging to the second and third category possess contrary opinion than that of the first category respondents and admit that more development has been taken place due to the implementation of the welfare measures on the tribal communities. It is so because of the difference of the ecological settings of the respondents, their educational standard, world view, level of awareness and the aspirations which jointly induce the tribal people to acquire all the potential benefits from the Government.

Resultantly, the tribal people who are aware with their privileges, and reside inaccessible areas as the respondents from second and third categories do, avail the maximum benefit, while the tribal people who are unaware, conservative, self-centered, uneducated and reside in the inaccessible, isolated and the remote areas can not achieve any positive results of the welfare measures and thus, remain illusioned that the developing process has almost stopped. In fact, the government machinery has almost failed to approach the people really meant by the tribals due to their inaccessible places of residence and thus has been unable to awaken them from the never ending traditionalistic lethargy. A motivational vacuum amongst the tribals living in the remote most areas has made their inertia still more static and compelled them to follow their conventions blindly and happily on account of which they could not make any aspiration for betterment nor they make any effort in the direction of development. Hence, in order to know the attitudes of the respondent units of the three categories towards the statutory provisions and the development plans, the sampled units have been asked, whether the statutory provisions and the development plans are essential for the welfare of the Scheduled Tribal Communities? The reactions thus achieved through the respondent units, have been presented in Table 21.

Table 21

The Statutory Provisions and Development Plans are Essential for the Welfare of the Scheduled Tribal Communities

Reactions	*Bhotiya*	*Buxa*	*Tharu*	*Raji*	*Jaun.*	*Total*	*%*
First Category							
Completely agree	13	—	14	02	01	30	8.10
Agree	11	03	06	07	06	33	8.92
Uncertain	32	42	42	09	08	133	35.95
Disagree	41	18	07	01	07	74	20.00
Completely Disagree	35	40	13	04	08	100	27.03
Total	132	103	82	23	30	370	100.00
Second Category							
Completely agree	55	02	07	—	07	71	56.80
Agree	14	04	—	—	01	19	15.20
Uncertain	03	03	02	—	02	10	8.00
Disagree	05	02	04	—	06	17	13.60
Completely Disagree	03	01	—	—	04	08	6.40
Total	80	12	13	—	—	20	125
Third Category							
Completely agree	98	11	11	—	17	137	66.83
Agree	20	01	05	—	05	31	15.12
Uncertain	02	01	02	—	01	06	2.93
Disagree	—	03	08	—	06	17	8.29
Completely Disagree	—	04	04	—	06	14	6.83
Total	120	20	30	—	35	205	100.00

The tabulated data shows that the majority of the respondents i.e. 100 (27.03%) out of the total 370 sampled units belonging to the first category completely disagree with the statement that, "the statutory provisions and the development plans are essential for the welfare of the scheduled tribal communities. "While 74 (20.00%) respondents disagree and 133 (35.95%) are uncertain in regard of the above mentioned statement. But there are contrary reactions of the respondents belonging to the second and third categories. Since in the second and third categories respectively the majority of the respondents i.e. 71 (56.80%) out of the total 125 and 137 (66.83%) out the total 205 completely agree with the statement. Moreover, 19 (15.20%) and 31 (15.12%) respondents have also agreed respectively from the second and third categories while only a nominal numbers of the respondents, i.e. 8 (6.40%) and 14 (6.83%) respectively from the second and third categories completely disagree with the statement. Thus, it may be said that the respondents in general who belong to the first category are not aware with the statutory provisions and development plans and their impacts hence they conceive any sort of the plans as well as the provisions unavailing rather more imaginary which arise only the false hopes among the native tribal people and thus put them in a mental predicament. While the respondents in general appeared more aware with statutory provisions and development plans specially formulated for them and hence they consider these plans and provisions necessary for the welfare of the community as a whole. Moreover, the reactions are almost the same in regard to the reservation policies made for the tribals to provide them more better opportunities in services. The data collected in this regard are being presented in Table 22.

Table 22

Reservation Policies are Helpful in Providing More Opportunities to Scheduled Tribe Persons in Services

Reactions	*Bhotiya*	*Buxa*	*Tharu*	*Raji*	*Jaun.*	*Total*	*%*	
First Category								
Completely agree	02	—	17	—	03	22	5.95	
Agree Partly	18	05	03	04	04	34	9.19	
Uncertain	35	58	46	14	13	166	44.86	
Disagree	56	23	09	04	05	97	26.22	
Completely disagree	21	17	07	01	05	51	13.78	
Total	132	103	82	23	30	370	100.00	
Second Category								
Completely agree	41	05	06	—	06	58	46.40	
Agree Partly	27	02	01	—	02	32	25.60	
Uncertain	04	04	02	—	03	13	10.40	
Disagree	02	—	01	—	07	10	8.00	
Completely disagree	06	01	03	—	02	12	9.60	
Total	80	12	13	--	20	125	100.00	
Third Category								
Completely agree	103	12	27	—	23	165	80.49	245
Agree Partly	17	08	03	—	12	40	19.51	106
Uncertain	—	—	—	—	—	—	—	179
Disagree	—	—	—	—	—	—	—	107
Completely disagree	—	—	—	—	—	—	—	63
Total	120	20	30	—	35	205	100.00	700

The data depict that the maximum 166 (44.86%) respondents out of the total 370 belonging to the first category are quitely unaware with the reservation policies and therefore uncertain to express any clear cut opinion about the reservation policies and their impacts on the tribal communities. This number of the respondents is succeeded by the 97 (26.22%) respondents who disagree with reservation policies and their implementation while 51 (13.78%) respondents completely disagree and prefer to avail the subsidized money for purchasing the live-stock and other subsidiary purposes that can instantly provide them the economic relief. While 34 (9.19%) respondents partly agree and 22 (5.95%) completely agree with the statement that the reservation policies are helpful in providing more opportunities to scheduled tribe people in services. In the second category most of the respondents i.e. 58 (46.40%) completely agree, 32 (25.60%) partly agree, 13 (10.40%) are uncertain, 10 (8.00%) disagree and the rest 12 (9.60%) completely disagree.

The results show that the social ecology play an important role in the determination of the attitudes and the awareness of the people. The respondent units related to the second and third category are in the frequent contact of the out groups and also in the state of availing the benefits of the communication media for getting the latest knowledge about different policies of the Government formulated time to time for tribals and thus make every possible efforts to acquire them. But the respondents belonging to the first category have constantly been confined within the social isolation completely away from the impact of the civilized world, untouched from the means of communication and transportation resultantly they have formed a stereotyped mental set up and outlook towards the life and the life values and thus they have neither felt the necessity for knowing about the outer world activities, whether they are beneficial for them, nor they ever wish any alteration in their social set up. Consequently, they are still unaware with their ownself and also of the spectacles through which the Government is viewing, and the scales by which the Government is measuring them. Hence, they neglect every thing which is either thrusted upon them from the outside world or apart from their traditional patterns of living.

Thus, it may be concluded that most of the respondents are

however, of the opinion that the statutory provisions framed for the overall development of the Scheduled Tribal Communities are essentially important to induce them to come out of their traditional surroundings to move the civilized and the cultured social life and also as an incentive to the tribals and their welfare. The educated tribal people and that part of the tribal population who is engaged in some sort of non-traditional occupations agree and admit the significance of the Government welfare schemes and the reservation policies for the eradication of the centuries old backwardness of the tribals.

Today almost all the educated tribal people, as the result of the present study prove have constantly been availing the facilities of reservations and alike of the other development plans made for the tribals in general. Under the statutory provisions a number of incentives have been given to make the tribals educated. Simultaneously, the educated tribal youths are also being given the maximum opportunities in government services so that they may lead economically a smooth life and also acquire honourable status in the broad spectrum of the society. Thus, the Government policies have not only make the tribals aware of their interests but also provoked them to lag behind their traditional life pattern and to follow the newly developed patterns of socio-economic life as to flow in the main stream of the Indian social life. Today they are trying to make their children more and more educated, and the educated ones come to urban or town areas to get education do not want to go back to their remote most villages and thus try to get some employment and also prefer to keep their wife and children with themselves.

Thus, the traditional domicile becomes the place for causal visit for them. In the town or urban areas they avail all the facilities pertaining to the modern life and also try to adopt the same patterns of life as the common people i.e. the civilized non tribal do. Thus, the literacy among tribals, their representation in government and other private or semi-government concerns, their migration to urban, their adherence with the non-traditional occupations with the result the detachment of the educated tribal people towards their own traditional style of life, laxity of the traditional norms, and to become flacid the control of the traditional family system, council of elders or the tribal council and also the changing form of the various social institution such as marriage, family, dormitory etc., all are the direct or indirect consequences of government welfare schemes which enabled the tribals to be educated, to be employed, and to boost up their traditional professions with the implementation of the new techniques and subsidized economic assistance and also provide them the most suitable opportunities to come in contact with the non-tribal groups by making available the transportation facilities unto the nearest most contiguous tribal regions. Thus, it may be concluded that hypothesis No. (a) i.e. "The statutory provisions are positively correlated with the process of cultural transformation of the Scheduled Tribe Communities of Uttarakhand", is proved to be true.

Hypothesis (b) "Education, means of transportation and communication have brought about changes in the social organization and the occupational structure of the scheduled tribal communities of Uttarakhand." To verify this hypothesis the impact of the above mentioned variables has been tested by knowing the reaction of the respondents about the following statements:

Statements	Reactions
(i) The expansion of education and the means of transformation and communication have helped the tribal people to come in contact with the non-tribal groups.	(i) Completely agree, partly agree, uncertain, completely disagree, disagree.
(ii) The contact with the non-tribal groups have induced the tribal people to follow the alien cultural traits.	(ii) Completely agree, partly agree, uncertain, completely disagree, disagree.
(iii) In what type of family would you like to live in?	(iii) Joint, nuclear.
(iv) On what consideration would you like to select the life partner of your children?	(iv) On the basis of the job, according to the choice of the children, according to the decision of the family head.

Table 23

Statement: Expansion of Education, means of transportation and communication is helpful in bringing about the Tribals in the contact of the Non-Tribals

Reactions	*Nos. of respondents of the first category*						*Nos. of respondents of the second category*						*Nos. of respondents the third category*						*Grand Total*
	Bho	*Bux*	*Tha*	*Raj*	*Jau*	*Total*	*Bho*	*Bux*	*Tha*	*Raj*	*Jau*	*Total*	*Bhu*	*Bux*	*Tha*	*Raj*	*Jau*	*Total*	
Completely agree	10	07	11	01	03	32 (08.65)	48	07	09	--	14	78 (62.40)	90	17	24	--	31	162 (79.02)	234 (33.43)
Agree	03	04	07	02	01	17 (04.59)	32	03	03	--	04	42 (33.60)	30	03	06	--	04	43 (20.98)	102 (14.57)
Uncertain	15	22	19	08	07	71 (19.19)	--	02	01	--	02	05 (04.00)	--	--	--	--	--		86 (12.29)
Completely disagree	75	44	33	09	13	174 (47.03)	--	--	--	--	--	--	--	--	--	--	--	--	186 (26.57)
Disagree	29	26	12	03	06	76 (20.54)	--	--	--	--	--	--	--	--	--	--	--	--	92 (13.14)
Total	132	103	82	23	30	370 (100%)	80	12	13	--	20	125 (100%)	120	20	30	--	35	205 (100%)	700 (100%)

Further, in order to know the changes occurred in the occupational structure, the respondents were asked about the traditional occupation of their forefathers, father's occupation and the present occupation of the respondents.

The reactions about the above mentioned statements of the respondents belonging to the different categories are being presented in Table 23.

Table 23 throws light on the reactions of the respondents belonging to the different categories. In the first category out of the total 370 respondents, the maximum number of the respondents i.e. 174 (47.00%) completely disagree with the statement that the expansion of the education and the means of transportation and communication is helpful in bringing about the tribal people in the contact of non-tribal groups. 76 (20.54%) respondents disagree with this statement, while 71 (19.19%) are uncertain to make any comment the favour/disfavour of the statement. Yet, there are 32 (8.65%) and 17 (4.59%) respondents who respectively completely agree and agree with the statement. Thus, it is clear that the majority of the respondents of the first category show their ignorance towards the education and the means of transportation and communication. For them the education and the means of transportation and communication have no meaning since they are still beyond the impact of all these factors. Infact, most of the respondents belonging to the first category are the domicile of the remote most rural areas where neither the educational institutions are established within the approach of the highly dispersed tribal villages nor the road transportation facilities are available in those area due to the hard and difficult geographical conditions. The means of communication like radio, newspapers, television have also no meaning for them because they are too illiterate to understand the use of all these things and also too poor to afford all these things. Yet some literate persons wish to keep at least the radio-set, through which they only listen the music programmes.

The education for the most of the respondents of the first category is uneconomic and therefore useless because every family member spontaneously become the earning member as soon as he or she attains the age of six years. The parents are the elderly members of the family therefore prefer to engage every family member belonging to the six and more years of age in some sort of economic pursuits. However, a handful respondents, who are literate admit the importance of the education and the means of communication and transportation which jointly can enable them to come in contact with the more civilized non-tribal groups and also can make them familiar with outer world activities. But the unavailability of all these medias and the acute poverty have altogether deprived them from the direct and indirect contact of the out groups and confined them within the ever-ending isolation and the gloom of ignorance. Thus, the illiteracy has interrupted the path of cognition of the respondents while the unavailability of the transportation facilities have obstructed their spatial mobility and the communication gap has broaden the gulf of the social distance with the modern society. On the contrary the majority of the respondents belonging to the second and third categories respectively 78 (62.40%) and 162 (79.02%) completely agree with the statement "The expansion of education and the means of transportation and communication have helped the tribal people to come in contact with the non-tribal groups." Moreover, 42 (33.60%) and 43 (20.98%) respondents respectively from second and third categories also agree with this statement. While a nominal numbers of the respondents i.e. 5 (4.00%) belonging to the second category and none from the third category are in the state of uncertainity. They could not express their views exactly towards any of the reactions already outlined in regard of the statement and presented before the respondents.

Thus, it may be concluded that the expansion of educational as well as the transportation and communication facilities have played an important role in bringing out the tribal people in the contact with the non tribal people. As a matter of fact, the respondents related particularly to the second and third categories reside in urban or town areas appeared to be familiar with the necessity of the education and the means of transportation and communication for their own development and also admit that the education is one of the powerful media for the overall development of the tribals. Hence, the awakened tribal people are giving education to their children and availing the facilities of reservation and thus trying to profess the non-traditional professions by going out of the traditional places of residence as well as the traditional pattern of living. In this regard the road transportation which linked atleast the different hill towns with the big cities has sped up the spatial mobility among the wilful tribal people. Alike of it, the means of communication such as; newspapers, radio, television which are available atleast in the town areas where the respondents of the second and third categories live and work have also helped the tribal people to know about the day to day news, activities and the plans in particular of the Government. Moreover, the intra-tribal interaction process has also awakened latently and indirectly the tribal people to protect and to secure their socio-economic as well as the constitutional interests. Thus, it is clear that education and the means of transportation and communication have helped the tribals and the non-tribals to come together on the one hand and also make them aware with their position in the national scene of the present day context on the other.

Besides this, the reaction in regard of the statement "The contact with the non tribal groups have induced the tribal people to follow the alien cultural traits" have been presented through Table 24.

It is clear from the Table 24 that the maximum 173 (46.76%) respondents out of the total 370, belonging to the first category completely agree with the statement and 58 (15.68%) respondents partly agree, 50 (13.51%) are not in the state of making any remark about the statement while 48 (12.97%) expressed their complete disagreement and the remaining 41 (11.08%) respondents disagree with the statement. Thus, it can obviously be asserted that the tribal people residing even in the villages also admit that with the contact of the non-tribal groups the tribal people have started to follow the same cultural traits as are observed by the latter ones. They further state that, the tribal people who go outside either for getting education or in search of jobs or engaged in some sort of business pursuits, have almost changed their life patterns, consequently, whenever they come back from outside they appeared to be an outstanding figure in the community particularly in their latest costumes, style of talking, behaving and even in ideologies. Alike of the first category, the most of the respondents i.e. 74 (59.80%) out of the total 125, belonging to the second category also completely agree with the statement and 28 (22.40%) respondents partly agree, 8 (6.40%) uncertain, 8 (6.40%) are completely disagree and the remaining 7 (5.60%) are disagree with the statement.

Table 24

Statement: The Contact with the Non-Tribal Groups has Induced the Tribal People to Follow the Alien Cultural Traits

Reactions	*Nos. of Respondents of the First Category*						*Nos. of Respondents of the Second Category*						*Nos. of Respondents of the Third Category*						*Grand Total*
	Bho	*Bux*	*Tha*	*Raj*	*Jau*	*Total*	*Bho*	*Bux*	*Tha*	*Raj*	*Jau*	*Total*	*Bho*	*Bux*	*Tha*	*Raj*	*Jau*	*Total*	
Completely agree	65	41	42	12	13	173 (46.76)	45	09	08	--	12	74 (59.20)	98	13	16	--	27	154 (75.12)	401 (57.29)
Partly agree	15	19	13	02	09	58 (15.68)	15	03	04	--	06	28 (22.40)	17	07	12	--	08	44 (21.47)	130 (18.57)
Uncertain	20	13	10	04	03	50 (13.51)	05	--	01	--	02	08 (06.40)	--	--	--	--	--	--	58 (08.28)
Completely disagree	18	17	08	03	02	48 (12.97)	08	--	--	--	--	08 (06.40)	05	--	02	--	--	07 (03.41)	63 (09.00)
Disagree	14	13	09	02	03	41 (11.08)	07	--	--	--	--	07 (05.60)	--	--	--	--	--	--	48 (06.86)
Total	132	103	82	23	30	370 (100%)	80	12	13	--	20	125 (100%)	120	20	30	25	35	205 (100%)	700 (100%)

In the third category out of the total 205 respondents, 154 (75.12%) are completely agree, 44 (21.46%) partly agree while only 4 (3.41%) have expressed complete disagreement with the statement. Thus, it may be concluded that with the result of the contact of the non-tribal groups, the tribal people under study have begun to imitate the cultural traits of the latter group. Today they appeared to be greatly influenced by the alien cultural groups with whom they frequently come in contact. Almost all the material cultural traits prevalent in the present day context are being used by the tribal people who have got their settlement in urban areas by virtue of the salaried jobs or the business engagements. Moreover, the respondents belonging to the third category, particularly who have been living outside of their native places since long are trying to get acceptance in the Hindu society by accepting the non-material cultural traits of the latter group. For instance, the Bhotiyas of Johar valley in Pithoragarh and the Khasas of Jaunsar-Babar have started to call themselves respectively as the Kumauni and the Garhwali Thakurs. However, they have not been absorbed so far, nor have they any position in the Hindu caste hierarchy.

Alike of the respondents related to the third category, the respondents belonging respectively to the first and second categories who in the close contact with the non-tribal groups also claim to be Hindus by religion and therefore make the false display of the abandonment of the unclean-non-Hindu habits, non-Hindu deities, major elements of tribal social customs, viz., animism (Khasa), youth club i.e. Ran-ban (Bhotiyas), polytheism (Rajis) etc. Though they are not in the state of complete abandonment of the non-Hindu habits, yet the gradual adoption of Hindu style of life may be considered as an indication towards the process of sanskritization. For instance, the tendency of taking the services of the Brahmin priest in the ritualistic performances by almost all the tribal communities under study, as well as the worship of the Hindu deities by them may be taken into account in the direction of sanskritization. The consolidated data of the three categories make it clear that the majority of the respondents i.e. 401 (57.29% out of the total 700 completely agree with the statement that, "the contact with the non-tribal groups have induced the tribal people to follow the alien cultural traits 130 (18.57%) partly agree, 58 (8.28%) are in the state of uncertainty, 63 (09.00%) completely disagree and the rest 48 (6.86%) disagree with the statement. Thus, it may be concluded that the tribal communities are in the process of absorbing the non-tribal cultural elements and simultaneously lagging behind their own traditional tribal cultural traits.

Moreover, in order to know, how far the impact of the various factors viz., education, means of transportation and communication and the occupational changes as powerful media of the modernization process have brought about changes in the attitudes of the respondents towards the social organization of the tribal communities, the respondents have been asked, "In what type of family would you like to live in." The following Table 25 throws light on the types of the families in which the respondents of the different categories prefer to live.

It is obvious that the majority of the respondents i.e. 350 (94.59%) out of the total 370 from different scheduled tribe communities belonging to the first category prefer to live in the joint families while only a nominal numbers of the respondents i.e. 20 (5.41%) of the same category prefer to live in the nuclear family. On the contrary most of the respondents of the second category i.e. 81 (64.80%) out of the total 125 prefer to live in the nuclear families and the rest 44 (35.20%) respondents still desirous to live in joint family. In case of the third category almost all the respondents, expressed their preferences for the nuclear families. Thus, it may be concluded that the occupational structure and the family types are invariably inter-related with one another and the occupational background of the respondents virtually determines their attitudes towards setting up of the family types they prefer to live in.

The respondents included in the first category are agriculturists and dwell in villages, hence they prefer to live in joint families because the agricultural economy particularly in rural hills need more manpower to carry out the agricultural jobs. Moreover, they are more traditional in ideology and therefore bear many sorts of hardships but never think about the separation from the joint family. The prevalent illiteracy has strenghtened their traditional feelings while the poverty has coerced them to cling with the joint family system since it has taken up the liabilities of all the family members and their necessities to be filled up.

On the contrary, the respondents relating to the second and third categories are respectively the businessmen and service men

Table 25

Attitudes of the Respondents Towards the Types of the Family

Types of Family	*Nos.of Respondents of the First Category*						*Nos. of Respondents of the Second Category*						*Nos. of Respondents of the Third Category*						*Grand Total*
	Bho	*Bux*	*Tha*	*Raj*	*Jau*	*Total*	*Bho*	*Bux*	*Tha*	*Raj*	*Jau*	*Total*	*Bho*	*Bux*	*Tha*	*Raj*	*Jau*	*Total*	
Nuclear	04	03	05	08	--	20 (05.41)	47	07	09	--	18	81 (64.81)	120	20	30	--	35	205 (100.00)	306 (43.71)
Joint	228	100	77	15	30	350 (94.59)	33	05	04	--	02	44 (35.20)	--	--	--	--	--	--	394 (56.29)
Total	232	103	82	23	30	340 (100%)	80	12	13	--	20	125 (100%)	120	20	30	--	35	205 (100%)	700 (100%)

eventually they live in town outside of their native places and away from the original families. Since, it is neither possible to keep the whole of the joint family in towns due to the lack of the housing facilities, nor it is possible to meet out smoothly the needs of all the members of the joint family and nor it is posible to live alone for a man engaged in any service or the business pursuits because he also felt the necessity of the family atmosphere, resultantly he always prefers to keep his wife and children with him. Besides this the business and the service based economy by nature develops the materialistic and subsequently, the individualistic feelings within the person concerned. Hence, he takes up only those responsibilities which are immediately concerning to him. Thus, alike of the occupational factor, the education and the literacy percentage also determines the attitudes of the people in regard of the different elements of their social organization.

The respondents belonging to the third category are almost educated and employed in different government services and express their preferences in favour of nuclear families. Thus, it may be concluded that the high percentage of literacy is positively correlated with the nuclear family system. The same findings have also been extracted in regard of the respondents towards the considerations in selecting the life partner of their children. Table 26 throws light on the results.

It is observed from Table 26 that out of the total 370 respondents relating to the first category 275 (74.32%) respondents are of the opinion that the decision of the head of the family will be considered as final for the selection of the life partner of their children because it is only the head of the family who is supposed to carry out the liabilities of the weddings of the children of the family. 68 (18.38%) respondents give importance to the choice of the children, while the remaining 27 (7.30%) prefer to consider the status of the family as the basic consideration for selection. Since, the respondents of the first category are quite away from the impact of the education and the means of transportation and communication, they are still away from the impact of urbanization and alike of the other factors of planned change, hence they prefer to follow the same route as has been followed by their forefathers since long. Their consideration are, therefore, appeared to be traditionally motivated, because in closed and traditional soci-

Table 26

Considerations in Selecting the Life-Partner of the Children

Considerations in selecting the life partner of the child	*Nos. of Respondents of the First Category*						*Nos. of Respondents of the Second Category*						*Nos. of Respondents of the Third Category*						*Grand Total*
	Bho	*Bux*	*Tha*	*Raj*	*Jau*	*Total*	*Bho*	*Bux*	*Tha*	*Raj*	*Jau*	*Total*	*Bho*	*Bux*	*Tha*	*Raj*	*Jau*	*Total*	
On the basis of educational standard	--	--	--	--	--	--	16	03	03	--	04	26 (20.80)	65	09	13	--	17	104 (50.73)	130 (18.57)
On the basis of family status	16	05	06	--	--	27 (07.30)	22	03	03	--	04	32 (25.60)	07	02	05	--	04	18 (08.78)	77 (11.00)
On the basis of the job	--	--	--	--	--	--	38	05	06	--	09	58 (46.40)	35	07	09	--	09	60 (29.27)	118 (16.86)
According to the choice of the children	32	08	18	03	07	68 (18.32)	02	01	01	--	03	07 (05.60)	13	02	03	--	05	23 (11.22)	98 (14.00)
According to the decision of the family head	84	90	58	20	23	275 (74.32)	02	--	--	--	--	02 (01.60)	--	--	--	--	--	--	277 (39.57)
Total	132	103	82	23	30	370 (100%)	80	12	13	--	20	125 (100%)	120	20	30	--	35	205 (100%)	700 (100%)

eties the choice of the head of the family and the status of the family counts more in decision making particularly in regard of the settlement of the marriage relations. In the tribal communities under study, the mutual consent and elopement is considered a way of acquiring mates and hence the choice of the children, to some extent has some weight in selecting the life partners.

On the contrary the maximum respondents related to the second category i.e. 58 (46.40%) give importance to the jobs of the person concern with whom they wish to settle the marriage relation of their children. 32 (25.60%) respondents give preference to the status of the particular family, 26 (20.80%) to the educational standard, 7 (5.60%) to the choice of the children while only 2 (1.60%) give the importance to the decision of the family head. In fact, the respondents of the second category are businessmen and therefore give preferential importance respectively to the jobs of the person concern, status of a particular family, the educational standard, the choice of the children and lastly to the decision of the head of the family in the selection of the life partner of the children.

But the attitudes of the respondents belonging to the third category towards the different considerations vary from the rest of the respondents. As most of the respondents i.e. 104 (50.73%) out of the total 205 prefer the high educational standard as the main consideration in selecting the life partner, while 60 (29.27%) prefer to the jobs, 23 (11.22%) to the choice of the children and the rest 60 (29.27%) to the family status. But none of the respondents prefer to the decision of head of the family. In fact, the respondents included in the third category are educated and employed in government services, they frequently come in contact with the non-tribal people and also look on their cultural patterns and subsequently try to absorb and assimilate them in their own life. Thus, it is clear that the changing occupation of the tribals and the growing education have simultaneously been replacing the traditionally prevalent old tribal considerations i.e. the decision of the head of the family as well as the methods of acquiring the mates i.e. the mutual consent and elopement (the choice of the children).

At present, every educated tribal individual give first priority to the educational standard of the person with whom he wishes to settle the wedding relation of the children, the second priority is given to the jobs of the person, third preference is given to the

Table 27

Occupations	Nos. of Respondents of the First Category						Nos. of Respondents of the Second Category						Nos. of Respondents of the Third Category						Grand Total
	Bho	Bux	Tha	Raj	Jau	Total	Bho	Bux	Tha	Raj	Jau	Total	Bho	Bux	Tha	Raj	Jau	Total	
Traditional Occupation																			
Hunting/Fishing	--	22	35	07	07	71	--	01	01	--	01	03	--	01	11	--	08	20	94
Food gathering	--	56	42	16	05	119	21	01	01	--	03	26	24	11	16	--	04	55	200
Cultivation	14	25	05	--	15	59	23	07	08	--	12	50	21	06	03	--	18	48	157
Animal Husbandry	18	--	--	--	03	21	14	03	03	--	04	24	30	02	--	--	05	37	82
Business	100	--	--	--	--	100	22	--	--	--	--	22	45	--	--	--	--	45	167
Govt. Service	--	--	--	--	--	--	--	--	--	--	--	--	--	--	--	--	--	--	--
Total	132	103	82	23	30	370	80	12	13	--	20	125	120	20	30	--	35	205	700
Father's Occupation																			
Cultivation	--	44	52	17	05	118	--	04	05	--	08	17	--	02	06	--	04	12	147
Animal Husbandry	--	--	--	--	--	--	--	--	--	--	--	--	--	--	--	--	--	--	--
--																			
Both Cultivation and Animal Husbandry	30	59	30	06	25	150	35	07	06	--	09	57	50	14	18	--	23	105	312
Business	102	--	--	--	--	102	45	01	02	--	03	51	40	--	--	--	--	40	103
Govt. Service	--	--	--	--	--	--	--	--	--	--	--	--	30	04	06	--	08	48	48
Total	132	103	82	23	30	370	80	12	13	--	20	125	120	20	30	--	35	205	700
Present Occupation																			
Cultivation	--	12	17	09	--	38	--	--	--	--	--	--	--	--	--	--	--	--	38
Business	--	--	--	--	--	--	80	12	13	--	20	125	--	--	--	--	--	--	125
Cultivation and Animal Husbandry	132	91	65	14	30	332	--	--	--	--	--	--	--	--	--	--	--	--	332
Govt. Service	--	--	--	--	--	--	--	--	--	--	--	--	120	20	30	--	35	205	205

choice of the children and the last consideration to the status of the particular family but it seems none of the educated tribal prefer the traditionally motivated decision of the head of the family. It appears that the educated tribal people and those who are engaged in some sort of non-tribal occupations have become more rational, awakened and therefore their attitudes are changing even in regard of the different aspects of the tribal social organization particularly to those which obstructed their socio-occupational mobility. Hence, more effort has also been made to observe the occupational mobility among the different tribal communities. Table 27 throws light on the different occupations of the different generations so that the occupational changes occurred in tribal communities may be understood.

As regards the traditional occupations of the forefathers, the respondents of the Bhotiya community belonging to the first category express their views on the basis of their memories and the sayings transmitted to them by their past generations. In this regard most of the Bhotiya respondents i.e. 100 (75.76%) out of the total 132 state that the business i.e. the trade of woolen stuffs, salt and other commodities was the traditional occupation of their forefathers. While 18 (13.64%) respondents said that the animal husbandry was the traditional occupation and the remaining 14 (10.61%) expressed the views in favour of the cultivation as the occupation of their forefathers. In case of the Buxas, the maximum 56 (54.37%) respondents out of the total 103 belonging to the first category admitted the food gathering as the main traditional occupation of their forefathers while the 25 (24.27%) and 22 (21.36%) respondents respectively indicated the cultivation and the hunting/fishing as the traditional occupation of their forefathers.

Alike of Buxas, the majority of the Tharu respondents i.e. 42 (51.22%) out of the total 82 stated the food gathering as the traditional occupation of their forefathers, while 35 (42.68%) and 5 (6.10%) respondents respectively indicated towards the hunting/fishing and the cultivation as the traditional occupation of their forefathers. Among Rajis the maximum 16 (69.57%) respondents out of the total 23 admitted that their forefathers were the food gatherers and 7 (30.43%) respondents stated the hunting/fishing as the main traditional occupation of their forefathers. In case of Jaunsaries, 15 (50%) respondents have stated the cultivation as the traditional occupation of their forefathers, while 7 (23.33%), 5 (16.67%) and 3 (10.00%) respondents respectively admitted the hunting/fishing, the food gathering and the animal husbandry as the main occupations of their forefathers.

Besides this, the respondents of the second and the third category have also expressed almost the same attitudes and the reactions towards the traditional occupations of their forefathers and on the basis of which it may be concluded that the hunting/fishing food gathering and the crude type of cultivation were the traditional occupations of the forefathers of the respondents belonging to the Buxa, Tharu, Raji and Jaunsari communities in particular. While the Bhotiyas, unlike of the rest of the scheduled tribal communities under study has been traditionally a commercial community since long.

Moreover, the respondents of the first category were further asked to tell the occupation of their fathers. In response of this question most of the respondents from Buxa, Tharu, Raji and Khasa community have stated that the cultivation and animal husbandry both, were the major occupations of their fathers. But in case of the Bhotiyas the majority of the respondents have again stated that the business was the main occupation of their fathers. There is however, some slight changes in the responses of the respondents related to the second and third categories. As Table 27 exhibits that the father of the majority of the respondents were although cultivators and cattle breeders both, yet some people have started to profess the business occupation particularly in Buxa, Tharu and Khasa community alike of the Bhotiyas. But none of the Rajis was found engaged in any sort of business pursuits. In the same way the majority of the respondents i.e. 105 (51.22%) included in the third category have also indicated that the occupations of their fathers were the cultivation and animal husbandry both. Moreover, there are respondents i.e. 48 (23.41%) and 40 (19.51%) in the third category who respectively stated that their fathers were the servicemen and businessmen but Rajis have still not any representation in the field of business and services. But in regard of the present occupations of the respondents of the different tribal communities belonging to the three categories, it may be said that the majority of the population dwell in the rural areas and subsist on the agricultural economy while some people have started the business or the service occupations. However, Raji is only the tribal community who absolutely subsist on the traditional type of crude cultivation and animal husbandry so far.

Thus, on the basis of the data shown in the Table No 27 it may be concluded that a marked change from traditional occupation to modern occupation is visible. For instance, the traditional family occupation of the Bhotiya respondents was the business but today with the ban on the international trade with Tibet and China, they have moulded themselves towards cultivation, animal husbandry and alike of the subsidiary jobs as well as the government services and a settled business. In the same way, the respondents of the rest of the Scheduled Tribal communities have also admitted that there is change in the occupational structure from the traditional tribal occupation to the occupations in the generation of their father and subsequently from father's generation to the present generation of the respondents. Because the settled cultivation, animal husbandry, business and the government services were not the part or the traditional occupational structure of the Scheduled Tribal communities under reference. But the occupational changes have invariably been the resultant of the statutory provisions formulated and implemented in tribal areas for their over all development. The modern education and the means of transport and communication have played an important role in bringing about the occupational changes. Thus, the foregoing analysis of the facts proved it that hypothesis (b) "The role of education, means of transport and communication have brought about changes in the social organization and the occupational structure of the Scheduled Tribal communities of Uttarakhand" is valid.

References

1. The Constitution of India, Article 46, Prakashan Niyantrak, Bharat Sarkar, Civil Lines, Delhi, April 1986, p. 15.

2. *Ibid.*, p. 80

3. *Ibid.*, p. 116.

4. *Ibid.*, pp. 90-91.

5. *Ibid.*, pp. 113-114.

6. *Ibid.*, p. 115.

7. *Ibid.*, pp. 4-5.

8. *Ibid.*, p. 115.

9. Government of India, Ministry of Home Affairs, Tribal Development Division, New Delhi, The News Letter, Oct. 1979, p. 1.

7

TRIBAL AND NON-TRIBAL INTER-RELATION SYSTEM AND THE PROCESS OF CULTURAL TRANSFORMATION

Inter-relations as practised and enforced in between the tribal dominant groups and of the minority non-tribal groups vis-Lvis differ significantly from one another. An objective analysis of the inter-relation system as it compares to the normative model will contribute to an understanding of the dynamics of stability and change in the tribal socio-cultural organisation as well as of the non-tribals. Though in its basic sense the tribals as such, with all its general characteristics, is a peculiar phenomena, yet with the course of time the process of absorbing the non-tribal cultural elements vis-a-vis the abandonment of the pre-sanskritized tribal elements, has paved the way to the tribals to get adimission into the caste hierarchy of the Hindu social organisation. In the present chapter the researcher is mainly concerned with the analysis of the inter-relation system in between the tribal and the non-tribal groups and also to observe, how and in what extent the tribal communities under reference are in the state of absorbing the alien cultural elements in order to acquire a distinct position in the Hindu caste hierarchy.

As a matter of fact, the tribal communities of today are not in the state of complete isolation. Because of the introduction of the various processes of planned social change, the tribal people are frequently coming in contact with other communities. The spatial and the occupational mobility, as well as the aspirations for the vertical social mobility have motivated the tribals to come under the influence of the non-tribal groups and made wider the scope of their social inter-relations. Today if we go through the various socio-cultural levels of the tribal communities in general, we find that the majority of the tribal population still confined within the traditional peripheries, while a small part of the tribal population have come out of their traditional socio-ecological surroundings and yet again, there is a middle group of the tribals which cuts across the two ends of the tribal socio-cultural system in general. The difference of the socio-cultural standard of the different groups determines the nature of their inter-relations with non-tribals, their psychology in regard to the alien cultural group and its various elements as well as the capacity of value judgment and self-appraisal in respect of the whole of the society.

Today the self-sufficient nature of the socio-economic, religious and political aspects of the tribal community have undergone a numerous drastic changes. They have comparatively more opportunities to be involved with the non-tribals and to interact with them. Thus, the interaction process eventually develops the inter-relationships between the tribals and the non-tribals which ultimately reproduce the different dimensions of the socio-cultural system which is of course inquisitive for the social scientist. Though a number of studies have largely been conducted by different scholars, in regard of the interaction process in between the tribals and the non-tribals, Mandaelbaum has studied the nature of interaction process among the Nilgiri tribals i.e. the Toda, Kota, Badaga and Kurumba and the non-tribals including the European and Hindus. In the study, the scholar has observed how the road communication has brought together the tribals in contact of the non-tribals and what type of the reactions have come forward.

Surjeet Sinha has also studied the interaction process between the Hindus and the Bhumij. The Bhumij are relatively simple by nature and an isolated tribal group while the neighbouring Hindus are the advanced peasant community. The close proximity of the both groups have led to the transformation of the Bhumij into the level of peasantry through gradual dissolution of ecological barrier of a forest and hilly lands between them and socalled Hindu peasantry. Moreover, there are studies conducted in the field of inter-tribal relations too. In this regard, Dube has completed a study of inter tribal relations in three cultural areas :

(i) the Gond Kumar-Bhumij, area of Chhatisgarh,

(ii) the Gond Kolam area of Adilabad, and

(iii) the Kaya hill Reddy, area of Warangal.

Saileshwar Prasad[1] has also made an attempt to identify the nature and extent of interaction between the three tribals i.e., the Maler, the Mal-Pahariya and the Santhal and also in between the tribals and the non-tribals. B.B. Goswami[2] has presented a paper on the topic entitled, "The Tribes of Assam: A Few Comments on Their Social and Cultural Ties With the Non tribes". The paper deals with the socio-cultural relationship between the tribes and non-tribes of Assam who live in varied ecological conditions, with their different economic organisations, linguistic groupings, social structures and religions. Thus, the scholar has tried to understand the nature and the degree of articulation/isolation of the tribal communities with/from the larger communities of Assam.

D.N. Majumdar[3] has also made a study of tribe-caste continuum and the process of sanskritization among the Bodo speaking tribes of the Garo Hills. In this study Majumdar has attempted to show that the transformation of a tribal group into a group in the greater Hindu society with a distinct position in the caste hierarchy may come about without any occupational specialisation within the group or by the group as a whole.

The present chapter has been focussed on the tribal and non-tribal interaction process and its spontaneous results which come particularly in two forms i.e. the articulation of the tribals with the non-tribals and the isolation of the tribal communities with the non-tribals. In this concern some hypotheses have been formulated to achieve the objective results. These are as follows:

(i) Inspite of the impact of the different cultural groups the tribal people of Uttarakhand, to maintain their own identity and self respect, are not in the state of complete abandonment of the pre-sanskritized cultural elements.

(ii) Economic, political, educational and the religious spheres are the main centres of tribal and non-tribal interactions with the result the tribals of Uttarakhand have begun to share the cultural traits and the dialect of the non-tribals of the respective regions they live in.

(iii) The cultural contact with the non-tribal communities has accelerated the process of cultural transformation.

(iv) Traditional taboos which play an important role in the determination of the nature of the commensal and connubial relations of the tribals with the non-tribals have interrupted the way of the cultural transformation of the tribe into the caste.

To verify the above mentioned hypotheses the respondents were asked a number of questions and the counter questions from the already structured schedule and also observed intensively their behaviour patterns and the mode of expression as to find out the psychological validation of the information collected through the respondents. Thus, in order to test the validity of the hypothesis No (i) the informants were asked various questions pertaining to their attitudes towards the pre-sanskritised cultural elements and the state of the tribalism in perspective of the cultural contacts of the non-tribals.

Attitudes Towards the Pre-sanskritised Cultural Elements and the State of the Tribalism

An attempt has been made to understand whether the tribal people want to maintain their traditional cultural elements as such for the maintenance of their tribal identity and also their reactions towards the utterance of the term 'tribe' used to denote them by the out groups as well as of the government machinery. They were further asked, how far the cultural originality is effective in the maintenance of the self respect and the identification of a given community. The following Table 28 throws light on the reactions and the information collected in regard of the above mentioned statements.

Table 28

Attitude Towards the Pre-Sanskritized Cultural Elements

Statement	Pre Sanskritized cultural elements are necessary for maintaining of the self respect of the tribals and their identification in broad canvas of the society.																	
Reactions	*Respondents of First Category*						*Respondents of Second Category*						*Respondents of Third Category*					*Grand Total*
	Bho	*Bux*	*Tha*	*Raj*	*Jau*	*Total*	*Bho*	*Bux*	*Tha*	*Raj*	*Jau*	*Total*	*Bho*	*Bux*	*Tha*	*Raj*	*Jau*	*Total*	
Completely agree	86	58	52	16	17	229 (61.89)	35	06	07	—	07	55 (44.00)	—	—	04	—	—	04 (1.95)	288 (41.14)
Partly agree	19	16	14	06	09	64 (17.30)	20	03	03	—	5	31 (24.80)	—	3	05	—	—	8 (3.40)	103 (14.71)
Uncertain	10	25	09	—	01	45 (12.16)	05	01	—	—	01	07 (05.60)	—	01	01	—	-	02 (0.98)	54 (07.71)
Completely disagree	08	01	04	01	—	14 (03.78)	15	02	01	—	04	22 17.60)	80	15	18	—	25	138 (67.32)	174 (24.86)
Disagree	09	03	-3	—	03	18 (04.87)	05	—	02	—	03	10 (08.00)	40	01	02	—	10	53 (25.85)	81 (11.58)
TOTAL	132	103	82	23	30	370	80	12	13	—	20	125	120	20	30	—	35	205	700

The table depicts that the respondents of the different categories have difference of opinion about the pre-sanskritised cultural elements and their preservation for the maintenance of the self-respect and also of the identification of the tribals in the broad canvas of the contemporary complex society. Here, the term 'pre-sanskritised' denotes to the cultural elements of the scheduled-tribal communities viz. the traditional patterns of living, costumes, food habits, religious rites, religious beliefs and practices, deities religious symbols, economy, occupational structure, the modes of the control of human behaviour, the non-Aryan language and the so-called unclean habits etc. by the observance of which a given community maintains not only its self respect but also the cultural originality for its identification amongst the diversified complex society of today.

The major percentage of the respondents belonging to the first category i.e. 61.89 percent (229) observe verbatim almost all their pre-sanskritized cultural elements, 17.30 percent (64) are partly agree and admit that they don't have the exact knowledge about their original forms of the cultural elements, yet they by seer nodding acquaintance try to present its picture but in some refined form as well as in the meaningful sense. For instance, the dormitory system among the Bhotiyas is still alive but as they assert it, has changed almost its traditional appropriateness, as well as the organisational form. However, there are 3.78 percent (14) respondents who completely disagree and the rest 4.87 percent (18) have expressed their disagreement with this statement that the pre-sanskritized cultural elements are necessary for the maintenance of the self respect of the tribals and their identification in the society as a whole. The rest 12.16 percent (45) respondents are uncertain to state any reactions in favour/disfavour of the statement.

In the second category, out of the total 125 respondents the maximum 44.00 percent (55) and 24.80 percent (31) have expressed respectively their complete and partial agreement with the statement, while 17.60 percent (22) and 8.0C percent t (10) respondents have respectively negative reactions towards the statement and the rest 5.60 percent (7) respondents were silent in this concern.

On the contrary, the responses of the respondents belonging to the third category are quietly adverse than the respondents of the previous two categories. As most of the respondents i.e. 138

(67.32%) completely disagree, 53 (25.85%) are disagree while the nominal percentage of the respondents i.e. 8 (3.90%), 4 (1.95%) and 2 (0.98%) are respectively disagree, completely disagree and uncertain in regard of the statement. Thus, if we analyse the category-wise attitudes of the respondent units, there we find that the majority of the respondents respectively from the first to the second category are conscious enough with their self respect and tribal identification and therefore wish to preserve almost all the pre-sanskritized cultural elements of the respective community they belong to. For instance, the "Ran Parishad", the "Tharu Parishad", "Buxa Parishad" and "Khasa Parishad" etc. are the cultural cum political organisations formed for the protection, preservation and development of the respective tribal culture as well as their socio-economic cultural and political interests. I still remember, a Bhotiya-respondent belonging to the second category (means from business class) offered a big amount for the composition of the 'Ran' script i.e. the non-Aryan dialect, and also proclaimed that whoever can compose and bring in existence the script of the 'Ran-dialect' will be awarded a big amount as a token of honour on behalf of the 'Ran-community'. Further, the Holi-dance without Holi festival by the so called shy and reserved nature Tharu men and women and their desire to come forward to present their special Holi dance before an outsider like me, in itself shows their love and mental attachment with their own culture and its preservation as well as the exemplary manifestation of it for their identification. Moreover, offering of the wine-cup by the virgin to every new comer or the visitor or the guest respectively in Khasa and Bhotiya community particularly only by those who still belong to the remote most traditional abodes (belonging to the first category in this study samples) and the tradition of washing the hands and the feet of the guest before and after meal by the lady of the family among Khasas and to seat even an unknown visitor on the cot covered with neat carpet by Tharu women are some exemplary manifestations of the cultural behaviour patterns of the different tribal communities and their adherence and attachment towards them.

On the contrary the respondents who are educated, employed in Government services, frequently come in contact with the more civilized non-tribal group and greatly influenced by the modernization process as well as the urban culture, (belonging to the third category) possess the contrary opinion than that of the rest of the respondents belonging to the first and second categories. Such a group of respondents appeared to be completely accultured, as the members of it claim to be 'Rajput' or 'Kshatriya' by caste and place the word 'Singh' with their name and wish to flow with the main-stream of the rest of the society by participating in almost all the non-tribal Hindu festivals and its celebration, abandonment of the so called unclean habits such as, to extract wine, and use of wine as a ritualistic commodity in the performance of the life cycle rituals as well as in the worship of the deities, abandonment of the traditional costume, the sharing of Aryan language, desire to use of the modern electric appliances as well as the means of communication and transportation within the capacity, the laxity in the rules/taboos of the commensality and connubiality are some common indications to show the desire for the articulation/ isolation of the tribal people belonging to the third category in this study with/from the non-tribal Hindus and their cultural elements. Yet it is strange that they are still keen to avail all the possible facilities under constitutional frame of reference in the name of the scheduled tribe and also wish to avail the reservation policies in future too.

However, the consolidated data pertaining to the attitudes of the total respondent units exhibit that the majority of the tribal population i.e. 41.14 percent (288) and 14.71 percent (103) respectively appeared to be completely and partly agree for the maintenance and preservation of their pre-sanskritized cultural elements as to make their different and outstanding identification in the society, while the rest of the respondents expressed their disagreement directly or indirectly with their pre-sanskritized cultural elements since they do not want to be a frog in the well any longer. In fact, the majority of the tribal population still reside in the same wave length as they were before while a little percentage of the tribal population is educated and engaged in some non-traditional occupations, resultantly their attitudes have gradually been changing with the change of their educational standard as well as the occupational and spatial mobility. However, it may be asserted that the majority of the tribal people are not in the state of complete abandonment of their pre-sanskritized cultural elements. Even the educated and the employed tribal people who have got their settlement in urban areas possess their tribal symbol in one form or the other. For instance, to set up the flag in front of house or the tying up of the flags in a rope around the periphery of the places of the residents is the symbol to denote the domicile at the Bhotiyas. Thus, it may be concluded that the tribal people inspite of their educational and occupational variations maintain their pre-sanskritized cultural elements as to make possible their identification in society.

The Articulation/Isolation of the Tribal Communities with/from the Cultural System of the Non-Tribal Groups

The respondents have also been asked whether the impact of cultural contact has made possible the articulation/isolation of tribal communities with/from the cultural system of the non-tribal groups. In this regard the responses of the respondents got through the direct contact are being presented in Table 29.

The consolidated data makes it clear that the maximum 176 (47.59%) respondents belonging to the first category are completely disagree, 78 (21.08%) have expressed seer disagreement and 41 (11.08%) were not in the state of making any sort of comment in favour or disfavour of the statement. Yet, there are 48 (12.97%) and 27 (7.30%) respondents who have expressed respectively the complete agreement and partial agreement with the statement. In fact, the respondents of this category are the cultivators and dwell in the aloof and the remote rural areas hence they occasionally come in contact of the alien cultural groups and therefore less articulated and more isolated from them. Yet, the frequency of articulation and isolation is not absolute, they are relatively articulated/isolated with/from the non-tribal groups.

In regard of the respondents relating to the second category the most of the respondents i.e. 76 (60.80%), 39 (31.20%) and 10 (8.00%) are respectively completely agree, partly agree, and uncertain while none of the respondents have expressed their disagreement towards the statement. The respondents of the second category who belong to the business class group and have their settlement in urban or the town areas, naturally have more opportunities to come frequently in contact with the non-tribal groups as well as to participate equally with the non-tribals and their cultural

Table 29

The Impact of the Cultural Contact has made possible the Articulation/Isolation of the Tribal Communities with/from the Cultural System of the Non-tribal Groups

Statement Reactions	*Nos. of the respondents of the First Category*						*Nos. of the respondents of the Second Category*						*Nos of respondents of the Third Category*						*Grand Total*
	Bho	*Bux*	*Tha*	*Raj*	*Jau*	*Total*	*Bho*	*Bux*	*Tha*	*Raj*	*Jau*	*Total*	*Bho*	*Bux*	*Tha*	*Raj*	*Jau*	*Total*	
Completely agree	10	12	10	07	09	48	48	08	07	—	13	76	95	11	14	—	32	152	276
						(12.97)						(60.80)						(74.14)	(39.43)
Partly agree	07	08	06	03	03	27	28	03	04	—	04	39	20	05	15	—	03	43	109
						(07.30)						(31.20)						(20.98)	(15.58)
Uncertain	15	08	11	02	05	41	04	01	02	—	03	10	05	04	01	—	—	10	61
						(11.08)						(08.00)						(04.88)	(08.71)
Completely disagree	76	48	39	06	07	176	—	—	—	—	—	—	—	—	—	—	—	--	176
						(47.54)													(25.14)
Disagree	24	27	16	05	06	78	—	—	—	—	—	—	—	—	—	—	—	—	78
						(21.08)													(11.14)
TOTAL	132	103	82	23	30	370	80	12	13	—	20	125	120	20	30	—	35	205	700
						(100%)						(100%)						(100%)	(100%)

activities along with the observance of their own cultural traits.

Alike of the respondents of the second category, most of the respondents belonging to the third category i.e. 152 (74.14%) completely agree, 43 (20.98%) partially agree and the rest 10 (4.88%) respondents are uncertain. Thus, it may be concluded that the tribal people, who are in frequent contact with non-tribal groups have comparatively more articulation with the cultural system of non-tribals while the uneducated and the isolated tribals who live in hills and valleys away from the contact of the alien groups have comparatively more isolation from the non-tribal cultural system.

Today mostly the educated tribals, as is observed in regard of the Bhotiyas and the Jaunsaris are largely in the process of moving into the caste society. They are trying to be integrated with their neighbouring larger Hindu community. Among Jaunsaris, we can observe a particular system of caste hierarchy. There are Brahmins, Kshatriya, Vyashya and Sudra, the social statuses and roles are well defined, yet the prevalent forms of 'Anuloma' and 'Pratiloma' marriages are the remaining traces of their tribalism. Among Bhotiyas of Johar, the tribal people posted in some Government posts are not ready to identify themselves as the scheduled tribe. On the contrary, the uneducated tribal population belonging to every tribal community under study have broadened socially, economically, politically the gap between them and the non-tribal Hindus. For instance, the Rajis of Pithoragarh Hills and the Tharus and Buxas of Tarai and Bhabar abstain the usual salutation and the normal social dealings with the neighbouring Hindus and the alien groups.

On the basis of some undesirable incident in past the tribals, it seems, have made the negative conviction towards the non-tribals that always induce them to keep themselves away from them. Thus, the degree and nature of articulation/isolation of tribals with/from the cultural system of the non-tribals is greatly influenced by the standard of the education which ultimately enabled the tribals to come in contact with the non-tribals and subsequently to profess the emerging new professions, modern ways of life and the alien cultural traits and vis-a-vis. Thus, it may be concluded that the tribal people whether educated or uneducated business class, service class or cultivators are not in the state of complete abandonment of the pre-sanskritized cultural elements inspite of the impact of the different cultural groups and thus, they have still maintained their identity and self respect.

The Spheres of Interaction with Non-Tribal Groups

The tribe population have all along been the important part, rather indifferent segment of the Indian society. On the cultural and linguistic plane, the tribes have never been markedly different from the neighbouring non-tribes. The eminent social scientist Ghurye has also admitted that the "so called aborigines" in India share the culture and language of the non-aboriginal Hindu rural communities of the respective regions they live in. Since long, the tribe people have been in close contact of their more civilized neighbours. Ethnically and culturally they were not distinct from the rest of the population. But gradually with the passage of time the gap between the tribe and the non-tribe groups was broadened by the imperial colonial power and it has widened in recent years after 1947.

Today the politically. motivated interest group seems to locate socially, economically, culturally, the tribal people in a distinct position and also demands for the distinctive treatment for the tribals on behalf of the government. On the other hand, the welfare government in India seems to be committed to treat equally, in its slogan, developmental objects, welfare policies and so on for all the sections of the society. The introduction of various processes of modernization have provided better opportunities to the tribal people to come in contact with their neighbouring more civilized groups and also caused them to move out of their isolation, remote hills and jungles and also provoked to get enterance at least in the contiguous plains and the groups of the people and their cultural patterns. The changing economy of the tribals as well as their aspirations for better living have simultaneously brought them in close contact with the non-tribals.

Today there are number of spheres of social life where the tribals and non-tribals come closer and interact with each other. This interaction process has developed the different dimensions of the inter-relation system. Yet there are tribal groups who have still maintained their isolation in the remotest hills and jungles, never-

theless the barriers of their isolation are being cracked by their unsatisfied economic needs and the longings to transform the patterns of living.

In regard of the Scheduled Tribal communities under reference, an effort has also been made to observe the degree and the nature of interaction process in between the tribals and the non-tribals. The following table depicts the data pertaining to the different spheres of the interaction process.

Table 30

Scheduled Tribes and the Spheres of Interactions with Non-Tribals

Spheres of inter-action	*Bhotiya*		*Buxa*		*Tharu*		*Raji*		*Jaunsari*	
	Yes	*No*	*Yes*	*No*	*Yes*	*No*	*Yes*	*No*	*Yes*	*No*
First Category										
Economic sphere	132	-	103	-	82	-	23	-	30	-
Political sphere	40	92	60	43	56	26	16	07	07	23
Educational sphere	05	127	11	92	22	60	04	19	04	26
Religious sphere	84	48	45	58	41	041	04	19	05	25
Second Category										
Economic sphere	80	-	12	-	13	-	-	-	20	-
Political sphere	80	-	12	-	13	-	-	-	20	-
Educational sphere	47	33	09	03	09	04	-	-	12	80
Religious sphere	69	11	07	05	08	05	-	-	20	-
Third Category										
Economic sphere	120	-	20	-	30	-	-	-	35	-
Political sphere	120	-	20	-	30	-	-	-	35	-
Educational sphere	120	-	20	-	30	-	-	-	35	-
Religious sphere	120	-	20	-	30	-	-	-	35	-

It is observed that there are four major spheres of social life of the scheduled tribal communities where they come in contact with the non-tribals and interact with one another. Almost all the respondents of all the three categories admit that in economic sphere they have more opportunities to interact with the non-tribals, because the tribals have not the economic sufficiency as it was before. They are not satisfied with their traditional type of economic subsistence pattern. They are more aware with the latest techniques of cultivation as well as the extra agricultural economic persuits viz. business, and the services (both the government and non-government) and their socio-economic importance in contemporary society. Thus, on the one hand, the increasing economic dependency has compelled the tribal people to come out of their traditional economic system and on the other the attraction of the white collar jobs and the status and power implies with them have also motivated the tribals to come in contact with the non-tribals. Even the cultivators go to sell the agricultural products in market places. For instance, the Bhotiyas, who were the traditional traders, even today prepare some particular woolen stuffs i.e. the blanket, 'Thulma', 'Chutaka', 'sweaters', 'shawls', 'woolen carpets' etc. and also go to sell them in market places in local fairs and in the adjoining non-tribal villages. They have the best technique to make bargaining with non-tribals and to trap them to purchase the goods prepared by them.

The Rajis also prepare some wooden vessels and the agricultural appliances and go to sell them in the nearest market place and the neighbouring villages. Moreover, as an agricultural labourer they are all related with the neighbouring Kumaunies. The Tharus and the Buxas have rather better opportunities as they seasonally go for selling food grains in market and the other group i.e. the contractors, Banjaras themselves come to their places to purchase the agricultural products.

Alike of the rest of the tribal communities, the Khasas of the Jaunsar Bawar are the best producer of the edible roots or the root vegetables such as the ginger, Ghuiyan, Tarurha, Gaderi, turmeric, onion etc. and sell them in the nearest markets. Khasas are the best milkmen but they only prepare 'Ghee' and sell it in markets. Moreover, almost all the tribal people belonging to different communities used to visit to markets to purchase the provisions for daily purchase. Thus, they avail a very good opportunity to interact with non-tribals. Today, almost all the tribal people can speak the dialect of their neighbouring non-tribal communities. They are in the process of following the non-tribal cultural elements.

Besides this, in political sphere too, the tribal people also come in contact with the non-tribal people particularly as a voter and participate in Parliamentary and Assembly elections. The Rajis, Tharus and Buxas and somewhere the Bhotiyas and Khasas have both the tribal and non-tribal population in their village who participate even in the local panchayat election. Recently in panchayat elections held in 1986 the first 'Raji' belonging to the Kimkhola village in Dharchula Tehsil in Pithoragarh contested the election for village chief (Sabhapati in village panchayat) against a non-tribal candidate. It shows not only the political awareness in the most backward community but also their lively participation with the non-tribal people. However, the percentage of political interaction process among the tribals and the non-tribals is comparatively low, because in the remote areas the tribal people formulate their own tribal council, as well as their own tribal rules and execute them by themselves, hence they neither formulate any mixed panchayat with non-tribal nor think it necessary to participate in General Elections conducted by the State Governments for Assembly and Parliament. For instance, in the first category only 40 (30.30%), 60 (58.25%), 56 (68.29%), 16 (69.57%) and 7 (23.23%) respondents belonging respectively to the Bhotiya, Buxa, Tharu, Raji and Khasa communities admitted that they participate in political activities with the non-tribals during elections.

But the political participation of the second and third category respondents from all communities have stated that they fully participated in political activities with the non-tribal people. In the educational sphere a little percentage of the respondents related to the first category participate with the non-tribals. It is so because of the separate educational institution of the tribal people in their tribal areas where generally the tribal children are enrolled. For instance, the "Ashram Padhyati Schools" and the "Agan Badi Schools" permit only the tribal children to get enterance as an eligible student. This system of education has at least deprived the tribal children to come in contact with the non-tribal children. Yet there are a nominal percentage of the respondents in the first category who have opportunity to interact with the non-tribals in educational sphere. For example only 5 (3.79%), 11 (10.68%), 22 (26.83%), 4 (17.39%) respondents respectively from Bhotiya, Buxa, Tharu, Raji and Khasa communities admitted that they avail the opportunity to interact with the non-tribals particularly in educational institutions.

On the contrary, the most of the respondents belonging to the second category admitted that educational institutions have been the centres of tribal and non-tribal interactions. For example, 47 (58.75%), 9 (75.00%), 9 (69.33%) and 12 (60.00%) respondents respectively from the Bhotiya, Buxa, Tharu and Khasa communities have reacted in favour of the interaction process possible in educational institutions. While in case of the third category, the hundred percent respondents admitted that the educational sphere of the social life is one of the most important spheres that not only enabled the tribals to come in contact with the non-tribals but also made their proper socialization and politicalization, and resultantly motivated them to flow in the main stream of national life.

Alike of the political and educational spheres, the respondents from different categories also expressed almost the same responses in regard to the interaction pattern with non-tribals in religious sphere too. Thus, it may be concluded that in the rural areas the tribal people are more confined within their own style of life. They have comparatively less opportunities to interact with non-tribal communities. But as soon as the tribal people are professing the alien professions so as they are getting more better opportunities to participate with non-tribals in different spheres of life and also absorbing their cultural traits. Hence, it may be asserted that the hypothesis, i.e. "Economic, political, educational and the religious spheres are the main centres of tribal and non-tribal interactions with the result the tribals of Uttarakhand have begun to share the cultural traits, the dialect of the non-tribals of the respective region they live in", is valid.

Traditional Taboos and the Nature of Commensality and Connubiality Among the Tribes

As regards the various aspects of cultural transformation, the two aspects i.e. the commensality and connubiality, can be taken into account as the important attributes, as to determine the nature of the inter and intra-tribal relations. In fact, the strict observance of the commensal and connubial rules has been the inseparable characteristic, particularly in traditional societies. However, the strictness of the rules in proportion of the different stages of the cultural transformation differ. Though the scholarly observation of the anthropologists exhibit that, a tribe, as such does not observe any rules of commensality, while it is quite contrary in case of the connubiality. Thus, the strict prohibition of inter-dining with out groups, particularly with those who have not abandoned the unclean habits, may therefore be considered as the first stage of cultural transformation. Simultaneously, the laxity in traditional taboos which ideally ascertain the nature of the commensality and connubiality and the desire for inter-dining with Savarn Hindus may, therefore be considered as the silent manifestations of tribals as to be accepted in the Savarn Hindu caste hierarchy. It is the second stage of cultural transformation in which the tribals not only permit their members to develop inter-dining and connubial relations with Savarn Hindus but also prefer to be called as Hindu Rajput by getting enterance into Hindu caste hierarchy.

In view of the scientific analysis of the different stages of cultural transformation among the Scheduled Tribal Communities of Uttarakhand, the opinion of the sampled units in regard of the acceptance/prohibition of inter-dining and inter-marriage relations with Hindus have been measured. It is also assessed that how far the role of the traditional taboos is effective in the ascertainment of the commensal and connubial relations of the tribals with Savarn Hindus. The following table depicts the reactions of the sampled units in regard of the role of the traditional taboos in the ascertainment to the commensal and connubial relations of tribals with Hindus.

Table 31

Role of Traditional Taboos in the Ascertainment of the Commensal and Commubial Relations of the Tribals with Hindus

	Bhotiya		Buxa		Tharu		Raji		Jaunsari	
	Yes	*No*	*Yes*	*No*	*Yes*	*No*	*Yes*	*No*	*Yes*	*No*
First Category										
Parity in interdining with Savarn Hindus	45	87	04	99	05	77	02	21	11	19
	34.09	65.9	3.88	96.12	6.10	93.90	8.70	91.30	36.67	63.33
Observance of traditional taboos in regards of the inter-dining with Savarn Hindus	87	45	99	04	77	05	21	02	19	11
	65.91	34.09	96.12	3.88	93.90	6.10	91.30	8.70	63.33	36.67
Observance of traditional taboos in regards of the inter-marital relations with Savarn Hindus	132	00	103	00	82	00	23	00	29	01
	100	00	100	00	100	00	100	00	96.67	3.33
Second Category										
Parity in interdining with Savarn Hindus	80	00	12	00	13	00	—	—	20	00
	100	00	100	00	100	00	—	—	100	00
Observance of traditional taboos in regards of the inter-dining with Savarn Hindus	00	80	10	12	00	13	—	—	00	20
	00	100	00	100	00	100	—	—	00	100
Observance of traditional taboos in regards of the inter-marital relations with Savarn Hindus	79	01	11	01	11	02	—	—	19	01
	98.75	1.25	91.67	8.33	84.62	15.38	—	—	95.00	5.00

Contd.

Third Category										
Parity in inter-dining with Savarn Hindus	120	00	20	00	30	00	—	—	35	00
	100	00	100	00	100	00	—	—	100	00
Observance of traditional taboos in	00	120	00	20	00	30	—	—	00	35
regards of the inter-dining with Savarn Hindus	00	100	00	100	00	100	—	—	00	100
Observance of traditional taboos in	116	04	18	02	27	03	—	—	30	05
regards of the inter-marital relations with Savarn Hindus	96.67	3.33	90.00	10.00	90.00	10.00	-	-	85.79	14.20

The data exhibits that the respondents belonging to the first category are not consensus in regard of the parity of inter-dining relations with Hindus. The majority of the respondents i.e. 65.91 percent from Bhotiya community, 96.12 percent from Buxas, 93.70 percent from Tharus, 91.30 percent from Rajis and 63.33 percent from Jaunsaris are not in favour to develop any sort of parity in regard of the inter-dining relations with Hindus. They asserted that the tribals have the distinct position in the broad spectrum of the Indian society so is their distinct line of commensality which indirectly governed by the rules of connubiality. Since the inter-marriage relations are not permissible among the tribals and the Savarn Hindus, hence they feel the inter-dining relations must be confined within the groups having the permissible connubial relations. However, a certain percent of the respondents i.e. 34.09, 3.88, 6.10, 8.70 and 36.67 respectively from Bhotiya, Buxa, Tharu, Raji and Jaunsari communities have the feeling of parity in regard of the inter-dining relations with Savarn Hindus.

Similarly, the same opinion has been observed in regard of the observance of the traditional taboos in maintaining the inter-dining relations with Savarn Hindus. As the majority of the respondents i.e. 65.91, 96.12, 93.90, 91.30 and 63.33 percent respectively from Bhotiya, Buxa, Tharu, Raji and Jaunsari communities belonging to the first category, are in favour of observing the traditional taboos in maintaining the commensality while the rest of the respondents from different communities have contrary opinion, as they are not in favour of observing the traditional taboos in determining the commensal relations. While, almost all the respondents belonging to the first category are in favour of observing strictly the traditional taboos in regard of the connubiality. Thus, it is concluded that the respondents who are still confined within their traditional abodes beyond the impacts of modernity, follow the traditional taboos in determining the marital ties in particular by following the rules of endogamy and connubiality in general. On the contrary almost all the respondents of different tribal communities belonging to the second and third categories have adverse opinion than that of the first category respondents. They are neither in favour of maintaining any sort of distance and nor in following of the traditional taboos in regard of the commensal and connubial relations with Savarn Hindus. In fact, the respondents respectively from second and third categories come constantly in contact with out groups and also, share equally the same opportunities for inter-dining without any feelings of differences as well as participate in different ritualistic ceremonies of each other. They have comparatively better opportunities to interact with the non-tribal people in different spheres of social life, consequently they deliberately lag behind the traditional taboos which broaden the gap between the tribals and the non-tribals.

Today a number of tribal people particular in Bhotiya and Jaunsari communities have developed commensal relations with non-tribal Savarn Hindus. In fact, the educated and the economically well-off tribal people seems to be wilful to enter into the Hindu caste groups and to hold a certain position in Hindu caste hierarchy. Thus, it may be concluded that the traditional taboos regarding to determine the commensal and connubial relations with Hindus are effective only in the traditional tribal areas where the people are absolutely cut off from the impact of the outer world and traditionally supposed to be governed by their own tribal laws, customs and traditions. On the contrary, these traditional taboos are least effective among those tribal people who have come out of their traditional peripheries either for professing the non-traditional professions or getting education to avail the reservation facilities in services and other fields. In other words, it may be asserted that the education, the impact of the intra-tribal contact have played an important role in bringing the laxity in the rigidity of the traditional taboos of the tribals.

References

1. Prasad, Saileshwar, Where the Three Tribes Meet, Indian International Publications, Allahabad, 1974.
2. Goswami, B.B., The Tribes of Assam: A Few comments on Their Societal and Cultural Ties With the Non-tribes, in Tribal Situations in India, By K.S. Singh, Indian Institute of Advanced Study, Simla, 1972, p. 271.
3. Majumdar, D.N., A Study of Tribe Caste Continuum and the Process of Sanskritisation Among the Bodo Speaking Tribes of Assam in Tribal Situation in India, by K. Suresh Singh., Indian Institute of Advanced Study, Simla, 1972, pp. 263-270.

BIBLIOGRAPHY

Adhikary, A.K., Status and Role of Women among the Birhor: A Nomadic Hunting and Gathering Community of Eastern India, in Tribal Women in India, Calcutta : Indian Anthropological Society, 1978.

Allport, Gordon W., The Use of Personal Documents in Psychological Science, Social Science Research Council, 1942.

Archer, W.G, Tribal Law and Justice (A report on the Santhal) Concept Publishing Company, New Delhi 1984, The Hill of Flutes —Life, Love and Poetry in Tribal India : A Portrait of the Santals, London, George Allen and Wnevin 1974.

Atkinson, E.T., The Himalayan Districts of the North-western Provinces of India, North Western Provinces and Oudh Press, Allahabad, 1984, Himalayan Gazetteer, Cosmo Publications, 1982.

Aurora, G.S., Tribe-caste-class Encounters: Some Aspects of Folk Urban Relations in Alirajpur Tehsil, Hyderabad, Administrative Staff College of India, 1972.

Bendict, Ruth, Patterns of Culture, Routledge and Kegan Paul Ltd., London, 1904.

Berreman, Gerald D., Hindus of the Himalayas, University of California Press, 1972.

Barnett, H.G., Innovation: The Basis of Cultural Changes, New York, 1953.

Bidney, D., Theoretical Anthropology, Columbia Press, 1953.

Bisht, B.S., Social Structure and Organization of Raji Tribe of Kumaun, Typed Thesis, Kumaun University, 1982.

Boas Franz, The Mind of Primitive Man, The MacMillan Co., 1911.

Bodley, J.H., Victims of Progress, California, The Benjamin Cuming Publishing Co., 1982.

Briffault, R., The Mothers, London, 1927.

Brown, Radcliff A.R., Structure and Function in Primitive Society, Routledge and Kegan Paul, London, 1979.

Burman, B.K. Roy, Tota Tribe of North Bengal, Ph.D. Thesis, Calcutta University.

Carr, Saunders, Morris A. and Wilson P.A., The Professions, London, Oxford University Press, 1933.

Chandra, Bimal, Hand Book on Scheduled Castes and Scheduled Tribes, Office of the Commissioner for Scheduled Castes and Scheduled Tribes, Govt. of India, New Delhi, 1968.

Chatterjee, B.B., Bhotiyas of Indo-Tibetan Border of Uttarakhand, Typed Project Report, 1975.

Chattopadhyay, P.K., Himalaya Pare Kailash Mansarovar, Calcutta Orient Book Co., 1934.

Chauhan, I.S., Cultural Change in Tribal Life, Economic and Political Weekly, 1970.

Crooke, William, Tribes and Castes of the North-West Provinces of Oudh Region, Calcutta, 1896. Races of Northern India, Cosmo Publications, New Delhi, 1973.

Dabral, S.P., Uttarakhand Ki Bhotantik, Dagadda Veer Gatha Prakashan, 1965.

Desai, I.P., Some Aspects of Family in Mahuwa, Asia Publishing House, New York, 1964.

Dube, S.C., Manav Aur Sanskriti, Raj Kamal Prakashan, Delhi.

Durkhein, E., The Division of Labour in Society, Translated by George Simpson, Free Press, Glencoe, 1947, Education and Sociology, Translated by S.D. Fox, The Free Press, 1965.

Desai, A.R., Rural Sociology (ed), Popular Prakashan, Bombay, 1969.

Doshi, S.L., Bhils: Between Social Self Awareness and Cultural Synthesis, New Delhi, Sterling Publishing House, 1971.

Process of Tribal Unification and Integration: A Case Study of Bhils, Delhi: Concept Publishing Co., 1978.

Doshi, J.K., Social Structure and Cultural Change in Bhil Village, New Heights, Delhi, 1974.

Elliott and Merrill, Social Disorganization, Harper and Bros. New York, 1950.

Elwin, Verrier, The Tribal World of Verrier Elwin, Oxford, 1965.

Festinger, L.,and Kats, D., (ed.) Research Methods in the Behavioural Sciences New York: Holt, Rinehart and Winston, Inc. 1953. Theory and Methods of Social Research, London, 1967.

Freud, S., New Introductory Lectures on Psycho-analysis, 1934.

Galtung, J., Theory and Methods of Social Research, London, 1967.

Gillin and Gillid, Cultural Sociology, The Macmillan Co., New York, 1950.

Goode, W.J., and Hatt P.K., Methods in Social Research, Mc Graw-Hill Book Company, Inc., New York, 1952.

Goswami, B.B., Traditional Religion of the Mizos, Calcutta I.A.S.P.E.R., 1976.

Tribe to Peasant, Not Caste: Some Comments on the Mizo Situation, Eastern Anthropologists, 1978.

Grierson, George A., Linguistic Survey of India, Superintendent of Govt. Printing, Calcutta, 1966.

Guha, B. S., Racial Elements in Indian Population, Oxford Pamphlet in Indian Affairs, Oxford University Press, Bombay, 1944.

Gulati, R.K., A Profile of Social Change Among the Bhils of West Khandesh, Tribe, 1970.

Hasan, Amir, The Buxas of Tarai, B.R. Publishing Corporation, Delhi, 1979.

Hasnain, Nadeem, Tribal India Today, Harnam Publications, New Delhi, 1983.

Herskovits, M.J., Cultural Anthropology, Oxford and IBH Publishing Co., New Delhi, 1958. Man and His Works, Alfred Knopt, New York, 1956.

Hoebal, E.A., Man in the Primitive World, Mc Graw Hill Book Co., New York, 1958.

Horsey, Anita, The Impact of Modernization on the Social Cultural Life of the Warli Tribe in Dehanu and Talasuri, Taluka Thane District, Maharashtra, University of Bombay, 1972.

Hutton, J.H., Census of India, 1931.

Jahoda, M., Research Methods in Social Relations, The Dryden Press, 1951.

Kothari, K.L., Tribal Social Change in Rajasthan.

Kroeber, A.L., Anthropology, Harcourt, Brace and Co., New York, 1948.

—— The Nature of Culture, The University of Chicago Press, Chicago, 1952.

Kulckhon, Clyde and Kelly, Willam, The Concept of Culture, Columbia University Press, New York, 1945.

Lal, Panna, Hindu Customary Law in Kumaun, Allahabad Govt. Press, 1942.

Lewis, R. and Maude Augu, Professional People, London: Phoenix House Ltd., 1952.

Lindman, Social Discovery, Republic Publishing Co., 1925.

Lundberg, G.A., Social Research, Longman's Green and Co., New York.

Mac-Iver, R.M. and Page C.H., Society, London : MacMillan, 1959.

Madge, John, Tool of Social Science, London, Longman's, 1965.

Majumdar, D.N. and Madan T.N.; Social Anthropology, Asia Publishing House, Bombay, 1963.

Majumdar. D.N., An Introduction to Social Anthropology, Asia Publishing House, Bombay, 1963.

—— Races and Cultures of India, Asia Publishing House Bombay, 1963.

—— Some Aspects of the Cultural Life of the Cis-Himalayan Region. Journal and Proceeding of the Royal Assiatic Society of Bengal, 1940.

—— The Frontiers of the Primitive Tribes, Universal Publishers, Lucknow, 1944.

Majumdar, D.N., Acculturation among Hajong of Meghalaya, Man in India, 1972.

Mann, R.S. and Vyas, N.N., Indian Tribes in Transition, Rawat Publication, Jaipur, 1980.

Mann, R.S., Leadership and Planned Change in Tribal Rajasthan, Bulletin of Cultural Research Institute, 1972.

Mohan, Hari, The Pahariya: A Study in Cultural Change, Patna: Bihar Tribal Welfare Research Institute, Mimeographed, 1969.

—— A Study in Acculturation, Patna: Bihar Tribal Welfare Research Institute, 1973.

Morgan, L.H., Ancient Society, New York, 1877.

Morris, R.T., The Two Mirrors: University of Minnesota Press, 1960.

Moser, C.A., Survey Methods in Social Investigation, New York, The Mac Millan Co.

Natrajan, N., The Missionary Among the Khasis, New Delhi, Sterling Publishers, 1977.

Narayan, D.L., An Appraisal of the Economic Conditions of Scheduled Tribes in Rayal Seema, 1976.

Northrop, P.S.C., The Logic of Science and Humanities; MacMillian, London, 1947.

Ogburn W.F. and Nimkoff, F., A Hand Book of Sociology, Routledge and Kegan Paul Ltd., London, 1960.

Palmer, V.M., Field Studies in Sociology, University of Chicago Press, 1928.

Pant, S.D., The Social Economy of the Himalayas, London, George Allen and Unwin, 1935.

Pareek R.N., Tribal Culture in Flux, B.R. Publishing Corporation, New Delhi, 1977.

Parmar, V.S., Polyandry in the Himalayas, Delhi, 1975.

Perry, W.J., Children of the Sun, London, 1923.

Piddington, Ralph, An Introduction to Social Anthropology, Cillian Boyd, London, 1952.

Prabhu, P.H., Hindu Social Organization, Popular Prakashan, Bombay, 1961.

Prasad, S., Where the Three Tribes Meet, Indian International Publications, Allahabad, 1974.

Rahul, R., The Himalyan Border Land, Vikas Publications, Delhi, 1970.

Rao, D.L. Prasad, An Analysis of Kinship, Economy and Religions of the Jatpus: A Scheduled Tribes in Andhra Pradesh Research Thesis, Andhra University, 1970.

Ray, B.D., Occupational Mobility among the Khasis of Shillong, Research Project, Sponsored by ICSSR, New Delhi, 1974.

Rayapa, R.S., Sauka, Rayapa Bros., Dharchule: Pithoragarh, 1974.

Risley, H.H., The People of India, Delhi, 1969.

Rivers, W.H.R., Kinship and Social Organization, Constable and Co., London, 1914.

Rizvi, Syed N., Nagar Haidar, Factors Influencing Health in Tribal Community : A Socio-cultural Analysis of Jaunsaris, Thesis, Lucknow University, Lucknow, 1982.

Robback, A.A., The Psychology of Character, London; Kegan Paul, 1952.

Sachchindanand, Tribe-Caste Continuum: A Case Study of Gond in Bihar, Anthropos, 1970.

Social Structure, Status and Mobility Pattern: The Case of Tribal Women, Man in India, 1978.

Sahay, K.N., Under the Shadow of the Cross, Institute of Social Research and Applied Anthropology, 1976.

Saksena, R.N., Social Economy of a Polyandrous People, Agra University, Studies Series No. 1, Agra, 1956.

Sheering, C.A., Notes on the Bhotiyas, Almora and British Garhwal, Calcutta, Asiatic Society, Bengal, 1907.

Singh, K.S., Tribal Situation in India (ed.), Indian Institute of Advanced Study, Simla, 1972.

Singh, Y., Modernization of Indian Tradition, Rawat Publication, Jaipur, 1986.

Smith, W. Robertson, Kinship and Marriage in Early Arabia, London, 1903.

Spencer, Herbert, First Principles, D. Applation and Co., New York, 1906.

Srinivas, M.N., Social Change in Modern India, Orient Longman Ltd., New Delhi, 1966.

Religion and Society among the Coorge of South India, Asia Publishing House, New Delhi, 1952.

Dimensions of Social Change in India (ed.), Allied Publishers Pvt. Ltd., Bombay, 1977.

Srivastava, N.P., Tribe Caste Mobility in India and Case of Kumaun Bhotiya, University of London, 1962.

Srivastava, S.K., Tharus: A Study in Cultural Dynamics, University Press, 1958.

Sutherland, and Wood Ward, Introductory Sociology, J.B. Lippin Cott Co., New York, 1748.

Thapar, Ramesh, Tribe Caste and Religion in India, MacMillan India Ltd., New Delhi, 1977.

Tharnwald, R., Nomades, Encyclopedia of Social Sciences, 1933.

Tylor, E.B., Primitive Culture, New York, 1874.

Vidyarathi, L.P., Aspects of Social Anthropology in India, Classical Publications, New Delhi, 1980.

—— L.P., Socio-Cultural Implications of Industrialization in India, New Delhi, Planning Commission, 1970.

Primitive and Vanishing Tribes of Bihar, 1977.

Vyas, N.N. and R.S. Mann, Indian Tribes in Transition, Rawat Publications, Jaipur-Delhi, 1980.

Wilke, Arthur, S., Pram French and Raj P. Mohan, Tribal India: Unintentional Acculturation, Bulletin of the International Committee on Urgent Anthropological and Ethnological Research, 1979.

Wissler, C., The American Indian, New York, 1922. An Introduction to Social Anthropology, Henry Holt and Co. New York, 1929.

——— Man and Culture, New York, Thomes Y., Crowell, 1923.

Yang, H.P., Fact Findings with Rural People.

Young, P.V., Scientific Social Surveys and Research, Prentice-Hall of India, New Delhi, 1982.